WE WERE *feminists* ONCE

ALSO BY ANDI ZEISLER

Feminism and Pop Culture

*BITCHfest: Ten Years of Cultural Criticism
from the Pages of BITCH Magazine* (with Lisa Jervis)

WE WERE
feminists ONCE

From Riot Grrrl to CoverGirl®,
the Buying and Selling of
a Political Movement

ANDI ZEISLER

PUBLICAFFAIRS
New York

Published in the United States by PublicAffairs™,
a Member of the Perseus Books Group

PublicAffairs books are available at special discounts for bulk purchases in the U.S. by corporations,
institutions, and other organizations. For more information, please contact the Special Markets
Department at the Perseus Books Group, 2300 Chestnut Street, Suite 200, Philadelphia, PA 19103, call
(800) 810-4145, ext. 5000, or e-mail special.markets@perseusbooks.com.

Library of Congress Control Number: 2016931950
ISBN 978-1-61039-589-2 (HC)
ISBN 978-1-61039-590-8 (EB)

First Edition
10 9 8 7 6 5 4 3 2 1

To my sweet Harvey—

May your generation be the one that

finally figures this shit out.

CONTENTS

INTRODUCTION

I didn't set out to write a book about the commodification of feminism, though I guess you could argue that I've been waiting for it to happen for twenty years.

As one of three founders of the magazine *Bitch: Feminist Response to Pop Culture*, I always believed that the realm of media and popular culture was where feminism would truly change hearts and minds. At the time we started making our black-and-white, stapled-together zine, it was 1995—a time when feminism had only recently reentered the pop-cultural imagination after the massive 1980s backlash that saddled the very word with a wealth of ugly baggage. We were omnivorous pop-culture consumers, and the point of *Bitch* was to take pop culture seriously as a force that shapes the lives of everyone, and argue for its importance as an arena for feminist activism and analysis. At the dawn of the dot-com revolution, there were no blogs about feminist film criticism, no Twitter feeds that mashed up Judith Butler and the Incredible Hulk. We had only each other as sounding boards for strong opinions and burning questions. Questions like: Why do daytime talk shows treat adolescent female sexuality like an epidemic to be contained? What's with men in sitcoms and commercials being portrayed as hopelessly bumbling ding-dongs who can't read a grocery list? Why are black people always the first to be killed in disaster movies? And, of course, the eternal query: Why must every female musician who makes the cover of *Rolling Stone* do so in her underwear?

We called the zine *Bitch* because we hoped to reclaim the word, and to make its verb form into something that could effect change just by speaking up and encouraging others to do the same. The word we were equally concerned with reclaiming, though, was in the subtitle: "A feminist response to pop culture." Born in the 1970s, we came of ideological age during the backlash, seeing and hearing feminism dismissed as, at best, a vexing political incident that had come and gone; or, at worst, a social experiment that had succeeded at the expense of a healthy society and left men hungry for home-cooked meals, children marooned in front of blaring televisions, and women bitter and love-starved. Feminism didn't have an image problem; it had an image catastrophe.

So we launched a zine, and the zine grew into a magazine. At the same time, the word "bitch" moved deeper into common parlance, becoming a staple of television and radio, a pangender casual greeting, and a signifier of female badassness. But the complexity of making "feminist" palatable remained.

The belief that there had to be other frustrated feminist pop-culture obsessives out there catalyzed *Bitch* as an activist project. Our content—essays about television and movies, critiques of ad campaigns, and interviews with feminists of all genders doing cool projects—were things we wanted to read, but had tried and failed to find elsewhere. As time went on, we found that we definitely weren't alone: Over the next ten years, pop culture began to be taken seriously. Very seriously. *New York Times* and *Wall Street Journal* seriously. Entire-Web-sites-devoted-to-television-recaps seriously. A decade after *Bitch* launched, we were one of hundreds of Web sites, podcasts, and blogs whose work plumbed the intersections of feminism and popular culture.

As part of a far-flung community of fellow pop-culture feminists that has bloomed over the years, I've seen pop culture and media transform feminism, for better and for worse—and feminism, in turn, change pop culture and media. But as I started to write this book, something weird happened: feminism got *cool*.

A current of excitement that had previously been humming just under the surface of mainstream culture suddenly amped up. In August 2014, Beyoncé commanded the stage at the close of MTV's Video Music Awards, the word "FEMINIST" glowing in neon lights behind her as her song "Flawless" sampled the words of Nigerian author Chimimanda Ngozi Adichie. ("We teach girls to shrink themselves, to make themselves smaller. We say to girls, 'You can have ambition, but not too much.'") The sample concludes with Adichie paraphrasing the dictionary definition of "feminist": "The person who believes in the social, political, and economic equality of the sexes." Though the song was already well known, and though Beyoncé's particular brand of business-minded feminism was threaded through lyrics dating back to her Destiny's Child days, the visual display served as her official flag in the ground. Bathed in spotlights, the biggest pop star in the world rocked the once-maligned label like a curve-hugging Met Gala dress, literally spelling it out for an audience of more than eight million.

Beyoncé staking her claim to feminism was the start of a media domino effect. Shortly after, Emma Watson, beloved for years as Harry Potter's Hermione, gave a speech on the importance of gender equality to the United Nations—noting, among other things, that "[i]t is time that we all perceive gender on a spectrum, instead of [as] two sets of opposing ideals." The pop singer Taylor Swift, who several years earlier had disavowed feminism, quickly changed tack with a media announcement that, in fact, she'd been feminist all along. At Paris Fashion Week, Chanel's runway-show finale took the form of a feminist rally, with models draped in the label's signature tweeds raising signs that read "History is Her Story" and "Women's Rights Are More Than Alright." Brands like Verizon, Always, and Pantene began centering feminist themes in their ads for wireless plans, maxi pads, and shine-boosting shampoos. And my Google alert for "women and feminism," which used to turn up lonely articles with headlines like "Feminism: Outmoded and Unpopular," began teeming with woman-power boosterism: "Beyoncé's Hip New Club: Feminism," "Emma Watson Gives Feminism New Life," "Why Male Feminists Are Hot." Seemingly overnight, almost every female celebrity—and a fair number of male ones—who walked a red carpet was asked whether they were feminists. References to Lena Dunham and Leaning In were suddenly cropping up in everything from gossip columns to in-flight magazines. The increasing presence of transgender women in mainstream pop culture—Laverne Cox, Janet Mock, the Amazon series *Transparent*—offered new opportunities to talk about gender as a limiting social construct. *Cosmopolitan*, the bible of man-pleasing sex tips, began embracing more explicitly political writers and subjects, though it will still teach you "40 Ways to Blow His Mind." Feminism, so long dismissed as the realm of the angry, the cynical, the man-hating, and the off-puttingly hairy, was officially a thing. It was hot. And, perhaps most important, it was sellable.

Theoretically, this was exactly the breakthrough my cofounders and I had always hoped to see in the media and pop culture we consumed. There's no question that feminism has in just the past few years made inroads into all aspects of culture, not simply in the numbers of female senators and CEOs but also in the ways that we talk about politics, about entertainment, about parenting, about art. Accusations of domestic violence, once considered extrinsic to the business of sports and its players, are now the subject of lengthy debates and press conferences. Offensive jokes from comedians that would have gone unremarked upon a decade ago are now the basis for micro-campaigns on social media, capable of gaining enough steam to create a lasting impact for the joker. Weekly entertainment magazines review new movies with a lens on how—or, for that matter, whether—female characters are represented.

Within a very short span of time, feminism has come to occupy perhaps its most complex role ever in American, if not global, culture. It's a place where most of the problems that have necessitated feminist movements to begin with are still very much in place, but at the same time there's a mainstream, celebrity, consumer embrace of feminism that positions it as a cool, fun, accessible identity that anyone can adopt. I've seen this called "pop feminism," "feel-good feminism," and "white feminism." I call it marketplace feminism. It's decontextualized. It's depoliticized. And it's probably feminism's most popular iteration ever.

By 2015, you couldn't swing a tampon without hitting someone or something that boasted its feminist import, in places you definitely wouldn't expect: nail polish, underwear, energy drinks, Swiffers. Things started getting a little weird. The Ms. Foundation for Women, in partnership with *Cosmopolitan*, closed out 2014 with a list of the "Top 20 Celebrity Feminists." Shortly after that, *The Daily Beast* enthused that "*Maxim* Just Became Your New Feminist Bible," hyping the new direction of the former lad magazine which, under a new female editor, no longer ranked the fuckability of famous women. (Well, no longer *only* ranks famous women—now, it also ranks vacation spots and restaurants!) Similarly, *Playboy*'s decision to stop printing nude photo spreads after sixty-two bodacious years was heralded as a bold pro-woman stance and attended by rose-colored remembrances with titles like "Playboy Bunny: Sexist Relic or Early Feminist Figure?"

In the summer of 2015, everyone's favorite karate-chopping Muppet, Miss Piggy, was awarded the prestigious First Award by the Brooklyn Museum's Sackler Center for Feminist Art, an honor previously bestowed on the likes of Toni Morrison and Chief Wilma Mankiller. Sure, Miss P had previously rejected the F-word, but with feminism in the news (and, perhaps more relevant, a new Muppets sitcom on the way) it was the ideal time for her to sit down with Gloria Steinem and announce that "*Moi* is a feminist pig." By the fall of 2015, when an issue of *InStyle* featured pop star Katy Perry describing her signature fragrance, Killer Queen, as "royal, rebellious, and feminist," it seemed like the word had become a catchall that media and pop culture were deploying like a kicky new seasoning for content.

But while "feminism" has become a buzzword everywhere from Madison Avenue to Hollywood, the actual issues crucial to feminism's forward movement are as threatened as ever. Here's the Supreme Court, which placed a hold on a Texas law that aimed to close every women's health clinic in the state by demanding that each one meets the medical standards of ambulatory surgery centers. Here's a feminist video game critic who has been forced to cancel a campus speaking engagement because of a note that threatened "a Montreal Massacre–style attack"[1] carried out against feminist supporters. Over here is Daniel Holtzclaw, the Oklahoma City cop who repeatedly profiled and targeted marginal black women in order to sexually assault them, and was put on paid administrative leave for almost a year before being fired. (Holtzclaw was sentenced to jail in late 2015.) And ooh, here's Microsoft's CEO telling a group of female professionals that women shouldn't ask for raises, but instead "trust the system"—you know, the system that has for decades paid women less than men—and be rewarded with "good karma."

It's become a constant game of Good News/Bad News. As we celebrate the increasing number of female TV showrunners and writers, Senate Republicans have twice unanimously voted against an act designed to close the gendered wage gap. As our tabloid magazines documented every blessed step of Caitlyn Jenner's transition, an anti-discrimination ballot measure in Houston, Texas was defeated thanks largely to TV ads that painted transgender women as child predators, warning, "Any man at any time could enter a women's bathroom simply by claiming to be a woman." As we excitedly binge-watch a Netflix series about life and love in a women's prison, dozens of black women have died in police custody in recent years, with no satisfactory explanation as to why.

These are problems that can't and won't be solved by marketplace feminism. They are impervious to our "feminist as fuck" necklaces and "I Blame the Patriarchy" unicorn t-shirts. (Nothing against those, they're cute as hell.) They don't care what a big deal it is that *Inside Amy Schumer* beat out all those late-night network sausage parties for an Emmy. They don't care what new thing Taylor Swift said about feminism. And now I can't help but worry that those of us that the marriage of pop culture and feminism would yiel progressive fruit might have a lot to answer for.

The aspects of feminism currently given voice in pop culture are the most media-friendly ones, the ones that center on heterosexual relationships and marriage, on economic success that doesn't challenge existing capitalist structures, on the right to be desirable yet have bodily autonomy. Watson's speech to the UN was centered on "inviting" men to get invested in feminism, in order to better legitimize it. Sheryl Sandberg's much-heralded Lean In philosophy is about women conforming to workplaces that increasingly see them not as human beings but as automatons with inconvenient biology. The feminism they espouse is certainly reasonable, but it's not particularly nuanced. It doesn't get to the root of why men might not be invested in feminism or why corporate culture forces untenable choices. It doesn't challenge beliefs or processes or hegemonies so much as it offers nips and tucks.

Despite every signal boost for feminism, every spot-on viral video about beauty standards, every badass, take-charge female film or TV role, and every catchily named nail polish, the beliefs behind the word "feminism" remain among the most contested in political and social life. The question that has always been at its heart—Are women human beings, with the same rights, access, and liberties as men?—is increasingly posed in spheres where it should have been resolved decades ago. This increasingly looks not like a world that has finally emerged into fully realized feminism, but like a world in which we are letting a glossy, feel-good feminism pull focus away from deeply entrenched forms of inequality. It's a feminism that trades on simple themes of sisterhood and support—you-go-girl tweets and Instagram photos, cheery magazine editorials about dressing to please yourself. The fight for gender equality has transmogrified from a collective goal to a consumer brand.

It's undeniable that media and pop-culture representations—even surface-skimming ones—of social movements can change attitudes.

As someone who honestly believes that pop culture is a force that can, and has, changed the world, I want to at least entertain the thought that a culture half-changed by feminism can harness that power to finally go the whole nine. After all, if we can have feminist television shows, feminist publishing houses, and feminist pop stars, why *not* a feminist underwear line? Feminist toys? A feminist energy drink? A feminist strip club? If feminism sells in the form of a movie or an album, why couldn't it sell as a nontextual product as well?

This book is an exploration of how the new embrace of marketplace feminism—mediated, decoupled from politics, staunchly focused on individual experience and actualization—dovetails with instilled beliefs about power, about activism, about who feminists are and what they do. The first half looks at the ways that feminism's past and present have informed the media and pop culture that represents and broadcasts feminism. The second half faces down the projects that remain unfinished. Both are a place to take the measure of marketplace feminism, to look at what a social, political, and still-radical movement becomes as it is filtered through the pop culture and media that serve as its contemporary translators.

There are those who argue that the measure of cultural change is the degree to which that change is assimilated into existing society, those who would say that the media co-optation of a movement (say, with a slideshow of "The 8 Best and Worst Feminists in Entertainment") is proof that it has truly made its mark. This is about the ways that modern feminism has changed *and* assimilated, and it's about what happens next in this strange new marketplace world.

PART ONE

The New Embrace

CHAPTER 1

The Corridors of Empower

"In a village chapel in upstate New York, 150 years ago, the initial bold steps in a revolution that would ensure women the right to vote were taken at the first women's rights celebration at Seneca Falls. And now you can celebrate the anniversary of this milestone in women's rights, and the strength and conviction of the courageous suffragettes involved whenever you use your First USA Anniversary Series Platinum Mastercard®. Celebrate women's rights. Apply today."

It wasn't the first time that women's liberation had been connected to our power to spend money we didn't have, and it wouldn't be the last. But First USA's linking of women's enfranchisement and their freedom to go into debt, in the form of a 1998 credit card come-on, was an almost admirably shameless co-option of the language of feminism in the service of capitalism. (The bank even promised to send a free "women's almanac" to cardholders after their first purchase.)

One of the many preliberation factoids that regularly makes the rounds to illustrate just how far women have come is that, up until the mid-1970s, women were unable to get credit cards in their own names. Married women needed a male cosigner—a husband or father—in order to use a card that was then issued in his name; single, divorced, 3 and even widowed women were denied altogether. (Very often both of these standards applied to library cards as well.) So when 1974's Equal Credit Opportunity Act was passed, it was a marker of liberation realized: marital status was no longer a bank's business where credit was concerned, and women were granted the right to buy whatever, whenever, with money that was theirs, and to go into debt right alongside men.[1] But the idea that purchasing itself was a feminist act became a key tenet of emerging marketplace feminism.

It's not a stretch to say that modern feminism was co-opted by the market almost as soon as it was born. The white, middle-class "new woman" of the late nineteenth and early twentieth century, who had leisure enough to chafe against the Victorian ideal of the "angel in the house," was an early target of advertisers seeking a fresh demographic. Those advertisers constructed ideal female consumers as mothers and wives who, like the late-blooming heroines written by Henrik Ibsen, were full of unmet potential, longing to buck convention and participate in public life. For this woman, consumer goods were positioned as one route to autonomy: Shredded Wheat wasn't just a cereal product, it was "Her 'Declaration of Independence.'" Meanwhile, the breezy, pompadoured "Gibson Girls" created by illustrator Charles Dana Gibson came to embody the spirit of the younger New Woman, and were often shown bicycling, playing tennis, and serving on juries. Both the New Woman and the Gibson Girl were more palatable commercial versions of the dreaded suffragists of the era, whose zeal to have their message heard was widely lampooned. ("At the suffragette's meetings you can hear some plain things—and see them too!") And both were depicted as refined and educated, but not so much so that they were out in the streets, agitating and hunger-striking for the right to vote.

The importance of women as a new target market at the turn of the century necessitated the inclusion of actual women within the advertising industry, and because many of these women were also active in the suffrage movement, they found themselves in a bind: they were

valued for their ostensibly innate sense
resented validating such an essentialist
copywriter at the J. Walter Thompson ag
New York State Suffrage Party, urged h
women an amorphous blob of suggestib
in mind the suffrage slogan "Women
1918, J. Walter Thompson's Women's Editorial Depa...
sponsible for more than half the agency's business.[2]

But while "Women Are People" seemed like a commonsense strategy, it was at odds with a growing mass-market culture whose profit motive not only emphasized gender divides but codified them, with manufacturers, retailers, advertisers, and magazine publishers all invested in establishing two discrete but reliable groups of consumers: men and (white) women. In fact, it was the women ignored by this sector who built some of the era's most successful businesses with women-as-people in mind: entrepreneurs like Madam C.J. Walker and Annie Turnbo Malone, for instance, both became pioneers of the direct-sales model in creating and selling products for black women's hair. Rather than structure their almost instantly successful businesses as top-down profit maximizers, they instead constructed them as sites of training, education, community building, and philanthropy.

The Sweet Smoke, Smells, and Sweaters of Freedom

Cigarettes were one of the first products that allowed the commercial realm to align itself—in market potential, if not political commitment—to emerging women's movements. In the late nineteenth and early twentieth centuries, smoking was considered such an unseemly activity for women that they were often explicitly prohibited from doing so in public. So it made sense that the American Tobacco Company saw capturing this emerging market as akin to "opening a gold mine right in our front yard."[3] ATC deftly exploited the first wave of feminism when it hired Edward Bernays (now

d the "father of public relations") to craft campaigns that
get more women smoking, and buying, cigarettes. Bernays
ally appealed to women's vanity by proposing cigarettes as slim-
ing aids—"Reach for a Lucky instead of a sweet," urged print
advertisements—but his hunch was that appealing to their growing
sense of autonomy might be the real mover of product. In 1929,
Bernays and ATC orchestrated a walk for equality down New York's
Fifth Avenue, hiring female participants to hold aloft Lucky Strikes
as "torches of freedom," while encouraging bystanders to "Fight another sex taboo!" by joining them in inhaling the heady smoke of
gender equality. In an early example of contrived media virility, the
photos of the march caused a national sensation and, as expected,
nudged the percentage of female cigarette buyers up by more than
half, from 5 percent in 1923 to 12 percent post-march. Lucky Strike
rivals quickly followed suit, with Philip Morris even organizing a
U.S. lecture tour in which cigarette experts instructed women on the
finer points of lighting up.

A similar view of symbolic liberation was the basis for Maidenform's
long-running "Dream" campaign. Devised by a female copywriter,
Kitty D'Alessio, and launched in 1949, it was both less wordy than
suffrage-era advertising and more visually evocative. In the ads, ordinary (though exclusively white) women were granted entrée to exotic
places and fantastic careers via nothing but humble brassieres. "I
dreamed I climbed the highest mountain in my Maidenform bra"
mused the copy that accompanied a brassiered woman in a ski lift, St.
Bernard dog at her side. Other dreams included boxing ("I dreamed I
was a knockout . . .") and chariot-racing in ancient Rome ("I dreamed
I drove them wild . . ."), as well as playing chess and going to work in
an office. This had the perhaps unintentional effect of suggesting that,
for such women, going to work and playing chess were activities as
fantastical as going back in time to race a chariot.

Four decades later, Virginia Slims, the first cigarette explicitly marketed to young, professional women, furthered Lucky Strike's legacy

by trading on the idea that smoking was a pivotal site of liberation. As with First USA's later Seneca Falls Mastercard, Virginia Slims conjured up a historical past of such vivid, indignant subjugation that, really, any alternative would look like a giant leap in progress. The cigarette's print and TV ads, launched in July 1968, used slapstick, sepia-toned vignettes of Gibson-Girl types putting themselves in outlandish situations in order to sneak a smoke away from the disapproving eyes of their husbands: a face-off between stodgy, paternalistic men and freewheeling women. ("In 1915, Mrs. Cynthia Robinson was caught smoking in the cellar behind the preserves. Although she was 34, her husband sent her straight to her room.") The famous slogan "You've come a long way, baby" suggested that being able to inhale that formerly masculine smoke was liberation itself, rather than a byproduct of it: it's fitting that when *Mad Men*'s Peggy Olson leaves Sterling Cooper Draper Pryce, in the show's fifth season, her first task at her new agency is to come up with both a name and an ad campaign for "a cigarette for ladies." As the first cigarette that used women's images to appeal to women as customers, Virginia Slims was an unqualified success for parent company Philip Morris in the first two decades of its existence; by the 1980s, its market share had grown from 0.24 percent to 3.16 percent.[4]

As the second wave of the women's movement gained momentum and media notice, the opportunities to market products using aggrandizing sales pitches grew. Take the Liberated Wool Sweater, the 1970 brainchild of the American Wool Council. Ads in women's glossies heralded this garment as the "embodiment of the new freedom," touting its ability to give wearers "freedom of movement, freedom from wrinkles, and freedom to wear any hem-length you like."[5] Advertisers were careful not to explicitly name feminism or the current women's liberation movement: the whole point was to capture potential customers who believed enough in women's liberation to want to support companies that referenced it, but not enough to shun what feminists saw as tools of sexual objectification. Could this cynical approach be enough to sell Massengill "feminine hygiene" aerosol douche by using the tagline "Freedom Spray"? Apparently it could.

The business of marketing and selling to women literally depends on creating and then addressing female insecurity, and part of the revelatory potential of women's lib involved rejecting the marketplace's sweet-talking promises about life-changing face creams and shampoos—not to mention the entire premise of women as decorative objects. There was good reason for industries that sustained themselves on the self-hatred of women to dread the potential reach of feminist movements. Co-opting the language of liberation to sell their products allowed them to have it both ways, celebrating the spirit of the movement while fostering a new set of insecurities ("Natural-look" cosmetics, anyone?) and a new aspirational archetype.

Charlie, a perfume "for the new woman" that launched in 1973, was the first American fragrance to become a blockbuster, in part because it was Revlon's first to target women under thirty-five. Charlie's iconic ad was a major part of its appeal: in it, model Shelley Hack jumps out of a Rolls-Royce and strides confidently down the streets of New York City in a kicky pantsuit, embodying all the freedom and confidence of the women's movement with none of the baggy clothes or scowling. The accompanying jingle assured potential buyers that this was the *fun* kind of liberation: "Kinda young, kinda now, Charlie!/ Kinda hip, kinda wow, Charlie!" As Revlon's twenty-point marketing profile of the "Charlie girl" pointed out, their customer was "Irreverent and unpretentious," "Can be tough, believes rules are secondary," "Can be very soft, but is never passive," "Is very relaxed about sex," and, interestingly, "Is not a Jewish princess."[6] (Here's where I note that my own Jewish mother worked in product development at Revlon until shortly before Charlie's time.)

Indeed, the Charlie girl didn't so much reflect the new vision of young, liberated white femininity as it did present it as a superior alternative to actual feminist activism. In her 2013 book *Wonder Women: Sex, Power, and the Quest for Perfection*, Barnard College president and self-described former reluctant feminist Debora Spar testifies to the power of Charlie's decontextualized liberation: "Feminists were loud and pushy, strident, and unfeminine. Charlie, on the other hand, was gorgeous, ladylike, and successful, a working woman and a mom. Who needed feminism if you could have Charlie?" For women like Spar, Hack's embodiment of liberation was much more alluring than the real-life agitators who made her possible. And that attitude, goosed by the product and embraced by its consumers, helped lay the groundwork for today's marketplace feminism, in which image is removed from theory and the fun kind of liberation is the most valuable.

Revlon followed Charlie's success with the 1978 launch of Enjoli, which took the new-woman iconography a step further. If Charlie was a sassy, carefree symbol of the liberated American female, Enjoli referenced what it took to maintain that freedom with its tagline: "The 8-hour fragrance for the 24-hour woman." The Charlie girl was a playful girl; the Enjoli gal was a serious *woman*—an image that the advertising drove home with its Peggy Lee–adapted jingle: "I can bring home the bacon/ Fry it up in a pan/ And never never never let you forget you're a man/ 'Cause I'm a woooomman/ Enjoli!" Its print ad showed a blonde woman walking to work, swinging a child, taking a business call, and jogging, a montage that is almost exhausting just to look at, but which was meant to flatter the modern superwoman in all her multifaceted glory. If you wonder where contemporary mass media got the idea that "having it all" is the holy grail of female existence, just refer back to the print ad: "You can feed the kids and the gerbils. Pass out the kisses. And get to work by 5 to 9." This was the first time a cosmetic product hadn't relied on a static image of a woman, and the first time perfume acknowledged that, for many women, life was largely unglamorous. It was definitely the first and last time the word "gerbils" was used to advertise fragrance.

The late 1970s also brought the launch of Secret antiperspirant, which, like Virginia Slims before it, used a battle-of-the-sexes advertising campaign to sell an intrinsically unisex product, emphasizing that though Secret was "strong enough for a man," it was "made for a woman." In its print ads, pairs of men and women—both black and white, though never interracial—flirted over which one of them got to benefit from the antiperspirant's dude-caliber strength. "There's some heavy talk going 'round that Secret antiperspirant is strong enough for a man," says a buff bodybuilder to a Diahann Carroll–coiffed beauty. "That's right, but it's made for a woman. Sorry, muscles," she responds.

Male figures weren't the focus of ad campaigns that co-opted the language of feminism, but most of them included men in some way, either as part of a playful competition—as Secret's ads would continue to do through the 1980s—or as adornment. Their role was to act as reassurance that the Charlie girl, the Enjoli woman, the gal in the natural-look foundation, and others weren't taking their newfound freedoms too far. Shelley Hack's Charlie pats her man on the tush in broad daylight but makes sure to order a salad at dinner; Enjoli's 24-hour woman slips into a silky negligee after the kids and gerbils are fed, the better to give her man some loving before grabbing two or three hours of sleep. Ultimately, there was little that was threatening to the status quo in advertising's liberated woman. It wasn't until the supposedly postfeminist 1990s and beyond that men slipped quietly out of the feminist-consumer picture and the idea that women could do and buy things "for myself" took hold.

Subtext and the Single Girl

For decades, advertisers had spoken to women chiefly by emphasizing their roles in relation to others. Early ads for Listerine warned women that their "poor hygiene"—malodorous breath or, worse, genitals—would cost them their marriages, and tartly reprimanded mothers for not treating their baby's butts with only the best diaper creams and disposable nappies. The 1990s brought ads that served as a departure, explicitly acknowledging not only that women can be happily single, but that many women, in fact, choose that status, and, as consumers, revel in it. In a 1999 *Village Voice* article titled "Women Are Easy: Why TV Ad Agencies Take Female Viewers for Granted," journalist Mark Boal mused, "Today's marketer or media buyer may well be a woman in Prada, reflecting the profound shift in gender roles that is also being acted out on the tube. The stay-at-home wife in *Bewitched* has been replaced by Buffy the weapon-wielding go-getter." Yet his piece went on to surmise that even this brave new adscape was pulling from an outdated playbook in targeting women, one in which their identities are still built around love and romance.

To anyone with a pop culture habit, this wasn't exactly news. Even flattering consumer appeals to single women served to underscore their status as outliers. One 1999 ad for Diet Coke featured a woman filling out a video-dating profile, telling the matchmaker that she has "great friends" and a "great job." "Sounds like you have a pretty good life," responds the matchmaker. The would-be bachelorette takes a swig of her low-cal beverage as those words sink in, and then zips out of the joint before wasting any more of her abundant singleton time. Who needs a man when you've got this artificially sweetened and caffeinated soda in your life? The ad was part of a series that emphasized "empowerment," with a tagline ("Live Your Life") conceived as a 180-degree turn from Diet Coke's previous appeal, whose smirky tagline ("You are what you drink") prioritized physical appearance.

A 2000 ad for De Beers' diamond solitaire necklace, meanwhile, cast the single woman as looking for Mr. Goodbar in a sparkler form. The ad copy invoked the language of a bar pickup, reading, "It beckons me as I pass the store window. . . . We look at each other. And though I'm not usually that kind of girl, I take it home." Neither the Diet Coke nor the De Beers ad seemed entirely comfortable representing a single women; it seemed as though their makers were so hamstrung by not being able to depend on the old wife-and-mom prompts that they had to hammer home exactly what these women weren't to define what they were. But as more brands began marketing to single women, they realized that the language of liberation from just those old ideals was the right pitch.

"Your left hand says 'we.' Your right hand says 'me.' Your left hand loves candlelight. Your right hand loves the spotlight. Your left hand rocks the cradle. Your right hand rules the world. Women of the world, raise your right hand."

With its 1947 "A Diamond is Forever" ad, De Beers had single-handedly created the market for engagement rings, turning diamonds into as crucial a symbol of wedded bliss as the white dress or floral bouquet. But by the early 2000s, the company was looking to expand its market, and the proliferation of unmarried female consumers aged thirty to fifty was its target. The right-hand ring was born: a line of fanciful designs meant for that formerly lesser ring finger, and an ad campaign that set out to flatter their would-be wearers. In the language of the right-hand ring's sales pitch, marriage was for unimaginative yes-women who were sweet, traditional, and, let's face it, pretty boring. Why would you want to wear a plain old diamond solitaire given to you by some chump when you could pick out your own, even fancier model?

For a time, the campaign was a smash: "Nonbridal" ring sales increased 15 percent in 2004, and in 2005 the campaign won the Gold EFFIE award from the New York American Marketing Association for "exceeding its objectives of bringing ring growth into line with total diamond jewelry growth."[7] The founder of consumer behavior–tracking organization America's Research Group told NBC News in January 2004 that the key to the rings' success was the sense of empowered entitlement among female consumers. "The days of getting permission are really over, and that's what's really expanded the buying power of women over the last 10 years."[8]

It turned out to be a short run. The brisk trade in right-hand rings was slowed down in part by the rising awareness of the blood-diamond scourge in Angola, Sierra Leone, Zimbabwe, and the Democratic

Republic of Congo, where children as young as five were forced into mining labor in order to fund civil wars in those countries. But stateside, things had changed as well: in the years after 9/11, there was a new emphasis on stability and domesticity, much of which envisioned a re-centering of traditional gender roles. Magazines theorized that the terrorist attacks had been a wake-up call for men emasculated by American culture, and declared the return of the cowboy as heartthrob; George W. Bush played at comic-book fortitude with his florid references to "evildoers" and chest-pounding entreaties to "Bring 'em on!" Publishing houses and women's magazines were suddenly all about the "art of domesticity"; sleek scouring tools and aromatic floor cleaners became stars of a new prestige-housekeeping category of consumer goods. Marriage was on the country's mind: the Bush administration, egged on by conservative-Christian advocacy groups, dedicated $1.5 million toward encouraging low-income couples to marry, but was quick to note that the push was for straight couples only. At the other end of the spectrum, splashy celebrity nuptials like those of Jennifer Lopez and Marc Anthony, David and Victoria Beckham, and Ben Affleck and Jennifer Garner were obsessively chronicled in a glut of new wedding-industry media, and even credited for bumping up the overall marriage rate. And despite Bush's fierce "protection" of heterosexual marriage, the wedding-industrial complex welcomed gay marriage with open arms and a slew of rainbow-themed product. By 2014, the new trend in "nonmarital" rings, according to *Vogue*, was single women wearing wedding band–esque baubles on their left-hand ring finger for a psychological sense of belonging. So much for upending tradition.

I Am Strong. I Am Invincible.
I Am Good for the Bottom Line.

"If you let me play," said the little girl, "I will like myself more." "I will have more self-confidence." "I will be 60 percent less likely to get breast cancer." "I will be less likely to get pregnant before I want to be." "I will be more likely to leave a man who beats me." "I will learn to be strong."

It was 1995, and Nike was reaching out a well-muscled hand to female consumers with its heart-tugging "If You Let Me Play" campaign, which turned the studied benefits of young girls playing team sports into a girl-power salvo. Using research collected by the Women's Sports Foundation, the brand packed decades of rebuttal to sports as a "boy thing" into thirty seconds of airtime. The spots featured a multicultural array of preteen girls one by one voicing these statements to the camera, as though addressing viewers' complicity in marginalizing girls' sports. It was one of Nike's most successful campaigns ever, and served to align the brand with feminism, education, and progressivism without compromising its bottom line.

"It wasn't advertising. It was truth," said Janet Champ, who served as Nike's chief copywriter during the campaign.[9] Either way, it was a new move for a buzzy brand whose cutting-edge ads featuring characters like Spike Lee's Mars Blackmon ("It's gotta be the shoes!") were definitely cool, but not usually quite so earnest. And the plaintive, fourth-wall-breaking dialogue worked even better than Nike had hoped. Mary Schmitt, who covered the campaign for *The Kansas City Star*, reported:

> The ad has been running on television for about a month, and the phones in the Nike headquarters have been ringing off the hook the whole time. . . . Many of the callers are mothers whose voices break when they say they want their daughters to have the opportunities they never had. Some are fathers whose girls are entering those arenas previously reserved for boys only. Some are coaches or teachers who have seen the differences sports can make in the lives of young girls. And some are women who never had the chance to find out.[10]

But despite Champ's heartfelt description, this was advertising, and very successful advertising at that. Unless you're a soulless pod person or an actual robot, you've probably been moved to tears by an ad or two. (I don't care what your product is, if the TV commercial makes use of Fleetwood Mac's "Landslide," I will be a soggy heap by the end of it.) Still, no matter how many hankies the ad necessitates, it doesn't change the goal: to make you buy things.[11]

Nike followed up a year later with a twist on "If You Let Me Play" called "There's a Girl Being Born in America." Over a similar montage of young, multicultural girls mugging for and staring down the camera, the copy's straightforward narrative again invokes sports as a means for girls to thrive in the world: "There's a girl being born in America/ And someone will give her a doll/ And someone will give her a ball/ And then someone will give her a chance." In a way, the ad's power came from depoliticizing the very reason that girls were (still grudgingly, in many cases) given a chance to play sports: Title IX, the 1972 bill that, among other things, mandated that schools receiving federal funding provide equal support for men's and women's sports. In both Nike ads, the copy turned demands into requests, appealing to invisible men— the "you" and "someone" referenced in the copy—and effectively blurring the role that feminist agitation played in the rise of women's sports. Women and girls may have fought for and won the *right* to play sports, but "There's a Girl Being Born in America" was effective in pointing out that the social stigma still, often, involved asking for permission.

The sister campaigns signaled a move on Nike's part to honor the female experience in sports by simply normalizing it—a smart move given that, at the time, the pop culture playing field was in a place of flux with regard not only to women's images, but to those of girls. (By 1997, the company's prioritizing of the female demographic was rewarded with 43 percent of the athletic-footwear market.) If the 1970s and '80s leveraged women's lib into a marketplace of self-actualized femininity, the following decade found it with younger consumers in mind. The 1990s brought media focus to a simmering "girl crisis" articulated in bestselling books like Mary Pipher's *Reviving Ophelia*, Peggy Orenstein's *Schoolgirls*, and Lyn Mikel Brown and Carol

Gilligan's *Meeting at the Crossroads*, all of which warned of a precipitous drop in girls' self-esteem at puberty and a host of damaging results. Study after study found that even smart, sporty, confident girls with plenty of familial support hit puberty and with it a wall of insecurity, self-doubt, and body shame. Suddenly, girls' lib seemed just as crucial as women's lib—and, incidentally, just as simple to market.

From Xena the Warrior Princess and her younger sidekick (and maybe-lover?), Gabrielle; to Buffy the Vampire Slayer and the tiny, animated PowerPuff Girls; to bodacious video game explorer Lara Croft and a ballsy new breed of Bond girls, action heroines were on the ascent in the mid- to late 1990s. An uptick in smart, self-sufficient, and justice-minded heroines wasn't meant to be a magical bridge for the real-life confidence gap written about by Pipher, Gilligan, and others, but it did fill a crucial void of visibility. Young women likely weren't that interested in reading the dog-eared books of feminist theory and popular psychology that may have bolstered the awareness and self-esteem of their mothers and aunts. But they could, and did, have access to characters on TV, in comics, and in movies that modeled strength in the quotidian, no-big-whoop way that boys had always had.

They also had new iterations of old advertising messages. Take Barbie, that pink plastic vessel for cultural assumptions and expectations about women. Since her debut in 1964, she'd been a lounge singer, a career woman, a bikini model, even a mother. In 1992, as Teen Talk Barbie, she became embroiled in controversy: each Teen Talk doll was preprogrammed with a limited number of phrases, several of which underestimated both the intelligence and the interests of teen girls. In a time of both the girl-crisis narrative and the flowering Riot Grrrl movement, no one had time for toymakers who programmed Barbie to say things like "Math class is tough!" and "Let's plan our dream wedding!" The American Association of University Women promptly issued a statement to Mattel noting that "preteen girls most likely to play with Teen Talk Barbie are at the highest risk for losing confidence in their math ability," and requesting that the phrase be struck from the dolls' lexicon. An even better response came from a group of guerrilla culture jammers calling themselves the Barbie Liberation Organization, who subverted somewhere between three hundred and five hundred Teen Talk Barbies and G.I. Joe "Talking Duke" dolls by switching their voice boxes so that Barbie growled "Eat lead, Cobra!" while Duke exclaimed "Let's go shopping!"

By 1999, Barbie's fortieth-anniversary year, the doll was talking a whole new game. The impossibly stacked fashion plate (she was originally based on a sexy German cartoon character) was rejiggered as a "lifestyle brand for girls," and a new series of ads did the impossible, selling Barbie without an actual doll. The campaign featured black-and-white photos of human girls playing hockey and basketball, with taglines including "Girls Rule" and "Become Your Own Hero." Only the unassuming pink Barbie logo in the corner of the ads revealed Mattel's involvement.

The campaign wasn't the only deliberate move away from Barbie's math-challenged past. The year 1999 also brought the launch of Mattel's official partnership with Girls Inc., a then-new nonprofit whose mission statement is "inspiring girls to be strong, smart, and bold." In exchange for a donation of $1.5 million from Mattel, Girls Inc. shared insights and expertise gleaned from their work with real-life girls that would, in theory, make Barbie less likely to remain a ditzy PR nightmare. Isabel Carter Stewart, the executive director of Girls Inc., announced that the organization was "delighted to have Mattel—a corporation that has such a tremendous impact on the lives of girls—as our partner. Their products help girls dream about the future, and our programs help girls prepare and plan to meet their goals."

On Mattel's part, there was initial reluctance to enmesh the corporate vision of Barbie with the tacit feminism in Girls Inc.'s language. As a spokeswoman admitted to the *Washington Post* in March 1999, "There were a lot of people [at Mattel] who bristled at the [phrase] 'strong, smart, and bold.' They thought that was too strong for Barbie."[12] But as former *Hues* and *Adios Barbie* editor Ophira Edut pointed out at the time, Mattel had recently seen both dwindling sales figures and a rise—thanks in part to the Internet—of feminist writing that positioned Barbie as a bane of female self-esteem. A grab for relevancy, not to mention some of the sweet girl-power cash that was changing hands during that decade, must have seemed like a winning move; though, as Edut pointed out, "Ads telling girls they can 'be anything' or 'become their own hero' are only wrapping the Mattel message—buy our products now!—in a vaguely girl-positive package."[13] (One of the partnership's first results was President Barbie, who was available in Latina and African-American versions in addition to the blonde-bobbed Caucasian one, and came with both a blue power suit and a red formal gown in order to emphasize her bipartisanship.) Things got rocky when the ever-alert fundamentalists of the American Family Association decided that American Girl dolls, also owned by Mattel, were tainted by association; the AMA petitioned American Girl to disassociate, calling Girls Inc. a "pro-abortion, pro-lesbian advocacy group." The partnership ended, and though presidential-candidate Barbie was revived briefly in 2008 and 2012, becoming her own hero took a backseat to becoming a fashion model, a princess, and a "pet stylist."

Your Body, Your (Consumer) Choice

The history of drawing on feminist language and theory to sell products has been driven by the idea that female consumers are empowered by their personal consumer choices—indeed, that choice, rather than being a means to an end, is the end itself. The idea that it matters less *what* you choose than that you have the right to choose is the crux of "choice feminism," whose rise coincided with the rapid, near-overwhelming expansion of consumer choice that began in the 1980s. Consumption, always associated with status, became elevated as a measure of liberation and swelled with the self-obsession of the privileged but insecure. Tom Wolfe identified this dynamic in his coinage of the term "Me Decade," and later satirized it in his 1987 novel *The Bonfire of the Vanities*. Historian Christopher Lasch, author of the 1979 bestseller *The Culture of Narcissism: American Life in an Age of Diminishing Expectations*, laid the enshrinement of a cycle of consumption and neediness at the doorstep of the advertising and marketing industries, but also excoriated left-wing movements, feminism included, as enablers. (The temperamentally antifeminist Lasch would later target burgeoning marketplace feminism in his posthumously published collection *Women and the Common Life*, writing that "the feminist movement, far from civilizing corporate capitalism, has been corrupted by it. It has adopted mercantile habits of thought as its own.")

The feminist cultural historian and media critic Susan J. Douglas has noted, for instance, that the success of advertising to women in the 1980s hinged on its effective pairing of status and power with liberation. As neoliberal, greed-is-good, if-I-have-an-umbrella-it-must-not-be-raining rhetoric became the common tongue of the overclass, luxury beauty products, designer labels, and exercise regimens (*Buns of Steel*, anyone?) became liberatory achievements, rather than mere consumer goods. "For women in the age of Reagan," wrote Douglas, "elitism and narcissism merged in a perfect appeal to forget the political already, and get back to the personal, which you might be able to do something about."[14] The representations of choice in a time of tacit postfeminism translated neatly into what could be called "empowertising"—an advertising tactic of lightly invoking feminism in acts of exclusively independent consuming.

Take the infamous 1994 billboards for Wonderbra that featured model Eva Herzigova looking down in delight at her suddenly pneumatic breasts swelling out of a scalloped black bra, alongside the words "Hello Boys." The Wonderbra had been sold in the UK since the mid-1960s, but sales rocketed up thanks to the billboards. The ads worked so well in part because they were tongue-in-check (others in the series read "Look me in the eyes and tell me you love me" and " . . . Or are you just happy to see me?"), but also because they assumed a level of what feminist theorist Angela McRobbie calls "feminism taken into account"—a belief that the movement's success has rendered it irrelevant as something to be considered in shaping culture. You can almost hear the rationale proffered in the Wonderbra billboard concept review: "This would *seem* sexist if we didn't know better, but we do know better, and because women *know* we know better, this is, in fact, empowering." If Herzigova, Kate Moss, and the millions of other women who sent Wonderbras flying out of department stores were making the choice to wear this underpinning, and they're exhibiting sexual agency in doing so, such logic went, what's more feminist than that?

There are no concrete numbers on how many consumers indulged that postmodern reading of the ads, but based on Herzigova's own reflections twenty years later, probably not a ton. Recalling the billboards (which, in 2011, were voted the most iconic ever by Britain's Outdoor Media Centre), she initially told the UK's *Mail Online*, "My Wonderbra campaign empowered women. . . . It didn't degrade them like some said."[15] But in the same article, Herzigova complained that when she tried to shift from modeling to acting, Hollywood executives wanted to check out her underthings first: "I met people who said, 'Yes, we can talk about the movie over dinner.' I was, like, 'What dinner? I can just read the script here.'" The fact that the supposedly empowering ad did nothing to chip away at the routine sexualization of women—that it might have further galvanized it, even—didn't seem to register.

By the mid-2000s, the theme of consuming as liberatory seemed to have gone full-on absurdist, typified by diet-frozen-entrée purveyor Lean Cuisine's 2004 pitch for its new frozen pizza: "The vote. The stay-at-home-dad. The push-up bra. The Lean Cuisine pizza." Implying that the push-up bra is a women's-rights development on par with political enfranchisement—and that a diet frozen pizza is equivalent to a revisioning of domestic gender roles—makes it seem like there'd be nowhere left to go in the shameless-sales-pitch department. And yet, there was always more to co-opt for fun and profit: that same year, an ad for Barely There lingerie posited that if Betsy Ross had been invited to sign the Declaration of Independence, she would definitely have wanted to do so in well-fitting undergarments. In the TV ad, model Shalom Harlow, as Ross, announces, "I want panties that don't ride up so I can sign the Declaration of Independence and then go to the fireworks. I wasn't invited to those events. I was home upholstering a chair. But if I were there, I'd be Barely There," an assertion that was apparently on-brand enough that no one involved in its creation realized that it was also batshit nonsensical.

And, in 2006, as a wave of state restrictions on both abortion and contraception rolled across the United States (including a controversial statewide ban in South Dakota), Gardenburger decided to debut its new tagline, "My Body, My Gardenburger." It was part of a winky campaign that borrowed famous progressive slogans ("Make Gardenburgers, Not War," "Peace, Love, and Hominy"), but there had to have been *someone* working for the company aware that it was a particularly terrible time to be conflating consumer choice with bodily autonomy.

Empowertising not only builds on the idea that any choice is a feminist choice if a self-labeled feminist deems it so, but takes it a little bit further to suggest that being female is in itself something that deserves celebration. The ego, already so key to effective advertising, is indispensible to empowertising, with its emphasis on the "personal sell" that takes the focus off objective value and places it firmly within the buyer's sense of individual mythology. What Douglas pinpointed as liberatory narcissism wears a different guise than it did in the 1980s—one that's less concerned with status or possessions than with the very state of womanhood.

Let's consider chocolate ads, since we all know that women's love for chocolate is rivaled only by our passions for shoe shopping and scented candles. Ads that portrayed women as constantly fiending for it, rationalizing it, and sexualizing it were part of the monetization of women's lib in the 1960s and '70s—the new, independent woman, ads implied, could get almost everything she needed from chocolate. But both sexual double standards and the belief that women should remain restrained in all appetites have held fast, so in the 1990s and early 2000s, the empowerment potential of chocolate hinged on both transgression—portraying both chocolate and its female eaters as "sinful" and "decadent"—and absolution. In the former category, there were ads that featured women draped in yards and yards of rippling brown silk, as well as lots of references to "melting." In the latter, there were chocolates who played the role of the cheerleading best friend in a romantic comedy, assuring you that everything was great. The individually wrapped Dove Promises, for instance, each contain an almost aggressively peppy affirmation: "Keep your chin up and a stiff upper lip. Maybe stick your ass out a little," advises one. "Draw yourself a bath," urges another. (Because if there's anything a woman likes more than chocolate and shoe shopping, it's a bath. Can I get an amen?) A third simply says, "You go girl! You deserve this"—since there's always the chance that even on the brink of popping a wee chocolate square, women will be consumed with so much self-doubt and anxiety that an extra push from a candy wrapper is required.

Seems harmless enough—but these messages are one part of the larger picture of female consumers encouraged to think of consumption as striking a blow for women's equality rather than just, you know, being hungry and eating some chocolate. Yogurt advertising and marketing has worked a somewhat similar angle in positioning what should be a gender-neutral snack as deeply, essentially feminine. The fervor with which women in yogurt commercials bond over their love of fruit-flavored dairy has made for excellent satire, including comedian Megan Amram's viral "Birth Control on the Bottom" satire and a *Saturday Night Live* skit in which Kristin Wiig played real-life Activia spokesperson Jamie Lee Curtis as a yogurt fanatic who can't stop pooping. It remains an irresistible target because even when actual yogurt ads address their own feminine myths—non-yogurt foods are guilty pleasures, yogurt is a "good" substitute for sweets—they do nothing to change them. One memorable Yoplait ad of the mid-1990s featured two disgruntled bridesmaids turning to yogurt for solace, soon exclaiming that the yogurt was "not-catching-the-bouquet-good" and "burning-this-dress-good." It was an attempt to subvert gendered beliefs (wait, don't women *love* weddings?) while deftly pressing others (yogurt is something that women just naturally crave completely apart from its associations with dieting).

Sell It, But Don't Yell It

Advertising's pitch to feminists has changed over time, from "liberated" versions of feminine standbys (the personal douche, the pushup bra, the low-cal frozen food) to the liberation inherent in consumer choice itself. But recently, the pitch has become a bit more nebulous. Two thousand fourteen introduced a new breed of empowertising with an ad for Verizon called "Inspire Her Mind." In it, a girl in various stages of child- and teenhood is discouraged at every juncture by an offscreen voice—when she's stomping through a creek ("Don't get your dress dirty!"), when she's examining marine life in tidepools ("You don't want to mess with that"), when she's building a rocket in the garage ("Why don't you hand that [drill] to your brother?"). The final scene finds the girl stopping in front of a science-fair poster in a school hallway, pausing, and then dejectedly using the window's reflection for that most stereotypically girly act: applying lip gloss. The voice-over: "Our words can have a big impact. Isn't it time we told her she's pretty brilliant, too?" appeared as statistics on how girls are often steered away from STEM (science, technology, engineering, and math) fields bloomed on the screen.

Another ad, for Always menstrual products, involved filmmaker and longtime girl-culture chronicler Lauren Greenfield asking adults to pantomime running, fighting, and throwing "like a girl." They did so with exaggerated, simpering steps and rubber-wristed movements. Greenfield then asked actual girls to do the same activities, and they followed directions with a fierceness untainted by stereotype—throwing, running, and fighting with their entire bodies engaged and their faces full of intent. Afterward, Greenfield followed up with both the kids, who were genuinely confused by the idea that doing things "like a girl" was meant to be an insult, and the adults, who were well aware. The text in the ad then noted that girls' self-confidence drops dramatically at puberty, and urged viewers to redefine what "like a girl" means.

The "Inspire Her Mind" ad centered on drawing more girls to STEM fields, an issue that's gained a lot of cultural traction, outreach, and funding in the past decade. For the campaign, Verizon partnered with MAKERS, the digital initiative aimed at showcasing the stories of women globally; its voiceover was done by Reshma Saujani, founder of the organization Girls Who Code. A section of Verizon's Web site called "Responsibility" elaborates on the company's efforts to raise awareness about girls' STEM education and showcases its partnerships with women's-and-girls' advocacy organizations. It's hard not to be moved by the evocative photos and videos of young, multicultural GWC graduates on the Web site—one holds a hand-lettered sign that reads "Great ideas STEM from diversity"—and it helps that nothing in either the Web site or the ad itself is explicitly selling a product to its audience. The unspoken message is, "Hey, we're the carrier who cares about your (or your daughter's) potential, so choose us."

Likewise, Always's "Like a Girl" spot wasn't pegged to any new product in the brand's line, but seemed simply to have been created to position the brand itself as one that's conscious of how stereotypes and beliefs about girls and women affect their lives. A section of the Always Web site titled "Fighting to empower girls everywhere" focuses on the brand's partnership with organizations like the Girl Scouts of America (for its #BanBossy campaign, a partnership with the Lean In Foundation launched in 2014) and UNESCO, with which Always works to deliver products to rural areas in Nigeria and Senegal where lack of access to pads equates to missed school days and decreased opportunities for girls.

Here's the thing we all know about advertising to women: the products aimed their way, from household cleaners to cosmetics to personal-care products, are pitched to solve a problem that in many cases the consumer might not ever know she had until she was alerted to and/or shamed for it. (Wait, I didn't *know* my armpits were supposed to be sexier!) What this new slate of commercials announced was that, finally, it seemed possible for the ad industry to reach women without making them feel totally awful about themselves. In 2014, after decades of women's movements, that was advertising's big breakthrough: don't make women feel like shit and they're more likely to buy your product. An incredibly low bar had been cleared, and everyone rushed to pat themselves on the back for it. Suddenly, there was a name for the phenomenon: "femvertising"— or, excuse me, #Femvertising. It was a hot topic on ad-industry trade sites, and panels on how to do this astonishing new thing of not insulting women became a draw for conference slates and seminars. A 2015 *AdWeek* roundup was titled "These Empowering Ads Were Named the Best of #Femvertising"; and that year's BlogHer—a yearly convening of lifestyle and brand-friendly women's media—featured a #Femvertising awards ceremony.

It is worth wondering what made the likes of Verizon and Always suddenly turn to the empowerment and well-being of women and girls as a strategy. After all, Always had been content to coast on its products' wings for years, with such bland, cheery taglines as "Have a happy period. Always!" and copy that focused on Dri-weave technology and "quick-wrap" packaging. Previous to 2014, Verizon's claim to fame was the cute, bespectacled "Can you hear me now?" guy. It probably sounds overly cynical to question the motives of a brand when their end result seems as genuine as the "Inspire Her Mind" and "Like a Girl" campaigns. But given the emphasis on the brands themselves and not the products, it's tempting to think that their pitches were, in a way, for feminism itself.

For a second, anyway. Empowertising can suck you in that way, and because there are so few commercials that celebrate, say, the athletic skill of preteen girls, of course they're going to stand out. But looking closer, it's the same old pitch—in Always's case, one that does everything it can to decouple girls' lack of confidence from the shame they're still taught to feel about their menstruating and developing bodies. ("Have a happy period, Always!" at least *mentioned* the word "period.") The ad seemed especially reticent in the context of a feminine-products market that has in recent years successfully harnessed humor and absurdism to send up the earnestness of the period-marketing past: Kotex, for example, marketed its U by Kotex line with commercials in which women mused, "When I have my period . . . I want to hold really soft things, like my cat . . . sometimes I like to run on the beach . . . I like to twirl . . . in slow motion." By the end, the spot just comes right out with it: "Why are tampon ads so ridiculous?" The upstart menstrual-product subscription service HelloFlo, meanwhile, has managed to make menstrual products downright delightful: their long-form ads incorporate nods to how young girls actually *feel* about their periods—excitement, fear, embarrassment, pride—and, as a bonus, dare to use the word "vagina" in pitching their service.

The Internet, social media, and the rise of rapid-response media criticism have undoubtedly played a substantial role in getting corporations to understand that even if a brand's bottom line is solid, it has to at least appear to care what its customers think. It used to be that a print ad or commercial that insulted women—think of those that wound up in *Ms.* magazine's "No Comment" section—might garner a stack of strongly-worded letters to a brand's corporate HQ, but there was little to keep the ad from continuing to run. More recently, it's a wildly different story: the same ad would very likely be the basis for well-placed blog posts at Forbes, the *Wall Street Journal*, and Copyranter, callouts on Feministing and Clutch and Autostraddle and

Bitch, an untold number of pointed tweets, and very possibly an online petition at Ultra Violet or Change.org. It's depressing that responses like this are consistenly necessary, but public shaming has turned out to be an incredibly effective way—and, in the case of ads offensive to women, perhaps the *only* way—to get brands thinking about the impact of their messages and imagery.

And at a time when audiences are choking on consumer choice, marketing with a purpose is no longer just a value-add for companies, but a crucial part of brand identity. In September 2014, a few months after both the Always "Like a Girl" and the Verizon "Inspire Her Mind" ads premiered, *Ad Age* reported on their effects as measured by the Advertising Benchmark Index. It found "that not only do a majority of consumers feel the ads promote a positive message for women, [but] they have a strong, positive impact on the brands' reputation. 'Given the subject matter, the call-to-action scores were higher than might be expected,' said ABX president Gary Getto."[16]

Advertising has one job to do, and it's not to reflect the nuances of social movements. But the staggering growth and spread of the medium in just the past two decades—from its slow creep into new physical spaces (shopping-cart handles, sports leaderboards, public-transit tickets) to its primacy in the digital realm (sponsored Tweets and Instagram posts, responsive Facebook ads) to its sneaky guerrilla and viral manifestations—has meant an attendant growth in power. If, as media scholars like Jean Kilbourne and Sut Jhally have spent decades arguing, advertising's power is both cumulative and unconscious, it will absolutely continue to play a crucial role in the ongoing project of gender equality.

Still, there's a vast difference between using the language of empowerment to suggest that being able to choose between three different kinds of diet frozen pizza is a radical accomplishment and helping to create a world where diet frozen pizza isn't something that needs to exist in the first place. (Or, at least, isn't something marketed solely to women.) And the difference between feminism and marketplace feminism is just as vast, which is why the designation of femvertising is useful, if not necessarily in the way it was supposed to be. Empowertising and femvertising are both ways to talk about the business of selling to women without conflating examples of that business with actual feminism. They're a gateway toward learning more about specific issues that impact women and girls; maybe they're a way to discover alternatives to mainstream products. But celebrating the ads themselves simply celebrates advertisers' skill at co-opting women's movements and selling them back us—and then rewards us for buying in.

CHAPTER 2

Heroine Addicts:
Feminism and Hollywood

"I talked to so many men. I walked into room after room after room of men who got to sit around and discuss whether they thought this movie was something that would appeal to women." —Jill Soloway, in *Entertainment Weekly*, 2014.

Just a smidge less inevitable than death and taxes is the summer Hollywood-blockbuster season. It's the time when the big studios roll out their "tentpole" franchises, so named because their behemoth profits finance the rest of the year's lesser-grossing output. It's the time when Spiderman, Batman, Iron Man, and other Mans take their rightful place in full surround sound and movie execs slide behind the wheels of their Teslas with dollar signs in their eyes. It's not, generally, a time when you hear a multiplex contender described as "an incredible feminist movie," and "the feminist action flick you've been waiting for." Except, in May of 2015, it was. The movie was *Mad Max: Fury Road*—the fourth installment, neither prequel nor sequel, to the Australian series about a former cop navigating the lawless realms of an unforgiving future wasteland. And the praise was near-universal: *Fury Road* garnered a coveted "99 percent fresh" score on the Tomatometer at film review site Rotten Tomatoes, and prompted the *New York Post*—a paper never known for taking any interest in feminism—to declare it "the feminist picture of the year."

I love big pointless explosions as much as anyone (I paid to see *Armageddon* in theaters. Twice.), but, like most feminists with a film habit, I've come to expect certain things from the female characters in big-budget action franchises that aren't called *Alien*. They're often presented initially as strong, smart, and steady—that is, until they're called into service as catalysts for the male hero's journey, at which point they're likely to be kidnapped, terrified, chained to a bomb, or whatever. Sorry I just spoiled a bunch of superhero movies for you!

Having grown up in a time when Mel Gibson wasn't yet a garbage person, and the *Mad Max* trilogy was the pinnacle of postapocalyptic cool, the idea that its dystopia could be a place where women seized power didn't seem too off-script, especially given Tina Turner's iconic portrayal of *Beyond Thunderdome*'s corrupt Aunty Entity. Still, encomiums like the ones being flung *Fury Road*'s way rarely come around in the realm of big-money Hollywood action franchises. Even more intriguingly, the movie's trailer and poster, which prominently featured star Charlize Theron, prompted a small but loudly aggrieved cluster of male bloggers to boycott the film on the grounds that it was some sort of pyrotechnic Trojan Horse freighted with feminazi propaganda. ("I'm angry about the extents Hollywood and the director of *Fury Road* went to trick me and other men into seeing this movie," complained one.) *Fury Road* hadn't been anywhere near my summer-movie to-see list; my husband, who has seen each previous *Max* movie approximately 250 times, didn't even realize there was another one. But hearing that the film's very existence was chapping antifeminists sent me off to the theater immediately, so thanks, guys.

Fury Road is indeed a movie that is explicitly about the damage caused, to women and men alike, by patriarchy, and about the desperate measures some will take to escape that system. Max (played now by Tom Hardy) has been so broken down by his past attempts to do right by his fellow humans that he's gone feral, mute and tortured by flashbacks to the deaths he's failed to prevent. So while he's the familiar character of the story, it's Theron's Imperator Furiosa who is its catalyst. Furiosa is the War Rig driver for Immortan Joe, a masked warlord who presides over The Citadel, where he wields his power over the starving masses, keeps women as breeding and milking stock, and uses Max and others as "blood bags." Furiosa is a buff survivor of untold atrocities with an Erector set of an arm and a plan for redemption that involves spiriting away the patriarch's prized harem and braving hundreds of miles of harsh terrain to get to the "green place" of her birth. Between Max's PTSD and Furiosa's grim single-mindedness, there's minimal plot exposition, so subtext does the talking. Male lust for power and control of resources has leached the land of its vitality; the warlord has spawned thousands of sickly boy-men who have been told, like the Vikings before them, that dying in battle is their one chance at glory. And the green place, it turns out, is gone, its only legacy a satchel full of seeds guarded by a motorcycle gang of elderly, gunslinging First Mothers.

I loved the movie, though that doesn't matter. Others didn't, which also doesn't matter. What does matter is that the most-feminist-picture-of-the-year accolades set the tone for a debate that wasn't so much about the movie itself but about feminism as an objective metric of quality. The many articles and blog posts touting *Fury Road*'s feminist bona fides were countered by an attendant raft of "well, actually . . ." rejoinders (one of which was actually called "Actually, *Mad Max Fury Road* Isn't All That Feminist, and It Isn't All That Good, Either"). For every person who enthused about Theron's stoic embodiment of Furiosa, there was someone who thought that she was too pert-nosed and perfect-looking to be realistic. Those who thought that a gross patriarch squirreling away the hottest women for his own pleasure seemed pretty on point as a postapocalyptic scenario butted heads with those who felt that a *real* feminist movie wouldn't feature a harem that resembled a Calvin Klein perfume ad.

This conversation wasn't particularly productive, but it deftly illustrated some of the disquieting facets of marketplace feminism. One is that the descriptor "feminist" now seems to be used to lavish praise on anything that isn't overtly degrading, demeaning, or exploitative to women. Another is that arguments over whether a movie is "feminist" or "not feminist"—especially when that movie never intended to claim either[1]—suggest that feminism is not a set of values, ethics, and politics, but merely an assessment of whether or not a product is worthy of consumption. *Fury Road* was undoubtedly a triumph of marketplace feminism. It was a boon to people who love big, dumb explosions but could do without the damsels in distress. It was a telling window into the mind of chauvinists and their fear of a world where women stand on equal footing with men. But it's not clear yet whether it will have any effect on what has for almost a century been one of pop culture's most openly unequal industries: Hollywood.

The Feminist Fallacy

Marjorie Ferguson coined the term "feminist fallacy" in her 1990 essay "Images of Power and the Feminist Fallacy" to describe the belief that representations of powerful women in media translate into "cultural visibility and institutional empowerment" for actual women, asking, "Do we . . . study depictions of women in literature, film, television, and print media as an end in itself? Or do we study those depictions as a means to an end?"

More than twenty-five years later, this question seems more relevant than ever. There's been no lack of what are now called, sometimes with the verbal equivalent of eye-rolling and/or air quotes, "strong female roles" in the history of cinema, and thanks to specialized film festivals, streaming services, and sites like YouTube and feminist video portal nist.tv, they're more accessible than ever. An incomplete list of movies often referenced on feminist blogs and listicles as feminist classics includes expected fare like *Queen Christina*, *The Color Purple*,

Thelma and Louise, *Born in Flames*, *9 to 5*, and the *Alien* franchise, but also *Clueless*, *Waiting to Exhale*, *Steel Magnolias*, *Fried Green Tomatoes*, *Set It Off*, *The Accused*, and *Real Women Have Curves*. In other words, the elements of what makes a film feminist can be as varied as the characteristics of the people who watch them.

But though there are endless forums where you can make a case for, say, the stealth feminism of *Legally Blonde*s 1 and 2, it's been frustratingly clear that there is indeed a glaring feminist fallacy in the big-screen realm itself. There is a difference between a movie offering a clear feminist lens on a subject—a way to "read" its text as something that reflects or is informed by feminism—and the film itself being feminist. After all, strong women on film—and resonant, powerful, nuanced stories about them—are not new. They've been in existence since film has been an industry. But their long-standing presence has done little to change the contemporary values and assumptions of that industry. In Hollywood history, cycles of women contributing to and then disappearing from central roles both in front of and behind the camera don't reflect the feminist movements of the time so much as they speak to an anxiety about the market for movies—anxiety that, over time, has become increasingly gendered.

In the silent-film era, Hollywood's film industry grew quickly to meet audience demand, and thus it was more pragmatically welcoming to women writers, editors, directors, and producers than it would be at any other time afterward. Directors like Dorothy Arzner, Lois Weber, and Alice Guy-Blaché (the latter widely considered to be the first true "auteur" of cinema), and actor-producers like Mary Pickford (founder of United Artists studios) and Clara Bow created films that weren't the escapist fantasies Hollywood would come to prize, but human stories that included complex relationships and forward-thinking subject matter: Weber's *The Hand That Rocks the Cradle*, for instance, was about the need for legalized birth control. At one point, women headed up dozens of production companies. But, as film journalist and historian Melissa Silverstein notes, "As it became more about money, the women behind the scenes disappeared." The expensive technology that turned silents into "talkies" beginning in the 1920s necessitated the involvement of Wall Street, which invested in young studios and became the big bosses of directors and producers, imposing a masculinized and increasingly sex-segregated workforce as part of the burgeoning corporate studio system. Women in powerful creative and decision-making roles were suddenly seen as amateurish and unprofessional; for the male-dominated financial forces that took charge of the Hollywood economy, and with larger and larger amounts of cash at stake, they were simply too much of a risk.[2]

Onscreen, representations of women followed a similar trajectory. In what's now known as the pre-Code era of Hollywood films, women were smart, professional, ambitious, forthright, opaque, tricky, even criminal. They blackmailed bosses, had babies out of wedlock, seduced other women—and the thrillers were even steamier. Jean Harlow's *Red-Headed Woman* was a brazen social climber more than willing to seduce any man to get what she wanted; Barbara Stanwyck, in *Baby Face*, was an exploited young woman who used sex to move from penniless to paid ("She had IT and made IT pay" leered the film's poster). And, of course, there was Mae West, the bombshell vaudevillian, playwright, producer, and model for every one of Samantha Jones's *Sex and the City* single-entendres, whose winking catchphrases—"Come up and see me sometime"; "When a girl goes bad, men go right after her"—have long epitomized pre-Code Hollywood's sassy repartee. It's not that the heroines essayed by these dames were *like* men; they weren't. They were simply as human onscreen as the men, as full of appetite and humor and stubbornness and fallibility. And that was part of the problem that the Hays Code was enacted to fix.

The Motion Picture Production Code of 1930 was created under former Postmaster General Will Hays to ensure that Hollywood no longer produced films that might "lower the moral standards of those who see [them]." The Code detailed ways in which films must be plotted and written so as not to tempt audiences into crime, revenge, or moral ambiguity, and it devoted special attention to issues of adultery, interracial relationships, "impure love" (including homosexuality and transgender relationships), and even dancing. Nudity was verboten, the mocking of religion a no-no. "Art can be morally evil in its effects," warned the Code. "This is the case clearly enough with unclean art, indecent books, suggestive drama."

Enforced from 1934 until 1968, the Hays Code's vision of right-minded filmmaking was an equal-opportunity wet blanket: the catalyst for it was the sensational manslaughter trial of silent-film star Roscoe "Fatty" Arbuckle, who stood accused of the lurid death of a young starlet in his hotel room. As dispatches from the trial buzzed out from radios and wire services, Hollywood's moral turpitude became a national obsession, and the industry realized that a program of self-regulation was necessary if it was to avoid harsher government meddling.

But there's no question that the rules laid out in the Code—among them, that "impure love . . . must not be presented in such a way to arouse passion or morbid curiosity on the part of the audience"—had much broader implications for representations of women than they did for men. In his 2001 book *Complicated Women: Sex and Power in Pre-Code Hollywood*, film critic Mick LaSalle noted that the Hays Code was especially preoccupied with the lives of women onscreen, seeing portrayals of fulfilling careers, sexual hungers, and lives that didn't depend on one man as unnatural and—that word again—"impure." It wasn't immorality so much as it was gender equality that put the Code's authors and administrators in a lather—or perhaps the two were indistinguishable. Either way, the fun and the freedom were effectively quashed; as LaSalle puts it, the Code "was designed to put the genie back in the bottle—and the wife back in the kitchen."

The Code's enforcement effectively kneecapped the possibilities for female characters and put in place a view of men and women that was literally and figuratively black and white. Its first and most powerful administrator, Joseph Breen, was a devout Christian, and his position and faith combined to make Hollywood films a place where the uncertainties of life and fallibility of human nature found no quarter. Under Breen's watch, nobody used birth control or got divorced. If a motion picture had a reference to a king-sized bed, Breen was there to suggest two twin-sized ones as a substitute. (That said, his directives did have their upsides: according to Thomas Doherty's 2007 book *Hollywood's Censor: Joseph I. Breen and the Production Code Administration*, Breen was also responsible for removing countless racial slurs from *Gone With the Wind*.)

This rigid belief in moral rightness and nuance-free humanity created a series of fictions that persist to this day. The belief that "good" marriages were made behind white picket fences, by white men and women who had only enough polite, procreative sex to produce two children—that was Breen's. The idea that the only truly "good" wife was one who tucked away her own dreams to further those of her husband and children—that was the vision of the Hays Code. The invisibility of and tacit disdain for people of color, homosexuals, transgender people, people with disabilities—that was Hollywood's neat, uncomplicated, homogenous reality. That these were all committed to celluloid for more than thirty years before the Code was lifted had a profound effect not just on Hollywood's imagination, but on that of America at large. Politicians campaigning on "family values" platforms have long invoked specters of a tragically lost Dick-and-Jane, Father-Knows-Best paradise to suggest that the country was healthier when women and other minorities knew their places. When talking heads and pundits sanctimoniously blame feminism for everything from divorce rates to child obesity to the death of chivalry, they're picking up where the Hays Code left off. When the likes of Mitt Romney and Paul Ryan blame single parents—specifically, single mothers—for America's epidemic of mass shootings and other gun violence, they're using talking points lifted from the Breen playbook, where marriage is a moral shield against untold evils.

The Code's corrective lens on the narrative possibilities for women was cemented in the late 1930s and 1940s, with the rise of so-called women's pictures. A brew of romance and melodrama that earned them the label "weepies," women's pictures were the original chick flicks, built from the ground up to appeal to what their creators had come to believe about female audiences: They sought out sap; they lusted not for sexual autonomy but for the snare of married love; and, with the advent of World War II and the departure of sons, husbands, and brothers overseas, they were looking for escapism.

The handprints of the Hays Code were all over the plots of women's pictures: where women had been the architects of their own lives, now they were the victims of them. The chief themes were abjection and self-sacrifice in the pursuit of love and motherhood, often to the point of sickness and madness; and the screen pulsed with a moralism that pitted women against one another, often in the form of doppelgangers. In motion pictures that were written and directed by men like William Wyler and Douglas Sirk, plot points that centered on women's suffering set the tone for decades of movies where the only sympathetic woman was a wronged wife or mother.

Nineteen thirty-seven's *Stella Dallas*, 1942's *Now, Voyager*, and 1945's *Mildred Pierce* remain three classics of the genre, united in their tacit approval of characters who all but erase themselves for others, no matter the cost. *Now, Voyager*'s repressed spinster, Charlotte (Bette Davis), emotionally abused by her mother, ultimately finds fulfillment in caring for the similarly scarred daughter of her unhaveable lover. Its most famous line—"Don't let's ask for the moon. We have the stars"—speaks to that lover's disbelief that Charlotte, unmarried and with no child of her own, could possibly be happy with her lot. And both *Stella Dallas* and *Mildred Pierce* center on women (played by Barbara Stanwyck and Joan Crawford) who do everything they can to make their respective daughters' lives an improvement over their own, yet are eventually shunned by the bratty, ingrate social climbers they've raised.

There was a pedagogical point to what film historian Jeanine Basinger called the "unquestionably demented" plots of many women's films: before women could make the right choice—the proper, self-abnegating one—they had to be sufficiently punished for making the wrong one. This is hardly different from the lessons for women scripted into contemporary chick flicks, which find their hapless heroines entertaining audiences with a series of cringeworthy mistakes. Bridget Jones embarrasses herself in front of Salman Rushdie and wears a Playboy Bunny outfit to a staid garden party; *What's Your Number?*'s Ally Darling pretends to be British and pratfalls all over the place in her attempts to hide from various ex-lovers; Katherine Heigl, in *The Ugly Truth*, unwittingly wears vibrating underwear to a business dinner, where the remote falls into the hands of a little kid. And so it goes, movie after movie, each woman rewarded with the right man and the promise of a happy future only after she's been appropriately mortified by her own terrible decisions. Then, as now, there's no success without a whole lot of abjection.

And yet the era of the women's picture remains an anomaly in American cinema. These weren't movies about women as supporting characters, written to better highlight the story of a leading man; the women themselves were the subjects. Probably no surprise, then, that film critics sniffed at them. Despite their industry recognition (Davis and Stanwyck received the Academy of Motion Pictures' Best Actress nominations, and Crawford won for *Mildred Pierce*) and financial success, the critics largely derided women's pictures as sappy melodramas whose main crime was that they were too, well, *female*. The minutiae of women's lives was irrelevant, charged critics. The plots were outlandish, the concerns of women solipsistic, the emotions overblown: over the years, critics used hundreds of words to issue a blanket sneer to women's films. This reception wasn't a new one, nor was it specific to the genre; these male critics echoed a disdain for female-targeted media that had been in place since the 1850s, when Nathaniel Hawthorne complained to his publisher about the "damned horde of scribbling women" whose books outsold his own. And those critical assumptions about the worth of female attention persist to this day, where it's alarmingly easy for both sexes to discredit entire cultural phenomena—Nicki Minaj, women's basketball, romance novels—by deeming them too "girly" for the discernment of critical eyes that are still, by default, male.

Indie-pendent Women

As with the era of silent pictures and that of women's pictures, the indie-film boom was one of the few points in Hollywood history where a critical mass of movies were made with a female gaze in mind. It's hard to think of a time when women had more of a diverse presence on the big screen than they did during the late 1980s and early 1990s, when a rapidly growing number of filmmakers working outside the big studios found their work in high demand thanks largely to the success of a Sundance hit called *Sex, Lies, and Videotape*. All of a sudden it was the age of the anti-blockbuster. Film festivals sprouted up across the country, and small development and distribution outfits focused on amplifying the voices and visions of filmmakers outside of Hollywood's baseball-capped boys' club were suddenly on the industry's radar. The result was that films not only about women, but also about radically varied groups of them, proliferated in small theaters and screening rooms across the country.

Lesbians loved, labored, and lost in *Desert Hearts*, *The Watermelon Woman*, *Go Fish*, *The Incredibly True Adventures of Two Girls in Love*, *Heavenly Creatures*, and *All Over Me*. Women grappled with race, love, and identity in *Just Another Girl on the IRT*, *Zebrahead*, *Mississippi Masala*, and *Eve's Bayou*. Tough and vulnerable girls navigated friendship, violence, and selfhood in *Girls Town*, *Ruby in Paradise*, *Trust*, *Mi Vida Loca*, and *Gas Food Lodging*. Women in remote places created magic in companionship in *Daughters of the Dust* and *Baghdad Café*. Punk girls wreaked havoc in *I Was a Teenage Serial Killer* and *The Doom Generation*, and femmes fatales vamped it up in *Bound*, *The Last Seduction*, and *La Femme Nikita*. With a rise in independent-minded media like *Sassy*, *Spin*, *BOMB*, and *Film Threat* pointing the way, it was a great time to be a feminist who loved sitting alone in the dark: I spent the years between 1990 and 1994 seeing these films, some more than once, in the art-house theater down the street from my college campus or at New York City's Angelika, feeling inspired and wildly lucky and blissfully ignorant of what was happening at the multiplexes.

Indie film of the 1990s didn't remain truly independent for long. Just as major record labels in the early '90s began snapping up the small imprints that gave us Nirvana and Guided by Voices, big studios sought out their own imprimaturs of cool via indie properties. With media conglomeration and vertical integration, indie film was co-opted almost as quickly as it had come on the scene. Time/Warner, Twentieth Century Fox, Disney, Universal, and Paramount bought up indies like Miramax (which has since regained its independence), brokered distribution deals, or started their own in-house concerns. By the latter half of the 1990s, most of the majors had independent divisions, like Fox's Searchlight Pictures or NBC/Universal's Focus Features; television's Independent Film Channel was launched by the Bravo network; and the Sundance Channel, created by Showtime, brought alternative goodness to film fans all over the country. And though the Independent Spirit Awards, or "indie Oscars" had been founded in 1984 (as the Friends of Independents Awards) to showcase films that were, as 1990 keynoter Martin Scorsese put it, "innovative out of inspiration as well as necessity," by 1996 IFC was broadcasting them as a low-key awards-show alternative.

As the profile of independent film rose and became part of the Hollywood machinery, though, the economics of the studio system began, just as they did in the early part of the twentieth century, to press out much of what made indie films a true alternative: namely, creators who didn't resemble the majority of big-time moviemakers.

Take *Just Another Girl on the IRT*, the 1992 film that told the story of Chantal, a smart and smart-assed high-school junior whose dreams of going to college and becoming a doctor are thrown into uncertainty when she gets pregnant. The story was notable not only for having a young, female, and black protagonist, but also for dealing with the issue of abortion and reproductive choice with a straightforwardness that was quickly becoming obsolete. Leslie Harris wrote, directed, and produced the film expressly to offer a fresh take on black women and girls in the movies. ("I was just tired of seeing the way black women were depicted, as wives or mothers or girlfriends or appendages," Harris told the *New York Times* in 1993. "She's the central character. There's no male character to validate her.") *Just Another Girl* was a standout at the Sundance Film Festival in 1993: indie hitmaker Miramax picked it up for distribution, Harris took home a special Jury Prize, and *Rolling Stone*'s Peter Travers raved about the film, calling it "artfully stylized, explosively funny," and identifying Harris as a "bracing new voice." The movie even turned a profit. The director could reasonably have expected to set off on a trajectory similar to that of fellow indie directors like *Sex, Lies, and Videotape*'s Steven Soderbergh, but she didn't. By 2002, when she was interviewed for an article in *Salon* about the lack of female directors, Harris had been trying for ten years to get a second movie funded, to no avail: "I've been told — a lot — that black women can't carry a film."[3] In 2013, Harris used crowdfunding to finance her new feature, *I Love Cinema*.

A 2013 study co-commissioned by the Sundance Institute and the nonprofit organization Women in Film confirmed that Harris's experience was consistent with a pattern of behind-the-camera stagnation for female film directors. The study found that, while the numbers of women and men graduating from film schools were nearly equal, from 2002 to 2012, women represented less than one-third of the more than eleven thousand writers, directors, producers, and cinematographers whose work has been shown at the festival, with little change in representation over those years. But women are *over*represented in

Sundance's list of one-hit wonders—films that, like *Just Another Girl*, were lauded at the festival only to languish upon release. The female directors of festival faves like *The Tao of Steve*, *The Woodsman*, *Blue Car*, *Girlfight*, and *Winter's Bone*, though embraced at Sundance (and, in Debra Granik's case, at the Oscars, where *Winter's Bone* was nominated for Best Picture in 2010), didn't get the kind of immediate support and industry mentorship necessary for a robust career—or even a second film.

It's worth comparing their careers and name recognition to the male directors who also debuted at Sundance and have since gone on to become some of the biggest names in Hollywood filmmaking—among them Soderbergh, Kevin Smith, the Coen brothers, David O. Russell, and both Andersons (Wes and Paul Thomas). Look at any list of "Sundance's Breakthrough Directors" and you're more or less guaranteed to see one male, white face after another. Do these guys just happen to make better movies, write more universally gripping stories, cast more appealing actors? Many people would likely argue that they do. But it's equally possible that the sure-footed appeal of their movies is the product of an undeniably gendered power structure wherein "the money" invests in male directors' potential from the start because executives already identify with them. (As director Mary Harron put it, "Male executives are looking for fantasy versions of their younger selves."[4])

The 2013 Sundance/Women in Film study asked fifty-one independent female filmmakers how their gender had affected their careers in films. In their answers, five key challenges stood out: "gendered financial barriers," "male-dominated networks," "stereotyping on set," "work and family balance," and "exclusionary hiring decisions." The first of these was the most overwhelmingly cited as having impacted the careers of women, with more than 43 percent of the respondents reporting having experienced gendered financial barriers, including lower production budgets, producers and investors being reluctant to trust female directors with big-budget features, "female" subject matter being deemed commercially unviable, and more. Discussing the findings of the study, Keri Putnam, executive director of the Sundance Institute, told *Entertainment Weekly* that female directors "do considerably better at Sundance than they do in the mainstream studio industry," noting that a more general lack of diversity in that industry makes executives and funders simply see women as outsiders—and thus, unlikely to make it into the hiring loop in the first place, particularly for big-budget projects. Put simply, "As budgets increased, the presence of women decreased."[5]

Alison Anders—who like many of her colleagues from the '90s indie boom, including Lisa Cholodenko, Lesli Linka Glatter, and Martha Coolidge, now works mostly directing television—made the point succinctly: "I've seen men who can't direct their way out of a paper bag make a film that bombs, and they turn around and get a huge studio film. . . . When our movies don't [succeed], we don't get a chance to make a second movie."[6] More recently, first-time director Desiree Akhavan, a young Iranian-American woman whose first film, 2014's *Appropriate Behavior*, drew instant raves, frankly noted on the podcast *Death, Sex & Money* that received wisdom about gender affected her sense of creative potential to begin with. "Two male filmmakers this year have told me, 'Why don't you just go ahead and make a B-minus second film?' . . . . I don't think I have the luxury of making a B-minus second film if I want to keep working. Who's going to finance the film after [the B-minus film]?"

At the root of this split is a fundamental difference in the way women's perspective is understood as a single entity standing apart from men's stories and visions. It's a perspective that's been devalued for much of history as canons of literature, film, music, and more have ingrained a tacit understanding of (white) men's stories as universal and women's as special-interest. (Back in 1996, David Foster Wallace tipped his hand when referring to any writers who weren't white and male as "tribal.") So when people complain—and they do—about surveys like Sundance's being "bean-counting," they're missing the point. It is about numbers, but more important, it's about what those numbers *mean*, about beliefs in the value of "men's stories" and "women's stories," not to mention an acknowledgment that—as *Fury Road* amply illustrated—these are not mutually exclusive categories. It shouldn't be a radical notion that the experiences of women have the potential to be as universal and as broadly felt as those of men. Yet two key beliefs—that women are only capable of telling women's stories, and that women's stories are still special-interest ones, tribal and uncompelling and even alien to men—hold particularly fast in Hollywood.

With much of the blockbuster business centered on international audiences, female directors' chances of breaching the gulf between indie and blockbuster may be getting even worse. Inkoo Kang, who covers film for *IndieWire*'s *Women in Hollywood* blog, notes that the studios are "quite aware" of the gender and race imbalance, but from a financial perspective, they'd rather take their chances on serving the international market than on serving the women here at home. "What they're banking on," she says, "is the status quo of racism and sexism that's already in the general public. And, unfortunately, the international audience is more racist and more sexist than mainstream American culture. So I don't really see much of it changing."

What Women Watch

Hollywood's long-standing woman problem has been so entrenched for so long in part because it's been kind of a family secret: Those who benefited from and invested in it saw it as the norm; those who might have wanted to protest risked their careers if they did so. And efforts to compel the motion picture industry to implement hiring practices that better reflect the demographics of filmgoing audiences are not new. Evidence of pattern race and sex discrimination in hiring practices in the 1960s prompted a series of hearings by the Equal Employment Opportunity Commission, which resulted in an investigation that found—what do you know?—discrimination in hiring practices.

A 1978 report issued by the California Advisory Committee to the U.S. Commission on Civil Rights reported in its findings that "despite claims to the contrary, minorities and women are poorly represented in decision-making positions in the motion picture studios," and, notably, that hiring practices make minimal use of official job descriptions, evincing instead "an overdependence on word-of-mouth recruitment."

Institutions like the New York Film Academy and the University of Southern California's Annenberg School for Communication & Journalism have funded studies that quantify inequality in everything from speaking roles (one USC study found that of 2009's one hundred top-grossing movies, only 30 percent of speaking roles were female) to how women are portrayed onscreen (in a survey of the top five hundred films from 2007 to 2012, for instance, the NYFA found that 28.8 percent of female characters wore sexually revealing clothing, as opposed to 7 percent of male ones). Surveys like this existed well before the advent of the Internet—Donna Allen's Media Report to Women, for instance, began chronicling women's participation in and creation of media in 1972; the Celluloid Ceiling Report has been published annually for almost twenty years by Martha Lauzen, executive director of the Center for the Study of Women in Television and Film at San Diego State University. But the blog posts, think pieces, and number-crunching infographics that regularly issue from these organizations and others have amplified them immensely. Online viral incubators like Upworthy send out bite-sized factoids, graphics, and videos like all-points bulletins, crafted for snacky shareability. Blogs like *Women in Hollywood*, *Shadow and Act*, and more report on nearly every aspect of the industry that relates to gender and race. And jaw-dropping anecdotes from the anonymous Tumblr called Shit People Say to Women Directors & Other Women in Film (Sample: "I'm not being sexist but it would be better to talk to a man in that meeting. Let's reschedule until [he] can make it") became a source of communal ire only hours after it debuted in the spring of 2015.

And yet, even as evidence of outright discrimination piles up like unsolicited scripts—even as the American Civil Liberties Union announced, in early 2015, a new investigation into the hiring practices of Hollywood's major studios—film-industry players regularly tell us that we're living in a time of unprecedented womanity at the movies, both behind and in front of the camera.

Take John Fithian, the CEO of the trade group National Association of Theatre Owners, who predicted at an industry convention that 2015 would be "The Year of the Woman" in movies, noting that female-identified moviegoers had already accounted for 60 percent of tickets sold to lady-friendly releases like *50 Shades of Gray*, *Insurgent*, and *Cinderella*. Fithian went on to add that he was "so pleased that my daughter can see more women in leading roles than ever before."[7] (As the key liaison between movie-theater owners and the film industry, one might rightly wonder why, if it was so important for Fithian's daughter to see more women, he hadn't made any previous overtures toward the industry, but okay.) A few months later, more year-of-the-woman accolades rang out from the prestigious Cannes Film Festival, where filmmaker Agnès Varda was given the festival's lifetime achievement award—the first time in sixty-nine years it had gone to a woman—and, in another first, the film chosen to open the festival, *Standing Tall*, was one by a female director.

According to the *Variety* article that reported on Fithian's address, his prediction departed somewhat from conventional wisdom. It noted that while "most analysts are betting that the domestic box office will exceed $11 billion for the first time ever, their confidence is largely based on a slate of fanboy fare such as *Avengers: Age of Ultron* and *Star Wars: The Force Awakens*." Meanwhile, the excitement over *Standing Tall* kicking off Cannes was a conscious PR move by its head, Thierry Frémaux, spun to downplay the reality that the festival, arguably the world's pacesetter for prestige films, has a dismal track record when it comes to showcasing those made by women. (*Standing Tall* was one of two films screening—out of nineteen total—that was helmed by a woman; the previous three years' respective totals were two, one, and zero.)

Declaring variations on "Year of the Woman" pronouncements in Hollywood has, over the past decade or so, become a very weird way in which the media continually lowers the bar on expectations. If, say, only 12 percent of lead roles in the hundred top-grossing Hollywood movies are women's roles—which was the case in 2014—then a few percentage points' increase the following year will be cause enough for effusiveness about how good things are getting. In 2012, despite noting that "it would be silly to proclaim, on the basis of a handful of roles, that some kind of grand role reversal has taken place," A.O. Scott's *New York Times Magazine* article on women's roles ("Hollywood's Year of Heroine Worship") was titled in a way that did just that.

I asked Martha Lauzen, who authors the annual Celluloid Ceiling Report, about the prevalence of what seems like an almost pathological optimism about women in the industry that insists, despite what the numbers say, on repeating that women have more power in Hollywood than ever before. It's a misguided notion, she agrees, that's fueled by two crucial things. "First, people see high-profile women succeeding—Kathryn Bigelow, for example—and assume that women have 'made it.' A few of these cases can dramatically alter people's perceptions of reality, which is why it is so important to actually count the number of women working in powerful behind-the-scenes roles and on screen every year."

The second thing, Lauzen offers, is that pondering the extent to which things haven't changed in decades is just *unbelievably depressing*, and Hollywood is nothing if not an aggressively feel-good business. "People have a very strong desire to believe that things get better every year," wrote Lauzen in an email, adding that "representatives for organizations with an investment in the status quo do their best to encourage this belief." She mentioned a statement that Cheryl Boone Isaacs, the president of the Academy of Motion Picture Arts and Sciences (the first African-American to hold the position, and only the third woman) had made in the wake of 2015's announcement of Oscar nominees, a list that had no nonwhite names in any of the acting categories and no women nominated for either writing or directing. Boone emphasized that the Academy was "committed to seeking out diversity of voice and opinion," but Lauzen wasn't convinced that this was anything more than an attempt to tamp down public derision like that of the #OscarsSoWhite hashtag that promptly scorched a path through Twitter.

There have always been wonderful, multifaceted, inspiring, funny female film characters (though admittedly most of them have been white). Likewise, there have always been robust female audiences, not to mention people of all genders who gladly vote with their dollars in favor of more female-directed, -produced, or -focused movies. But that hasn't changed the overall attitude of movie executives toward either female stars or female audiences: instead, the prevailing belief is often that if such a film succeeds at the box office, it's some kind of wild, unprecedented fluke. The same is true for movies with majority-non-white leads, a fact that nonwhite filmmakers have emphasized over and over, apparently unheard, as studio executives scratch their heads at "overperforming" recent films like *McFarland USA* and *The Best Man Holiday*. (Lee Daniels, director of *The Butler* and *Precious*, has been especially pointed: "What does it take for people in Hollywood to see that black people will come out to see a movie?")

When *Bridesmaids* was released to critical acclaim and crackerjack box office receipts in 2011, it was greeted by Hollywood critics and analysts as though it had literally never occurred to anyone in the industry that: a) a comedy starring a female ensemble cast could be funny; and b) that women would haul ass to the theater to watch such a thing, and not even on date night. The headlines everywhere, from trade papers to movie blogs, all seemed to ask variations on one question: *What kind of sorcery is this?* Sure, its raunchiness—in the form of anal-bleaching jokes, foul language, and, of course, the collective gastrointestinal meltdown in a bridal atelier—was a newish twist on the female-ensemble film. But was the concept of a female-ensemble film new? It shouldn't be, assuming you've heard of a few recent pictures called *Sex and the City* ($153 million), *Mamma Mia!* ($144 million), and *The Devil Wears Prada* ($125 million), to say nothing of past hits like *9 to 5*, *Waiting to Exhale*, *Steel Magnolias*, *Charlie's Angels*, and *Working Girl*.

Nevertheless, *Bridesmaids'* surpassing of box office estimates (it grossed $288 million worldwide) incited a flurry of studio and media interest that, much as it was supposed to be good news, highlighted just how regressive the industry is. *Business Insider* reported that "Studios were paying close attention . . . to see how it would do before they greenlit other female projects."[8] Producer David T. Friendly wrote an entire article in the *Hollywood Reporter* congratulating himself for actually calling up a female screenwriter to discuss a project. As with the aforementioned female-focused hits, *Bridesmaids* ushered in a spate of think pieces in which reporters (invariably, but not exclusively, male) tried to pinpoint just exactly where this nutty new women-going-to-the-movies trend had started; and along with those came a disquieting amount of people patting themselves on the back for supporting it.

The belief that women, as well as nonwhite people, are not an audience has been Hollywood's most naggingly persistent fiction. Nora Ephron noted, shortly before her 2012 death, "It is always a shock to people at studios that women do go see movies"; Nia Vardalos, whose *My Big Fat Greek Wedding* remains one of the most successful indie films in history, revealed in a 2009 *Huffington Post* article that she'd been asked by a studio executive to change the sex of the lead character in her next film from female to male because "women don't go to the movies." (The same exec, who apparently lives somewhere inside his own ass, called high-grossing female-fronted films like *Sex and the City* and *Obsessed* "flukes.")

Meanwhile, the idea that male audiences might possibly be expected to reciprocate the attention that women have always paid to their onscreen buddy capers, shoot-outs, space flights, romantic trials, existential struggles, car chases, and dick jokes is, in Hollywood, almost laughable. "Studio executives believe that male moviegoers would rather prep for a colonoscopy than experience a woman's point of view, particularly if that woman drinks or swears or has a great job or an orgasm," wrote the *New Yorker*'s Tad Friend shortly before *Bridesmaids* came out, in a piece that grimly laid bare the industry's lack of prospects for female comic actors. "Funny Like a Guy: Anna Faris and Hollywood's Woman Problem" brimmed with unconcerned statements from anonymous studio executives ("Let's be honest, the decision to make movies is mostly made by men, and if men don't have to make movies about women, they won't"), references to constant dieting, and anecdotes from women about being told to "get some tits." Everyone quoted in the article described this as business as usual, even when they knew it shouldn't be.

But let's back up: Did *Bridesmaids* work as a floodgate-opener for female-focused movies? Well, yes and no: a few female filmmakers—including *Bachelorette*'s Leslye Headland and Kay Cannon, who wrote *Pitch Perfect* and its sequel—noted that its blockbuster status success definitely helped their own films get made.[9] And *Bridesmaids'* gross-out factor might have made Hollywood more likely to get on board with something like Maggie Carey's raunchy 2013 sex comedy *The To Do List* (which, among other things, revisited *Caddyshack*'s famous poop-in-the-pool gag). But the flip side is that each one of these films, not to mention other post-*Bridesmaids* efforts, were inevitably compared to their predecessor and found wanting. The fear that *Bridesmaids* director Paul Feig articulated—"The whole time we were getting ready to do this movie, I had a lot of angst: if I screw this up, Hollywood is just waiting for an excuse to say, 'See, you can't do a movie with this many women in it'"—shifted to filmmakers who now had to worry about any female-friendly project they made being panned with negative comparisons. Attaching a male name to the project *and* invoking *Bridesmaids* is something of a fail-safe, as was made clear by the promotional posters for 2015's summer hit

Trainwreck, directed by Judd Apatow. Though it was written by and starred Amy Schumer, her name was absent from the posters: instead, they read "From the guy who brought you *Bridesmaids* . . . ," a reach that, while not technically *un*true—Apatow produced the film, but Paul Feig directed it, and the script was by star Kristin Wiig and Annie Mumolo—was meant as audience assurance. ("Don't panic, guys—this is kinda like that other thing you grudgingly concluded was 'pretty funny for a chick film.'")

There's even more cultural mulishness when it comes to action movies either directed by women or featuring female leads. When they succeed, as with the nail-biting war narrative *The Hurt Locker* (directed by Kathryn Bigelow) and the boxing drama *Million Dollar Baby* (starring Hilary Swank), they're brushed off as lucky breaks, shining exceptions to the rule that women and grit don't mix well. When such movies fail, however, their performance is used to buttress the belief that "women don't see action movies" or "female directors can't do war films," or any number of other industry maxims. In 2009, an internal memo from the desk of Jeff Robinov, president of production at Warner Brothers, surfaced on Hollywood reporter Nikki Finke's blog: the studio would no longer be doing any films with a female lead. It seemed that after the disappointing box office returns of the Jodie Foster action drama *The Brave One* and the Nicole Kidman thriller *The Invasion*, Robinov decided to put the onus for the studio's underperforming movies squarely on women—a move, noted Finke, that was reductive to a bizarre degree. ("I'm told he doesn't even want to see a script with a woman in the primary position.") After all, plenty of Warner Brothers films with male leads—in fact, with majority-male casts—had underperformed at the box office in roughly the same time period as *The Brave One*, including the George Clooney–starring, Steven Soderbergh–directed *The Good German*, the brotastic western *The Assassination of Jesse James by the Coward Robert Ford*, the sinking-ship remake *The Poseidon Adventure*, and the superhero reboot *Superman Returns*.

Duds like these were even noted in an October 2006 *New York Times* piece titled "After Big Flops, Warner Hopes for 'Sleeper' Hit in Smaller Films." And yet we can assume that none of these disappointments resulted in Robinov and his fellow executives deciding that maybe movies with male leads were the problem. That he felt comfortable decreeing that female-led movies were, though, was naked sexism of a kind that has long existed in Hollywood. Warner Brothers issued a statement reading, "Contrary to recent reports in the blogosphere, Warner Bros is still committed to women. . . . Jeff Robinov insists he is moving forward with several movies with women in the lead. Indeed, he is offended by rumors of his cinematic misogyny." But a look at the list of Warner Brothers films released between the time of the memo and 2013, when Robinov left the studio, suggests he was true to his original words.

In this realm—a place where 51 percent of the population is still disregarded as a troublesome niche audience not worth expending money and energy on—making what can be praised as the summer's or the year's or the decade's most feminist film means, in many cases, simply making a film that acknowledges women.

The Bechdel Baseline

"I'm *tired*," says Melissa Silverstein, the founder of Women in Hollywood. Silverstein is among a number of women who have parlayed their frustrations with the Hollywood status quo into producing a yearly film festival; the one she organizes, the Athena Film Festival, presents a slate of films that highlight "women's leadership" (though they need not necessarily be directed by women). We're talking on the phone shortly after her return from 2015's Cannes festival, and she's referring to the years after years of year-of-the-woman plaudits. While surely well-meaning, she emphasizes, they obfuscate how much hasn't changed while letting progressive-minded critics bask in the feeling that by even seeing a movie like *Spy* or *Trainwreck*, they're striking a blow for feminism. As it happens, a few days before we talked, the *New York Times* had featured two male columnists, Frank Bruni and Ross Douthat, talking about women's roles with the clubby pomposity of those who have the luxury to discuss women's equality as an occasional rhetorical diversion. "I can't even begin to read that," sighs Silverman. "I'm tired of praising people for doing what is right in [supporting] diverse films."

Marketplace feminism runs on that kind of artful hyperbole, and, to be very honest, it's easy to get caught up in it—especially if you want to at least attempt to be optimistic about the prospect of change. Let's say you read a story, as many of us did recently, about thirty-seven-year-old Maggie Gyllenhaal being informed that she's too much of a crone to play the love interest of a man twenty years older, and, right after it, a story about how *Bridesmaids* director Paul Feig is dedicating himself to directing and producing comedies starring women. It's likely the latter that you'll want to share on social media with a dancing-lady emoji and a bunch of exclamation points. Most of us are tired of not only the bad news itself, but of being made to feel like we're focusing only on the negatives and ignoring imminent positives like an all-female reboot of *Ghostbusters*. (Which I, personally, plan to see the shit out of.) I'll admit that I've often wondered if our complicity in this kind of smoke-and-mirrors display is part of why the industry has been so slow to change.

Silverstein doesn't think so, instead pointing to the lack of a critical mass of films by and/or about women all happening at once, a filmic version of a girl gang roaring toward the industry. "As [*Selma* director] Ava DuVernay said, 'The math is against us,'" she notes. "One movie by a woman or about women can always be dismissed. But six at one time can't. Critical mass is talked about as the key in politics, it's talked about in business. There have to be enough of these movies being successful enough at once that it can't be brushed off as a fluke."

If there's any kind of silver lining here, it's that more people than ever are talking about Hollywood's woman problem as pattern behavior, rather than movie-by-movie shortcomings. Feminist analysis of movies was for a long time a niche concern, with critics like Laura Mulvey, Molly Haskell, B. Ruby Rich, bell hooks, and others writing outside mainstream media to academic or otherwise self-selecting readers. But in just the past two decades, thanks mostly to the advent of the Internet, a wealth of feminist film criticism has emerged via blogs like Silverstein's own Women and Hollywood, as well as webzines, fan communities, and other participatory media. *Bitch*'s very first issue featured analyses of two then-timely films, *Kids* and *Sleep with Me*, whose representation of women and sexual themes we knew mainstream reviewers would gloss over; twenty years later, digging into feminist themes is itself, in many cases, mainstream fare.

What this means is that movie audiences, especially ones who are nonwhite and non-male, are in many ways speaking a completely different language than the people who create the movies. Hollywood's version of "feminist" content often feels like presenting a graduate student with a copy of *Pat the Bunny* and saying, "I heard you love to read!" Marketplace feminism, in the form of mainstream movies where women get to kick ass and take names, is increasingly responsible for a bridge across that gulf. But in a time when ostensibly "feminist" content has become a moviegoing trend, the bridge might be less sturdy than Hollywood thinks.

The Bechdel Test's swift glide into the lexicon of film criticism is a fascinating, if sometimes frustrating, dimension of marketplace feminism. For those who haven't heard of it, the test is named for graphic novelist Alison Bechdel, who started her career with a comic strip called *Dykes to Watch Out For* that followed the lives of a close-knit group of multicultural activist lesbians. In the 1985 strip "The Rule," the butch, acerbic Ginger and her date ponder what movie to see, and Ginger explains that she requires a movie to pass three basic tests: "One, it has to have at least two women in it, who, two, talk to each other about, three, something besides a man." The punch line ("the last movie I was able to see was *Alien*") underscores just how rare it is to find a movie that satisfies even these basic requirements. The test (though Bechdel credits the test itself to her friend Liz Wallace, it retains her name) began to be name-checked in blogging and online film criticism in the late 2000s, and, thanks to the power of the Internet, was a full-fledged meme by 2010, when the Web site bechdeltest.com began logging movies that passed the test.

As the Bechdel Test began to creep into the sightline of mainstream movie criticism, it was notable to see the surprise of some male critics that their favorite movies—*One Flew Over the Cuckoo's Nest*, *Goodfellas*, *The Princess Bride*, *Clerks*, the original *Star Wars* trilogy, the entire *Lord of the Rings* trilogy, and even *Tootsie*, when you get right down to it—so soundly flunked it. For many women, the reaction was more of a shrug, along with relief that, finally, there was a simple way to help writers and directors step over an embarrassingly low baseline. To be clear, applying the rule isn't about snatching away the well-earned status of *Raging Bull* or *The Godfather* or even *This Is Spinal Tap*. As Anita Sarkeesian, creator of the Web site Feminist Frequency, noted in a 2009 video about the rule, "It's not even a sign of whether it's a feminist movie, or whether it's a good movie, just that there's a female presence in it."

The latter point is something that many people fail to grasp when trying to explain away why their favorite movies don't pass the test ("But Batman is the hero of the movie! Of course the women characters are going to talk about him!"): the Bechdel Test is not a judgment of quality or nuance. After all, the beautiful, moving *Gravity* fails the test, while a formulaic rom-com like *27 Dresses* passes with no problem. But the test itself is a simple, bloodless assessment of whether female characters are deemed important to a story—and a way to conclude that, most of the time, they aren't.

Its simplicity hasn't kept the test from being denounced as politically correct nitpicking or, worse, a nefarious plot to make all movies conform to feminist dogma. In 2013, a small coalition of theaters in Sweden announced a pilot project that would rate movies according to the Bechdel Test, awarding passing films an A. One of the organizers, Ellen Tejle, told the Associated Press that seeing more women onscreen would mean opening up more imaginative possibilities for women themselves: "The goal is to see more female stories and perspectives on cinema screens." Naturally, this proclamation was greeted with outrage from other film-industry machers, who protested that the test prioritized a limited view of what makes a film meaningful, placing quantification above ineffable qualities of character development and plot; the CEO of the country's Ingmar Bergman Foundation called the new rating "the final sacrifice of meaningful cultural criticism at the altar of honourable stupidity."[10]

Feminist and antiracist film critics and fans have noted the limitations of the Bechdel Test and proposed further, similar kinds of measures: Shortly after the 2013 release of robot-battle movie *Pacific Rim*, one Tumblr user proposed the Mako Mori Test, named for one of the film's scarce but beloved characters. It tweaks the Bechdel criteria in small but specific ways, suggesting that the bar is cleared if a movie has "a) at least one female character; who b) gets her own narrative arc; that c) is not about supporting a man's story."[11] A rule named for TV critic Eric Deggans proposes that a show/movie passes the test when it features at least two nonwhite characters in the primary cast of a movie or TV show that is not about race. And former *Bitch* editor-in-chief Kjerstin Johnson suggested, after seeing 2015's *Ex Machina*, that assessing female nudity in films would also be a useful measure. ("How long [is she] naked? For whose pleasure are the shots? Is she a corpse?")

Part of the problem with the Bechdel Test is that its utility has been elevated way beyond the original intention. Where Bechdel and Wallace expressed it as simply a way to point out the rote, unthinkingly normative plotlines of mainstream film, these days passing it has somehow become synonymous with "being feminist." It was never meant to be a measure of feminism, but rather a cultural barometer. After all, the *Twilight* movies, which are essentially about a young woman in a semi-abusive relationship with a vampire and a slightly more autonomous one with a werewolf—squeaks over the baseline. *Bride Wars*, the 2010 movie in which Kate Hudson and Anne Hathaway play best friends who go full-bore Bridezilla when they schedule their nuptials on the same day, hurdles over it, as does *Sin City*, a movie in which almost every female character is either sexualized as a stripper or prostitute, or the victim of horrific male violence. Meanwhile, wonderful films like *My Dinner With Andre* (a movie that is literally just two men talking) or *Run Lola Run* (in which the titular character is onscreen, though largely silent, almost every second) are whopping Bechdel Test failures. And films by, say, a director with avowedly worrying attitudes toward women (waves to Woody Allen, my personal *bête noire*), can't be considered feminist by most stretches of the imagination, but are undeniably Bechdel-friendly.

In a marketplace-feminist world, it's all too easy to imagine writers and directors who essentially game the system, scripting in just enough named female characters and not-about-men conversations to clear the benchmark while doing nothing to alter the overall sexism. In some cases, it already seems to be happening: the 2014 Marvel blockbuster *Guardians of the Galaxy* boasted a female screenwriter and a trio of Strong Female Characters, but was also beset with what reviewer Gavia Baker-Whitelaw called "a miasma of douchiness" that included green-skinned assassin Gamora (Zoe Saldana) being called a "whore" by one of her male space colleagues and another one suggesting that she use sex to spring them all from prison.[12] As with the special-interest attitude toward female directors, it's very easy to dole out the Strong Female Character roles here and there to make sure there's an empowerment factor in otherwise formulaic films. It's much harder to actually commit to changing the attitudes of both moviemakers and audiences.

Still, as one part of what Silverstein calls the Film Equality Movement, the test is undeniably useful—not as an ending point, but as one producers, writers, and directors can jump off from. It offers a language for pointing out the pattern sameness of Hollywood product; it gives a framework and a context to story editors and producers who have been regularly ignored when they point out to their bosses what's missing from scripts and plotlines. The Bechdel Test has grown to be something of a standard for people who write about films, if not yet for those who make them.

Which brings us back, at least briefly, to *Mad Max: Fury Road*, the feminist fallacy, and what makes a cultural product feminist. It's not just a female writer and/or director, as we know from the oeuvres of Nancy Myers and Nora Ephron, delightful as kitchen-porn fare like *It's Complicated* and *Julie and Julia* might be. It could be a movie with a Strong Female Lead® doing stuff usually reserved for dudes, but it just as easily might not be. It's the job of Hollywood to be honest in its attempts to do better by diverse moviegoers—and if it takes an investigation by the ACLU to get that done, so be it—but it's also the job of invested audiences to help change the conversations and the standards. Getting beyond marketplace feminism requires that we reword the question of "Is *Mad Max* (or *Trainwreck*, or whatever) feminist?" because otherwise we're suggesting that what matters most about a movie is that people who identify as feminists can enjoy consuming it with a clear conscience.

Treating feminism as a fixed metric flattens out the narrative possibilities that make people want to see movies in the first place. Seeing a movie that's not feminist doesn't keep anyone from watching it through a feminist lens. *Fury Road* would be good, loud, manic fun whether or not it passed the Bechdel Test mainly because, like other dystopian films before it, looking closely at the narrative yields a stark condemnation of how patriarchy hurts everybody. The rush to laud the movie for simply not being the usual woman-sidelining fare dished up by Hollywood during those all-important summer months is far less rewarding—because, ultimately, it presses the conclusion that it's the most we should hope for.

CHAPTER 3

Do These Underpants Make Me Look Feminist?

"I am remembered as a hairdo. It is humiliating because it reduces a politics of liberation to a politics of fashion." —Angela Davis, 1994

Granny panties are the new feminism. That's not me talking, that's the *New York Times*, which, in early June 2015, featured an article on the front of its Styles section about the white cotton staple of the supposedly old and sexless. Apparently, they were on the comeback trail thanks to a new set of young, female entrepreneurs designing indie underpants, one style of which features the word "feminist" on the butt. "Young Women Say No to Thongs" presented sales figures indicating a declining market for thongs and an expanding one for fuller styles as evidence that we're in the midst of a feminist undie uprising. To quote one panty peddler, "Most lingerie is designed to appeal to a man. . . . For us, that's not even a consideration. This is underwear you wear totally for you." (Unless, as the piece pointed out, you display your undies to Instagram in "belfies," a word I'm very sorry to have just foisted on you.) Remember when we thought the next horizon of feminism was going to be wage equality or universal health care? Turns out, it's underpants.

The *New York Times* article was promptly picked up by multiple online outlets that parroted its claim: "Why Granny Panties are Cool Again" (*Refinery 29*), "Watch Out Victoria's Secret: Women are Abandoning Sexy Underwear" (*Business Insider*), "The Rising Popularity of 'Granny Panties' Could Be Tied to a Healthier Perception of Beauty" (*Huffington Post*), and the oddly grave "Young Women Opting for Granny Panties Over Thongs, According to Report" at the *NYT*'s own Women in the World blog were among headlines touting the granny-pants revolution.

There are a few things to say about this story. The first is that it was not a "report," but rather a trend piece. The second is that, as a trend piece, it was perfectly on-brand for the *NYT*'s Styles section: Draw attention to something that a very small group of privileged people are doing (deciding that something once uncool is now cool, building a business around that thing), and write about the thing as though it reflects a national shift in aesthetics. Downplay the rarefied nature of the product itself (the undies profiled sell for $25, $34, and $45 apiece). Overstate the facts. (Is a 7 percent downturn in thong sales really that significant?) Make sure the people making the products are young and cute enough to be photographed wearing their own product, in this case underpants with "Feminist" printed in pink across the butt. Encourage a tenuous connection with body or beauty politics that builds significant buzz for whatever's being sold.

But let's say that this granny-panties piece wasn't an opportunistic leap onto the current wave of feminism-is-cool media that also had the chance to grab readers with pictures of half-naked young women. If that were the case, the following would still be true: *Feminism has nothing to do with your underwear*, and anyone telling you it does probably wants to sell you something ($45 underwear, most likely). But the fact that the granny-pants story whirled through the news cycle as though it was an actual feminist breakthrough has everything to do with marketplace feminism's seductive infiltration of fashion.

There have certainly been periods in history that sewed a connection between liberation and undergarments. The Rational Dress reformers of the late nineteenth century sought to bring women out from under layers of wool petticoats, crinolines, and whalebone corsets that limited their movement and mobility; the women of London's Rational Dress Society, for instance, quite reasonably proposed that women shouldn't have to wear more than seven pounds of undergarments. These radical broads were among the many freedom-minded fans of the undergarment popularized in the 1850s by Amelia Bloomer, a Victorian-era feminist and avid bicycler who adapted "bloomers" as a version of the loose pantaloons worn by Turkish women.

Decades later, girdles were among the garments dumped in the Freedom Trash Can from whence the "bra-burning" myth came, at 1968's protest of the Miss America pageant in Atlantic City. Germaine Greer, in her zesty debut, *The Female Eunuch*, famously called the brassiere "a ludicrous invention." And let's not forget that thongs were once marketed as offering their own kind of liberation, if only from visible panty lines and unforgiving wedgies.

In contrast, no outlet that reported on the feminist granny panties that were purportedly sweeping the nation could agree on exactly what they stood for. Were they a nod to increasing body positivity? A response to the gaudiness and sweatshop-iness of Victoria's Secret and its ilk? A corrective to mass-media images that suggest only the young and thin deserve nice knickers? The 'undiepreneurs' profiled in the *New York Times* could only agree on two things: that big chonies are comfy, and that they aren't about what men think. (Which raises a whole other set of questions: Do these women think that only heterosexual and cisgender people wear underpants? Also, have they never heard of Jockey For Her 3-packs?)

As marketplace feminism has fully emerged, perhaps it's not surprising that feminist underpants have become kind of a thing. (There are several small companies that advertise their wares as feminist, as *Nylon* magazine noted in an online slideshow that enthused "Underwear shopping just got a lot more empowering.") Underpants are a safe consumer item to brand as feminist: everyone needs them, they're mostly kept under wraps, and they supply reassuringly normative associations. The rise of feminist underpants is a weird twist on Karl Marx's theory of commodity fetishism, wherein consumer products once divorced from inherent use value are imbued with all sorts of meaning. To brand something as feminist doesn't involve ideology, or labor, or policy, or specific actions or processes. It's just a matter of saying, "This is feminist because *we say it is.*"

This Is What a Feminist Looks Like

"Feminist fashion," for a long time, has been an oxymoron, publicly perceived as a bridge too far for those on both sides. An acknowledgment of style as a feature of feminism extends to acknowledging the trademark clothes and accessories of well-known figures—Andrea Dworkin's sacklike overalls, Bella Abzug's gigantic hats, Gloria Steinem's aviator glasses and concho belts. But very few people have ever presumed that feminists cared for or participated in fashion as an interest or avocation. The ideas key to different feminisms, after all, have historically been anticapitalist—questioning advertising messages, consumer imperatives, and commercialized, Caucasian standards of sex appeal. And besides, feminists were supposed to have weightier things on their minds: to admit that you cared about fashion, or even look like you cared, was to risk having your politics scrutinized. The miniskirts and tall boots that Steinem rocked in the 1970s were the source of a lot of side-eye from her comrades; years later, when feminist literary critic Elaine Showalter penned an article for *Vogue* in which she "came out" as a fashion fanatic and noted that her interest "can sometimes seem a shameful secret life," many of her academic and feminist colleagues, as if to prove the point, promptly turned their noses up at her. The 1990s term "lipstick feminist" always seemed like it was deployed with a barb of disbelief—as though anyone who truly embraced typically feminine trappings was a sham. And it's notable that the handful of fashion designers whose clothes inspire the descriptor "feminist"—including Miuccia Prada, Rei Kawakubo, and Maria Cornejo—are also described as "intellectual," which from what I can tell is a word people use for either very dark or very light-colored clothes that are quirkily draped or full of angles and deliberately show a minimum of skin.

In the past few decades, though, the relationship between feminism and fashion has become more pluralistic and more nuanced. There are body-positive independent designers and retailers whose dedication to selling well-made garments with precise tailoring in larger sizes has been a boon to women whose sizes or shapes most designers and retailers ignore. There are feminist fashion journals and blogs that consider a range of subjects from gender identity and sexual codes to fabric history and construction. There are blogs that offer "upcycling" how-tos designed to keep unwanted clothing out of landfills. And an increased awareness of the feminized labor force that makes fashion accessible—often unregulated, unethical, and dangerous—has kick-started public conversations that are as much about ethics as about appearance. The 2013 collapse of a Bangladesh factory that produced clothes for the likes of Walmart and Joe Fresh, for instance, was a moment of reckoning for a Western population that had come to depend on the "fast fashion" of H&M and Forever 21—cheap runway knockoffs meant to last only a season before being discarded for the next thing. Most of the almost 1,300 workers killed in the collapse were women for whom factory jobs are often the only available work. It was a sobering finger pointed at consumer liberation: it's awfully presumptuous, after all, to extol the feminist self-expression found in fashion when the women who actually make the clothes have no such luxury.

Writer, editor, and actor Tavi Gevinson started her fashion blog Style Rookie at the age of eleven, promptly becoming a media wunderkind who fielded Fashion Week invitations and interviews, and whose following comprised as least as many adults as peers. Style Rookie (which evolved into the online magazine *Rookie*) was precocious in its approach to discussing high fashion as art, but what was even more striking was Gevinson's approach to feminism: At an age when most preteens have about as much interest in gender politics as they do in retirement funds, she was far more articulate than many adults about the way that fashion is scorned as a site of liberation. When I interviewed Gevinson in 2013, she was a senior in high school, editing *Rookie*'s print annuals, fresh off her film debut in Nicole Holofcener's *Enough Said*, and, as she put it, less interested in the fashion world than she'd once been. ("I want to be comfortable.") But when our talk turned to the long-standing antagonism between fashion and feminism, she bristled with fresh annoyance when recalling how many people had brushed off her interest in both. "It was like, 'Won't she just give up this fashion crap and be smart already?' I just remember feeling, 'What, the only people who write about fashion should be stupid?'"

Though Gevinson acknowledged that the industry's obsession with youth and thinness, as well as the racism that has historically permeated it, makes it "deeply flawed," she dislikes the way an interest in fashion itself is dismissed as at odds with intellect and feminist potential. "There was a really stupid piece in the *Guardian*—I was in eighth grade when it came out—called 'Why I Hate Fashion,'" she recalls. "And it was, like, 'I hate ads for stores that tell me that shopping is good, I hate that models are skinny,' and all this stuff. And I was, like, 'Yes, but . . . that's like saying [that you] hate food, because there's McDonalds.' It's so *broad*."

Recent years have brought a sense of possibility that the self-expression found in clothing can be decoupled from the elitist, tone-deaf fashion industry itself. (This might explain why Chanel's "feminist" runway show in 2014 seemed like such a shameless attempt at trend-chasing.) So perhaps it's not surprising that the most visible feminist statement made by clothes these days is a literal statement. Slogans like "Feminist killjoy," "Crush the Patriarchy," or even just a simple "FEMINIST" have become staples of online retailers and independent t-shirt lines. I've never been a slogan t-shirt person myself, but when I saw the news story about an Ohio teen who sent a scathing rebuke to her middle school after someone there saw fit to Photoshop the "Feminist" off her t-shirt in a class picture, I gave her a silent high-five. With the amount of things that people broadcast via clothing—brands, designers, alma maters, sports teams, religious affiliations—taking offense to the word "feminist" just seems bone-headed. (Especially if you're old enough to remember the stretch of the 1990s when it seemed like half the young adults on the street were sporting shrunken baby tees with "Porn Star" and "Sexxxy" emblazoned across the chest.)

Slogan t-shirts have been part of the public face of almost every modern social movement, obviously. But the progenitor of this most recent spate of clothing-as-billboard was the humble white tee, sold by the Feminist Majority Web site starting in 2003, that proclaimed "This is What a Feminist Looks Like." When Ashley Judd wore hers to a *Glamour* magazine shoot, eyes lit up around the offices at *Ms.*, and soon Judd—along with Margaret Cho, Whoopi Goldberg, and Camryn Manheim—appeared on the magazine's cover, proudly representing for Team Feminism. Between 2005 and 2006, the shirts became the Feminist Majority's best-selling item: more than 650 different styles of shirts bearing the slogan were sold through the site, with bulk orders to be distributed or sold on college campuses accounting for many of the sales. The appeal of the slogan was easy to interpret: after all, too many people find the biggest roadblock to embracing feminism is in its unflattering optic legacy. Hags, dykes, ugly, unshaven, angry, finger-pointing, *furious* women—such adjectives and images have been encoded as the truth of what "feminism" represented for so long that it's begun, sadly, to feel natural. The women and men who embraced the shirts were embracing the idea of jarring loose those ancient expectations of who might proudly identify as feminist.

Feminists who weren't fans of the shirt argued that it was overly conciliatory, that the slogan actually seemed meant to reassure others that women could be feminist and still care about being normatively good-looking and attractive to others. The fact that the shirts came in a tight-fitting, shrunken baby-tee style and were expressly marketed to an audience of younger women, they argued, suggested that the point of the shirts was less about proclaiming that feminist stereotypes were pointless than it was about capitulating to the very same beauty standards that feminism wanted to banish. One such naysayer, journalist (and current *New York Times Book Review* editor) Pamela Paul, told *Women's ENews* that she thought the baby tees, in particular, "feed into anti-feminist rhetoric that says that women who stand up for their rights are somehow unattractive, not sexy, humorless and not getting any. . . . I think it's kind of a sad way to represent power." But younger women, in particular, couldn't care less: from just the number who called the *Bitch* office to see if we, too, sold the shirts, it was clear plenty of them were ready to make a simple, declarative statement into a small act of resistance.[1]

The power of "This is What a Feminist Looks Like" owed a lot to the political context from which it emerged. The George W. Bush administration had from its inception mounted an all-out attack on almost everything related to reproductive choice and access. Among the *Handmaid's Tale*–esque undertakings that Bush shepherded or signed off on between 2001 and 2004: Cutting funds for family-planning services while bulking up those for abstinence-only sex-education programs; proposing regulations that would offer health care coverage to fetuses but not to the fully-formed people growing them; establishing National Sanctity of Human Life Day (which, in case you couldn't guess, was not about people already living); curtailing federal funding for stem-cell research; and—my personal fave—appointing to the FDA's Reproductive Health Drugs Advisory Committee one Dr. David Hager, a zealously paternalistic evangelical gynecologist who refused to prescribe contraceptives to his female patients, much less help get FDA approval for Plan B.

And even though the scorched-earth situation going on with respect to women and their bodies was obvious to many people, it was also something of a taboo to discuss it, particularly while the terrorist attacks of September 11 were still so fresh and all-consuming. When I ask Gloria Feldt, the former president of Planned Parenthood Federation of America and the author of 2004's *The War on Choice*, to recall this time, she still seems a bit stunned by how mandatory patriotism threw a kind of invisibility cloak over the widespread dismantling of reproductive rights. "I wrote *The War on Choice* because there was no way in the normal political realm that you could actually lay bare what was going on with women's rights, in public," she explains, her bright voice laced with ire. "Because you would get creamed. You would be considered not credible. *Traitorous.* I wanted to just dispassionately document every single one of the things that the [Bush] administration and their buddies were doing. And when you put them all together, you saw that it was not random attacks. This [was] a pattern."[2]

The "This is What a Feminist Looks Like" t-shirt became popular again in 2014. By this time, it was just one of thousands of offerings in a consumer landscape where a young, Riot Grrrl–inspired feminist aesthetic was available to those who knew where to look: on Etsy, for instance, where you might buy anything from a cross-stitched sampler reading "Ask Me About My Feminist Agenda" to a plush uterus with a stitched-on happy face to wooden earrings bearing the image of Audre Lorde. Or in magazines like *BUST* and *Worn*, which showcased DIY clothing hacks and size-friendly indie lines, as well as throwback girl-culture icons like Jem and the Holograms. *Ms.* had already featured on its cover a picture of Barack Obama, pulling open the top of his button-up shirt, Clark Kent–style, to reveal a Photoshopped "This is What a Feminist Looks Like" t-shirt underneath. Bush-era champions were still giving their all to a rollback of women's bodily freedoms, of course. But in contrast to what Feldt described in the early 2000s, there were more people, connected and galvanized by social media, who seemed willing to come right out and call bullshit on fearful, regressive attitudes about what happens when women are autonomous, sexually confident people.

However, there was something different about the 2014 version of the "This is What a Feminist Looks Like" t-shirt. Created by Britain's Fawcett Society, in partnership with *Elle* UK and the high-street women's-clothing chain Whistles, the tees were part of a line that included sweaters, clutches, and phone cases emblazoned with the phrase. The slogan was no longer broadcast in big, blocky letters, but in arty, thin, hand-drawn type—a branding shift that involved making the words both less confrontational and more aesthetically attractive. "This is the vintage slogan tee to end all vintage slogan tees!" affirmed *Elle* in its September 2014 issue. "First worn by well-known feminists like Tracey Emin, Kirsty Wark, and Shami Chakrabarti, we have teamed up with the forward-thinking team at Whistles to reinvent the iconic tee for the modern feminist. Want one? Of course you do." After decades of knee-slapping hilarity about unkempt gals in Birkenstocks and baggy pants, feminism was finally in fashion. Sure, it now seemed to take the form of trendy, consumable objects for women rather than that of an ethic concerned with human rights, but at least people were talking about it. Right?

"Be a Feminist, or Just Dress Like One"

Author and civil rights activist Angela Davis was not the first black woman to sport an Afro. The radical Communist Party leader, Black Panther, and prison-reform agitator became a household name in 1970 when, as a fugitive, she was named to the FBI's Most Wanted List for her involvement in the assassination of a judge. Her hair, like that of many comrades and colleagues, was inherently political—an expression of the Black Pride movement that embraced natural hairstyles as part of a larger black-is-beautiful aesthetic—but hardly the most notable thing about her. So Davis was taken aback when, as she recalled in a 1994 essay, a woman "introduced me to her brother, who at first responded to my name with a blank stare. The woman admonished him: 'You don't know who Angela Davis is? You should be ashamed.' Suddenly, a flicker of recognition flashed across his face. 'Oh,' he said. 'Angela Davis—the Afro.'"[3] "It is both humiliating and humbling to discover that a single generation after the events that constructed me as a public personality, I am remembered as a hairdo," she wrote.

Twelve years later, Davis was among the icons celebrated in an issue of *BUST* magazine whose cover line announced "Be a Feminist, or Just Dress Like One." The fashion spread inside, titled "Our Outfits, Ourselves"—a wink to classic women's-health guide *Our Bodies, Ourselves*—featured models styled up to look like modern versions of Gloria Steinem, Bella Abzug, Elizabeth Cady Stanton, Kathleen Hanna, Camille Paglia, and Angela Davis, along with inset photos of the actual "fashionable feminists." *BUST* is an emphatically feminist magazine, and the feature was done in good faith; readers familiar with the magazine's cheeky, referential tone knew that the copy wasn't actually advocating for thoughtless co-optation. (The "Be a Feminist . . ." cover line was a reference to a famously cheesy ad for New York's Barbizon modeling school that promised, "Be a model . . . or just look like one.") It also wasn't the first time that *BUST* had paid homage to feminists with fashion sense; an earlier issue featured a two-page spread of real and fictional "feminists fatale" that included Frida Kahlo, Natalie Barney, Josephine Baker, and—you guessed it—Angela Davis.

Still, the fashion spread bothered me in a way I couldn't name at the time. Maybe it's as simple as this: there's a difference between admiring the great style of feminists who came before (but really, though: *Camille Paglia*?) and including fashion credit and store details, commodifying the women as though their clothing is the most salient thing we can learn about from them, as though aping their style is tantamount to activism. That skeptical feeling hit even harder more recently after taking in a spread in the Spring 2015 issue of *PORTER*, the thick, high-end glossy that's the house organ of the online luxury destination Net-A-Porter. "*PORTER* celebrates American feminist Gloria Steinem's clarion call to women, her liberating agenda, and her iconic 1970s style that still inspires and resonates today," announced the introduction to fourteen subsequent pages of color-saturated photos that featured a young Steinem manqué doing vaguely political-looking stuff like talking on the phone, kicking back in a lecture hall, and leaning against a wall with her mouth hanging open in front of handbills reading "MANIFESTO" while a long-haired male acolyte looked on. All clothing and accessories, from the $2,815 leather cape by Salvatore Ferragamo to the $10,610 Tom Ford suit—and, of course, the $1,300 aviators by Cartier for maximum Steinem verisimilitude—were available on Net-A-Porter.

There are some material differences between this fashion spread and *BUST*'s, as well as, say, Davis's inclusion in an online slideshow called "19 Moments in Hair History That Changed the World," which, while still leading with the world's most famous Afro, acknowledges right up front why its owner is legendary. The title of the *PORTER* fashion spread, meanwhile, is "The Way We Were," and, after its aforementioned introduction of Steinem, goes on to say literally nothing else about her. The copy is either clothing and styling credits or hackneyed instructional babble straight out of the Big Book of Fashion Cliché. ("Vamp up a buttoned skirt with knee-high boots to reveal just a flash of skin"; "Function meets femininity in a single-shade cape and skirt duo.")

But it's the subtext of "The Way We Were" that revealed its marketplace-feminist aim: here was a fashion magazine reclaiming a thing its industry never wanted to be associated with until that thing was both mainstream enough to be acceptable and vintage enough to be cool. The spread takes a movement that was in large part about liberating women from constricting societal representations and recasts it as a retro-chic magic hour of long, shiny hair and sharp pantsuits. And however unsettling the *BUST* fashion spreads were, they at least acknowledged feminism as an ongoing, collective movement that encompassed multiple figures, voices, and issues; for *PORTER*, the fight for women's liberation is presented as the work of a single person. This last thing is particularly relevant, both because Steinem herself caught so much flak for the way she was singled out by mainstream media as a spokesperson, and because she has since been outspokenly frustrated by the tendency to frame contemporary feminism solely in terms of palatable icons. (When asked by the *New York Times* in 2012 whether there can be "another Gloria Steinem," she answered, "I don't think there should have been a first one.")

I like fashion magazines. I buy and subscribe to fashion magazines. On early-morning flights, I am that person who looks like she ran straight from a house fire to the airport, but is nevertheless face-first in *Marie Claire* reading about new coat silhouettes. What I'm saying is that I don't have any illusions about what goes into a fashion magazine. I get that their makers are in the aspirational-fantasy business, not the social justice one, and I would not expect a magazine like *PORTER* (or even *BUST*, for that matter) to be, like, "If you want to dress like Gloria Steinem, try the jeans and black turtleneck that are already in your closet." That said, the most discomfiting thing about the "The Way We Were" was what it was showcasing: not smarts, not women's leadership, but something that's currently far more powerful than any of those—feminist branding.

Branding—the series of stories, images, and vocabularies associated with a company and its products—is a concept whose importance has grown, as neoliberalism has grown, to become what's arguably a global orthodoxy of success. We've come to talk and write not of the successes of people or their companies, but of their successes as brands. Everything is a brand: Oprah (obviously) and the Kardashians (inescapably); Apple and Microsoft; Hillary Clinton and Carly Fiorina; and even you, the everyperson, to whom the 1997 *Fast Company* article "The Brand Called You" addressed itself. "It's time to give some serious thought and even more serious effort to imagining and developing yourself as a brand," wrote branding expert Tom Peters at the time. And so we did.

Nicki Lisa Cole, a scholar who's currently at work on a book about the worldwide dominance of Apple, notes that branding has become more important as the labor that creates actual products is increasingly outsourced. "Companies used to stand on their product," she explains. "That was your name, the product that you made. But when you don't actually *make* the product, you have to create something else to sell to people." What becomes valued is the brand.

Until fairly recently, the idea of branding social movements probably would have seemed hideously cynical. Sure, political and social struggles including civil rights and gay pride had their attendant stories, images, and vocabularies, but they weren't considered products; that would suggest a motive that was purely mercenary, rather than about humanity and justice. But the language of branding is no longer native to companies: building your personal brand, branding yourself to appeal to employers and romantic partners, and "leveraging" your brand through social media are actual things people discuss constantly with a straight face. And with everything from Barack Obama's presidential campaign to one-for-one TOMS shoes to #BlackLivesMatter, social movements as branded entities have begun to seem far less cynical than they once might have.

So while previous backlashes against feminism have generally been called what they were—fearful responses to an ideology perceived as threatening to a status quo that works great for those it benefits—in the past several years that narrative has changed. It's not a backlash; it's a "branding problem." In 2013, British *Elle* partnered with three advertising agencies and three feminist organizations to "rebrand" feminism as something cooler and more relevant to young women than they perceived it to be—a sort of makeover for "a term that many feel has become burdened with complications and negativity," as *Elle* put it. Stateside, the women-in-advertising group The 3% Project, along with Vitamin W Media and Miss Representation, sponsored a similar contest shortly afterward, seeking creative visual "rebrands" and urging, "Give feminism some love. Make it relevant and meaningful to everyone." The *Elle* partnerships resulted in three graphically snappy posters: two that were specifically about the act of identifying as feminists, and one that urged women to draw attention to wage gaps by asking their male coworkers what they make. The winning entry of the 3%/Vitamin W contest was a set of posters that proclaimed "Feminism is Human Rights." And . . . that was it. That was the extent of the efforts to rebrand. People who already knew about the rebranding initiatives were encouraged to share the graphics that resulted from them, but there seemed to be no larger plan for spreading the good word of a new-and-improved, quick-dry, lemon-fresh feminism.

Branding as a new lingua franca aside, the idea that a single group or initiative can take a diverse social/political movement with no ownership and single-handedly "rebrand" it was fairly troubling. Rather than strengthening feminism from the inside—reiterating core values and amplifying the multiplicity of voices past and present that have contributed to feminist movements—a rebrand is outward-focused, a recruitment effort to make feminism appeal to as broad an audience as possible by distilling it down to an image and a few words.

That's impossible in a time of pluralistic feminism—a time, in fact, when it's no longer possible to refer to one feminism at all. But a brand, by design, is something of a club that attracts desirable buyers by communicating its unique value. (Mercedes-Benz doesn't want the same customer as Jeep, for instance.) In the case of *Elle*'s rebranding project, the posters visualized feminism as the province of middle-class white women in mainstream industries who want everyone on their team—which even middle-class white women like me, for the most part, know is a woefully insufficient description of feminism's lived realities. That brand of feminism is amply represented already. All the ostensible rebrand has done is reify the issues and images that have already lived in the mainstream for decades, making feminism more alluring only by continuing to erase its unsexy, uncomfortable complexities.

The Uncanny Valley

There's a phenomenon in aesthetics known as "the uncanny valley," which describes the sense of unease, revulsion, and even fear provoked by nonhuman bodies and features that move almost—but not quite— like human ones. Think of the soggy, long-haired girl-ghosts who lurch and scuttle through horror movies like *The Ring* and *Shutter*, or the computer-animated superhumans in films like *The Hulk*. It's not alien enough to be legible as inhuman, but it's not quite human enough to avoid giving you the willies. (Or, as *30 Rock*'s Frank Rossitano once put it, "We like R2-D2, and C-3P0 . . . but down here [indicates valley] we've got a CGI Stormtrooper and Tom Hanks in *The Polar Express*.") The Gloria Steinem *PORTER* spread is an example of feminism's own uncanny valley, where images that are recognizable because we know what they are meant to be become deeply unsettling when examined up close. It's not just that this ersatz version of a feminist isn't Steinem, it's that the magazine is urging us to see her as representing the whole of feminism past.

Marketplace feminism is in many ways about just branding feminism as an identity that everyone can and should consume. That's not a bad thing in theory, but in practice it tends to involve highlighting only the most appealing features of a multifaceted set of movements. It kicks the least sensational and most complex issues under a rug and assures them that we'll get back to them once everybody's on board. And it ends up pandering to the people who *might* get on board— maybe, possibly, once feminism works its charm—rather than addressing the many unfinished projects still remaining.

Feminism's uncanny valley brims with facsimiles of familiar ideas, objects, and narratives that are, on closer inspection, almost exclusively about personal identity and consumption. Sheryl Sandberg's

Lean In is so successful in part because of how seamlessly it leads women into what appears to be feminism in every way—except for the part where it asks those women to mold their individual selves to an existing, unequal corporate culture rather than collectively endeavoring to change that culture. Numerous news outlets, meanwhile, stumbled into the uncanny valley when they unquestioningly reported on the 2015 rebranding of *Maxim* magazine as "feminist" based on its new female editor putting a self-described feminist (Taylor Swift) on the cover and not even making her wear a bikini. In the uncanny valley, those granny panties are feminist because they say so on the butt.

The feminist uncanny valley is the result of a larger neoliberal framework that over the past five decades has come to unite politics, economics, and culture in a web of individualism, privatization, and decreasing focus on both community and compassion. As a theory, neoliberalism privileges free trade, corporate deregulation, and privatization; as a practice, it took specific hold in the 1980s, when Ronald Reagan and Margaret Thatcher joined forces to enact policies that shifted economic power from the government to the private sector. Neoliberalism holds that we don't need government because we've got the free market, in which we're all theoretically equal and which will sort out what's valuable and what's not. Its social message, meanwhile, is that underclasses—the poor and economically disenfranchised—are not oppressed, but just insufficiently motivated—or, less charitably, unwilling to do the bootstrap-pulling that's required to get ahead. American culture, perhaps more than any other, prizes individualism. Our narratives of art, politics, and business idolize the person who triumphs against the odds, with only himself or herself to answer to. The lone wolf. The stranger in town. The maverick. The plucky kid. The Final Girl. You've only got yourself, in the end. *It's all up to you.*

Neoliberalism is significant to contemporary feminism in quite a few ways, but one in particular is that both emphasize consumer choice and individual power in a way that can narrow to tunnel vision. Much as "trickle-down" economic theory was a linchpin of Reaganomics, "trickle-down feminism"—a term coined by sociologist Tressie Mc-Millan Cottom—has become central to mainstream feminism: both propose that entitlements and benefits will flow downward from the citizens richest in those resources, and ultimately benefit everybody. Trickle-down economics was a roaring failure for almost everybody but the already-rich; the stakes for trickle-down feminism are not that much more hopeful. "Powerful people," writes McMillan Cottom, "will act in the interest of power, not in the interest of gender (or, race, for that matter)."[4]

Where neoliberalism meets the feminist uncanny valley is in the unquestioning celebration of, for instance, women in powerful positions—even when they use their powerful positions in ways that do most women very little good. Former Secretary of State Condoleezza Rice, for instance, was a powerful woman in a powerful position, but did not use that power in the interest of other women. Ditto for the Republican women who voted, along with every one of their male colleagues in the Senate, against the Equal Pay Act—twice. Yahoo's Marissa Mayer took the helm of the tech giant and promptly cut the company's work-from-home policy, a decision that stood to affect families in particular. And the less said about Sarah Palin, the better. On the way down into the uncanny valley, we've decided that images of women in power, in the abstract, are as important as people of any gender who are actually working to make equality a reality for everyone.

One common response to the mainstreaming of consumer feminism is the question: Well, isn't this a *good* thing? Shouldn't we be psyched about a mass centering of anything that embraces the concept? "If feminism has to become a brand to make change, I'm all for it," asserted Lena Dunham in a November 2014 interview with the UK's *Guardian*. But again, the purpose of a brand is, like neoliberal feminism, deeply at odds with the necessary evolution of movements to address issues that are about more than what trickles down from the highest echelons. The diversity of voices, issues, approaches, and processes required to make feminism work as an inclusive social movement is precisely the kind of knotty, unruly insurrection that just can't be smoothed into a neat brand.

Powerful Women Wear Powerful Panties

And that, somewhat depressingly, brings us back to underwear. In the realm of fashion and product marketing, the slow shift in feminist branding from tacit to overt might best be illustrated by the prodigious success of Spanx, those bright, cartoony packages of gut-strangling spandex that became a pop-culture phenomenon seemingly overnight. Founder Sara Blakely began selling the stretchy "shapewear" ("foundation garments" are so 1950s) out of her Georgia apartment in 2000, but within a few years was presiding over a booming bum-slimming business. Spanx's success was cemented when Oprah Winfrey, whose yo-yo dieting has been a relatable feature of her own brand, spread the gospel via her annual Favorite Things special; by 2012, Blakely was one of the world's few female billionaires, raking in an estimated $250 million annually. The brand's "tummy taming," "thigh trimming," and "butt boosting" products are a friendlier cousin of the constrictive girdles of decades past; I've sported them myself and can testify to experiences that range from minorly pinchy to sweating lower-torso hellscape. They've become the Band-Aids of contemporary culture: imitators like Yummie Tummie have crept in to grab a piece of the shapewear market, but Spanx is the catchall name for what is now considered a women's wardrobe necessity.

Though Blakely noted in a 2012 profile in the *Guardian* that she was compelled to make Spanx in extra-large sizes once she realized that men, particularly in Hollywood, were wearing them, women remain the brand's prime target. (Blakely hasn't, to my knowledge, mentioned transgender women or drag queens as a tertiary market, but Spanx have definitely been name-checked as a staple item for both groups.) The company's motto is "Changing the world, one butt at a time," and part of its brand supremacy is the way that female celebrities are vocal about relying on them. On one episode of *30 Rock*, Liz Lemon bemoaned the fact that, with three weddings to attend in one day, "I'll be in Spanx for 12 hours." However, Lemon's creator, Tina Fey, told a red-carpet interviewer that the shapewear was "my dream come true," and while it's possible she was being sarcastic, the media ran with the quote. British superstar Adele copped to wearing four pairs of Spanx, one on top of the other, to the 2012 Grammy awards. She took home six awards for her album *21*, but the next day's headlines made as much reference to her multi-Spanx as to her musical triumph.

That Fey, Adele, Tyra Banks, and many other bold-name women with scrutinized bodies are open about their shapewear is a notable departure from more openly oppressive decades, when girdles were an unspoken necessity that became visible only when women of the second wave began shunning and disposing of them (and, more recently, when they've become prominent in fetish fashion). Part of what motivates today's women toward undergarment transparency is Spanx's feminist spin: rather than being constricting, they are *empowering*. With names like In-Power Panties and a tagline that reads "Powerful Women Wear Powerful Panties," Spanx has recast the subtext of foundation garments past (women's bodies and freedom of movement must be circumscribed by any means necessary) as a visible signpost of autonomy and progress (you can make your life better by *feeling* better about your otherwise unruly body). In 2015, Spanx made the sales pitch explicit in a *New York Times* piece on the company's attempt to reach those holdout consumers who don't want to be tortured by their underpants. Kicking off with the complaint of a New York City fashion stylist ("compression is just so 15 years ago"), the piece noted that the shapewear trend has been affected by the rise of "athleisure" looks—mostly yoga pants—that have slimming and lifting fabric construction, but also allow wearers to tie their shoes without risking nerve damage.

If you ask Spanx's new CEO—which the *Times* did—to explain the company's rebranding efforts, it's all about a new, feminist world where every kind of body is accepted and there's more public pushback on negative body conversations. Thus, the company's new packaging promotes "feminist inspiration" in the form of lady-to-lady affirmations like, "Don't take the rules too seriously." That would be great if changing the rules was actually what Spanx is about. But Spanx is a business, and its embrace of feminism isn't about women's equality. It's about a company boosting revenues that have fallen behind those of competitors offering less punishing undergarments and workout clothes. If emphasizing the comfort of "dig-free" and "soft touch" material is where the money is, that's where Spanx is going. After all, a "feminist" slogan like "Re-shape the way you get dressed, so you can shape the world!" literally dresses up an age-old standard in slightly roomier stretch fabrics—as though the only thing that's kept women from busting through pink-ghetto walls and glass ceilings isn't social expectations or institutional inequality, but insufficiently thigh-smoothing panties.

If Spanx had existed in the 1980s, the marketing message might have been something like, "The control you want as you control your destiny," paired with an image of a woman in a suit with enormous shoulder pads facing a conference room full of men. In the 1990s, the brand might have turned to a more Oprah-esque message of self-actualization, maybe "Shapewear that's as powerful as your own dreams." The current slogans about rule-breaking and reshaping the world nod to feminism in suggesting that women have big things to do for humanity and impatience with "the rules" that they have internalized. Spanx aims to have it both ways, paying lip service to the idea of rebellion against conformity while its very existence encourages its buyers to conform or risk inadequacy. (The underwear might be feminist, ladies, but that doesn't mean your ass isn't too big.)

This is a time-honored approach to marketing, one that's not worth remarking on when it's used to shill diet shakes or cars or tech gadgets by playing to the self-regard of potential consumers. Of course there's potential to feel powerful in a pair of Spanx, just as there's potential to feel powerful in a push-up bra or a killer dress or a soccer jersey or any other item of clothing that showcases what we like about our bodies. Does that make the product itself feminist? Or, more to the point, if it does, than what item of clothing *isn't* feminist?

So buy that feminist underwear. It's turning out to be a surprisingly robust market—not just granny panties, but also underpants with built-in menstrual pads, bras that lift and support without the aid of poky underwires, you name it. Because the truth is that while feminist apparel is having its trendy moment, there's no one way a feminist looks. But reinscribing feminism as something you dress in or consume, rather than something you do, accomplishes nothing—not for you as an individual, and not for how women as a whole are viewed, valued, and validated in this culture. Whatever it says across your butt, that's what matters.

CHAPTER 4

The Golden Age of (Feminist) TV

"Like, I am woman, hear me roar."
—Shoshana (Zosia Mamet) on *GIRLS*.

The smart folks at the American Civil Liberties Union knew an opportunity when they saw one. On a Monday morning in the spring of 2015, they blurred past and present, fiction and reality with a tweet to *Mad Men*'s beloved Joan Holloway-Harris, who the night before had faced down her new firm's top boss with stoic purpose. The former big fish in the small pond of Sterling Cooper and Partners was now swimming with chauvinist sharks in a vast, stinging ocean of corporate sexism, and when she took her complaints to the corner office, she had little choice but to invoke the holy trinity of 1970s women's rights: the Equal Employment Opportunity Commission, the ACLU, and Betty Friedan. Bright and early the next day, the ACLU's Twitter account addressed our head bitch in charge thus: "Joan, sexual harassment has no place at work! Contact us here." Though plenty of *Mad Men* watchers, many of them young men, hopped on Twitter to express skepticism that things could really have been that bad for women in the circa-1970s workplace, the ACLU's salient point was not only that they *were* just that bad—but, in many cases, they haven't gotten that much better.

That particular episode of *Mad Men* aired less than two months after Ellen Pao, a Silicon Valley venture capitalist, lost a landmark discrimination lawsuit against her former employer, VC firm Kleiner Perkins Caulfield & Byers. The case had been a flashpoint for an ongoing debate about just how bad sexism in supposedly meritocratic Silicon Valley was: like many female, transgender, and nonwhite tech workers, Pao believed that she was excluded from an overall office culture whose makeup was overwhelmingly white and male. Ski trips, private dinners, and other collegial events, she stated, were simply not open to office minorities; she was fired, she charged, because she accused a senior colleague of sexual harassment. Though plenty of stats on the larger landscape of markedly homogenous tech companies like Twitter, Google, and Apple and even less-diverse VC-firm slates would suggest that Pao's case might have merit, a six-man/six-woman jury found no grounds for discrimination and no basis for the claim that Pao was fired due to her sexual harassment claim. (Pao's next job, however, pretty much made her case about tech-world gender imbalance for her: as the interim CEO of notoriously douchey Internet man-cave Reddit, she shuttered some of the site's foulest hate-speech forums and triggered an avalanche of racist and sexist threats and abuse before eventually resigning the position.)

The *Mad Men* episode aired slightly more than a year after the *New York Times* published a guide to salary negotiations for women that underscored the perils of negotiating while female. The title "Moving Past Gender Roles to Negotiate a Raise" was misleading, given that the piece was all about what women in the workplace should do *differently* than men when advocating for better pay. Women were urged, for instance, to take negotiation-playbook tips written for men and "soften" them, given that employers often find it "unseemly, if on an unconscious level" when women talk up their merits. Elsewhere, female-identified workers were advised to approach salary talks as "dialogues," rather than negotiations, since asking for what they deserve—as men are expected to—would be sure to freak everybody out. "We are asking women to juggle while they are on the tightrope . . . it's totally unfair because we don't require the same of men," stated the founder of Carnegie Mellon University's gender-equity program. Almost every expert quoted in the piece, in fact, acknowledged that discrimination is very much a part of both workplace culture and individual workplaces. Yet the guide proceeded as though there were no possibilities other than those that asked women to submit to indelibly gendered expectations and reify them for future women in future workplaces.

The episode aired less than a year after the release of "The Glass Floor," a report on sexual harassment in the restaurant industry—a field identified by the Equal Employment Opportunity Commission as the largest source of sexual harassment claims. The report's findings were deeply upsetting, if not all that surprising: though restaurant employees of all genders experience unwanted sexual questioning, touching, bullying, and pressuring, women and transgender workers are the most affected, experiencing harassment from management, coworkers, and customers; tipped workers in states that pay a sub-minimum wage are most likely to be subject to regular unwanted sexual attention.[1] The assertion that echoed throughout the data was that sexual harassment is "endemic" to the industry, so much so that a majority of workers see it as simply part of the job.

And the episode aired just under two years after the Supreme Court's *Vance vs. Ball State* decision, which narrowed the definition of supervisory roles in sexual harassment complaints. By limiting the definition of "supervisor" to someone who has direct power to hire, fire, or promote employees, *Vance* set a precedent that markedly affected the chances for plaintiffs to see justice in workplace harassment cases. Cases in which retail, restaurant, and hospital employees, among others, were subject to ongoing harassment by a senior employee to whom they reported—in other words, a supervisory figure—were subsequently thrown out not on grounds that they didn't occur, but because the tailored definition of "supervisor" (defined only as someone with direct hiring/firing power over an employee) enabled employers to duck responsibility. And, as the EEOC's general counsel told Think-Progress, *Vance* also lessened the likelihood of lawyers even taking on cases that were likely to be contested on the technicality—by extension suggesting that victims of harassment really shouldn't bother seeking justice if the conditions to argue for it weren't airtight.[2]

So yes, skeptics on Twitter, things really were that bad, and, in too many cases, still are. But they've also gotten much better, in one especially crucial way: there is now a parallel sphere in which for every depressing real-life inequity there's a depiction of a different ending, and many of us have ready access to that sphere. On television, we see and hear women constantly. We watch and listen to them; we are influenced by them and encouraged to emulate them. The maxim that "You can't be what you can't see" no longer applies to an encouraging number of women in public life, because for almost anything we might want to be there's a woman somewhere on your television or computer who is already a shining example of it. There she is: She's a hard-charging political fixer, or a hotshot surgeon with a temper. She's the DA, the assistant DA, and the presiding judge. She's the president of the goddamn United States. She's a special agent, a lovelorn dowager, the Supreme of a coven of sassy witches. She's a clone, a cyborg, an alien. She's an awkward black girl, a clueless white girl, a pregnant virgin, a sex addict. She's a trans woman, a butch woman, a woman who's still trying to figure it out. She's finding love in unlikely places, ditching dead-end relationships to finally find herself. She's framing her enemies, overdosing on drugs, running a crime syndicate. She's using martial arts training to fend off a shitload of zombies. She's too stoned to peel herself off the couch.

Who knew that all those years of talk about having it all actually referred to TV?

Women in Boxes

As a medium that exists mostly at the whim of advertisers, television wasn't exactly the first industry to jump aboard the women's liberation train. TV executives knew what to do with women as a broad and undifferentiated category of humans who took care of babies, bought laundry powder, and heated up frozen dinners. But when faced with the prospect of actual female people who didn't see themselves represented on their living room screens, TV executives—a white, male bunch, mostly—were at a loss. Once it was clear that feminism was something that female audiences were interested in, these execs were faced with the task of telegraphing some of its core messages while not alienating their sponsors. By 1971, television had seen a small handful of single, independent career women in the form of *Julia*'s Julia Baker and *The Mary Tyler Moore Show*'s Mary Richards and Rhoda Morgenstern, but such women were initially presented as one-dimensional. *MTM*'s female writers (it was the first network offering to have more than one) understood that even the carefully crafted, wholesome Mary had to reveal the facets of her womanhood by slow degrees: they simply couldn't be as frank about essaying a single woman's freedom as they could with a man's. The chronically dating Mary didn't have her first overnight with a man until the show's third season (and that was offscreen); its major milestone came later that season with a reference to the Pill.[3]

The women who agreed with *Redbook*, in a 1972 poll, that "the media degrades women as mindless dolls," and wanted something a little juicier were the perfect audience for *Maude*, the *All in the Family* spin-off featuring Edith Bunker's sharp-tongued cousin Maude Findlay. A thrice-divorced feminist with a sensible, graying hairstyle, a Valium prescription, and a penchant for maxi vests, Maude was both a product of the women's movement and a send-up of it. It was okay to cringe at her often clueless, if well-meaning, efforts to be the best liberal in the room, but she could also be deeply sympathetic—especially important given that she was the first prime-time character to have a legal abortion.

Television in the 1970s that wrestled with feminist issues was effective in part because the landscape was evolving quickly and in real time: divorce, single parenthood, unemployment, coming out institutional sexism and racism, poverty, male chauvinism, and more were all part of the films, sitcoms, dramas, and talk shows of the decade. Furthermore, television had at least one producer—Norman Lear, of *Maude, All in the Family, Good Times, The Jeffersons, One Day at a Time,* and *Mary Hartman Mary Hartman*—who made a career of giving a voice to the social issues of the time in ways that didn't pander to audiences or attempt to end each half hour with a tidy, pat resolution. Lear, a self-described "emotional" liberal, was matter-of-fact about the groundbreaking material he brought to television, though its content often tied the networks in knots. *Maude's* discussion about abortion, for instance, "was conversation I'd heard a hundred times in family life—in my country and my culture," Lear told Terry Gross in a 2014 *Fresh Air* interview. "So I didn't see any reason why we couldn't open it up for a television family." (Lear, along with congresswoman Barbara Jordan, later founded People For the American Way, a civic advocacy organization meant to combat the growing cultural influence of the Religious Right.)

But by 1980, the perception was that women's liberation was a done deal, and nobody wanted to hear any more about it—particularly the TV networks. Contrast Maude's abortion dilemma with that of Christine Cagney of female buddy-cop drama *Cagney and Lacey.* The show's creators had battled with CBS executives over nearly every aspect of the women's roles since the start: they were too tough, too old, not "feminine" enough, and not sufficiently vulnerable, charged the brass. Making the denouement to Cagney's surprise pregnancy a miscarriage, it turned out, wasn't good enough. Instead, the script was rewritten so that the pregnancy was just a scare, which prompted a lecture from Lacey that conspicuously avoided the subject of abortion.[4]

By mid-decade, feminism had become so taboo on television that one popular work-around was to simply avoid writing roles for adult female characters, which brought about the popular subgenre of sitcoms in which a mother has either died or deserted: *Diff'rent Strokes, Gimme a Break!, Punky Brewster, Silver Spoons, My Two Dads, Full*

House, *Blossom*, *The Nanny*, and *Raising Miranda*. Most of these shows never even mentioned the missing mother after establishing her dead-or-deadbeat status and introducing the invariably wacky parental substitute who was either pressed into service by the bewildered dad or was the dad himself. One possible explanation for the disappearance of sitcom moms was that as divorce became more normalized—by 1983, no-fault divorce laws had been adopted in all but two states—these stories offered a reassuring way to contest the belief that a family wasn't a family without a mother present—all a dad needed, really, was a housekeeper, or a girlfriend, or at the very least, another dude or two. (See also the hit 1987 movie *Three Men and a Baby*.)

Two notable exceptions to TV's feminist blackout in 1980s TV were *Roseanne*, the blue-collar family sitcom whose Learian mix of humor and social import was anchored by standup comedian Roseanne Barr's no-bullshit brashness, and *Murphy Brown*, whose title character—a formerly alcoholic control-freak TV journalist—was arguably the closest thing sitcoms had seen to a female antihero. Both were variations on TV-comedy archetypes that would continue to be duplicated, and which spawned, over the next decade, sitcoms focusing on mouthy working-class women (*Grace Under Fire*, *Reba*) and privileged single ones grappling with dating, aging, and children (*Cybill*, *Suddenly Susan*, *Veronica's Closet*).

A bit more of an outlier was *Living Single*, whose twist on the awesome-foursome female-focused sitcom (*Designing Women*, *The Golden Girls*) was its four black professional women living together in pre-hipster Brooklyn, contending and commiserating with careers, beauty standards, sex, and gender roles. *Living Single*'s popularity was one of the few alternatives to feminism's televised face, which, much like its public one, had become increasingly homogenous. But it did share one key feature with its paler TV sistren in its firmly individualistic approach to choices. All of these women were living tacitly liberated lives—they made their own decisions, their own money, and their own mistakes; and they had no interest in being guilted or shamed for their independence, their sex lives, or their views. It was decentralized, decontextualized, and safely unaffiliated feminism. And, most important, it sold.

Mighty Big TV

That television, in particular, has emerged as a medium that regularly engages with, challenges, and re-envisions feminism seems all the more unlikely not only because of its history, but because of how the economics of the medium have changed over the past several decades.

In 1990s America, there was a Democratic president, a federal budget surplus, a tech revolution on the rise, a focus on multiculturalism, a reinvigoration of youth activism, and a feminist presence that, coughing on the rancid wind of backlash, was re-emerging into social and political discourse, often via music, indie film, and other pop culture. Antifashion was fashionable; indie and alternative youth cultures were being scouted by a new breed of corporate "cool hunters," and the *New York Times* was so eager to be down with the kids that it unwittingly printed a glossary of made-up "grunge" slang. (Harsh realm, lamestains!)

And as the underground became mainstream, TV audiences were becoming more carefully target-marketed than ever before. The industry's bread and butter had for decades been family viewing, with households gathering around their sets each night to watch the Walton, Ricardo, Cosby, or Keaton families do their thing. But starting in the 1980s, the advent of cable channels like HBO and Showtime, and independent ones like Nickelodeon, meant that shows could finally deviate, if only minimally, from the time-honored model of "least objectionable content" that had kept the Big Three networks robust. (Least-objectionable-content theory held that viewers didn't necessarily like everything they watched, but would reliably watch what offended them the least.) Meanwhile, niche marketing—

segmenting potential viewers by age, race, gender, household income, and more—replaced mass marketing as the primary strategy of audience building.

In pursuit of the prized 18-49 demographic, new television "netlets" were born from entertainment conglomerates that followed the example of Fox, the network launched by Rupert Murdoch's News Corp. in 1986 whose hits included *The Cosby Show* and its spin-off, *A Different World*, as well as *Beverly Hills 90210* and *Melrose Place*. With Warner Brothers debuting the WB (for teens and tweens); Paramount offering UPN (for young men and the audience known as "urban"), and Lifetime and WE aiming for the ladies (with the similarly targeted Oxygen debuting in 2000), the practice of "narrowcasting" was increasingly crucial for advertisers as long as such small audiences had big pocketbooks. In selling women to advertisers, the female-targeted netlets were careful to avoid the word "feminist," lest it conjure the image of an audience that shunned beauty products, household cleaners, and baby needs—though Lifetime would later describe its target viewer as "a woman in her early forties, she is probably a working mom. . . . a busy, multitasking women, very interested in a lot of different things: information about health, parenting, social issues, violence against women and how to break the cycles, so she's a multifaceted person." And Oxygen's president of programming offered advertisers a viewer who was "very interested in herself—moving herself forward . . . [she] feels like, 'I'm not getting older, I'm getting better; these are the goals I have for myself; this is what I want to accomplish.'"[5]

But the most significant shift for television was Bill Clinton's signing of the Telecommunications Act of 1996, a major piece of legislation designed to promote economic growth and competition between media companies by deregulating the communications industry, including radio, television, and the young Internet. The Telecom Act had positives, like its mandate that new televisions be manufactured with parental-consent V-chips and its plan to make sure that all U.S.

schools, libraries, and other learning institutions had Internet access. But the act's emphasis on deregulation led to the largest and most destructive wave of media mergers in history. For example, the limit on the number of radio and TV stations that could be owned by a single company was lifted, a policy that paved the way for behemoths like Clear Channel and Comcast to monopolize consumer access. Independent, local, and minority-owned entities were swallowed up; the giant companies who owned them were granted longer broadcast licenses that, among other things, rendered them far less accountable to the public.

If a movie is ever made of the aftermath of the Telecom Act, it could realistically just be another *Godzilla* remake, with the role of Godzilla filled by a series of multinational corporations stomping across the United States, snapping up thousands of locally-owned media companies and crushing them. The implied expectation of these mergers was that formerly independent broadcasting entities would still be able to hew to a standard of "television in the public interest"—a fairly roomy term that nods to "informational and educational needs," particularly those of children.[6] But the reality was that for the global entertainment conglomerates who now owned them—by the mid-2000s, more than 75 percent of prime-time TV viewing was controlled by five multinational entities—the only consideration was money. More television meant more advertisers, which meant more profits; making more television meant making it cheaper; making it cheaper meant fewer unions, fewer original scripts, and more product placement. And that's how we ended up with today's surplus of Bachelors, Bachelorettes, Survivors, Swans, Top Models, Basketball Wives, Storage Wars, Real Housewives, Dance Moms, Duck Dynasties, and more, as well as with approximately five million shows about flipping houses, hunting ghosts, lying in wait for Sasquatch, running tanning salons, and realizing way too late that breast implants don't belong in your butt cheeks.

Reality TV existed before the Telecom Act, of course. When MTV's *The Real World* debuted in 1992, it was a social experiment that mimicked 1973's landmark TV miniseries *An American Family*—cameras everywhere, no narrative, let's see what happens. For *The Real World*, the experiment was in how seven unrelated strangers would navigate their differences and learn from one another. Each season hinged on casting a likable, diverse set of regular-looking young adults that viewers could relate to; the show's attempts to create a balanced ecosystem of learning moments (AIDS, homelessness) and inevitable conflict (racism, unhygienic peanut-butter habits) was either well-meaning or cynical, depending on whom you asked. But there was no question about the moment when the show turned a corner: the Season 7 episode when Seattle housemates Stephen and Irene exchanged words, followed by Stephen slapping Irene in the face. The slap became the central focus of the rest of the season, and changed the tone of every one that followed. Current events and social issues were back-burnered, hot tubs and gallons of booze were rolled in, and shows were less likely to be about teachable moments than about using bad behavior to make good TV. It was in this context-free vacuum that reality television, with its narratives, tropes, and "journeys," became network gold.

The effect of the Telecom Act on news outlets, meanwhile, was transfiguring. In 1980, there was only one 24-hour news channel, CNN. When there wasn't quite enough round-the-clock news to cover, the network turned to entertainment and human-interest stories, one genre of which prefigured viral videos. (Watch this goat eat the morning paper right out of its owner's hands!) By the late 1990s, there were more than five national news channels and a multitude of regional ones, and none of those had enough actual news to fill twenty-four hours, either. By the early 2000s, as the Internet began increasingly to be a primary source of breaking news, televised news channels had to find a different way to appeal to viewers. "Infotainment"—health scares, ginned-up political scuttlebutt, celebrity gossip—became an ever-larger part of news broadcasting, and as time went on, the fluff padding out the hard news seemed to squeeze "info" entirely out of the picture. When Anna Nicole Smith died, I heard it first from CNN.

Ruling Reality

Media critic Jennifer L. Pozner has spent thousands of hours and an immense amount of patience watching both cable news and reality television, and understands better than the average person how alike they've become. "We treat stories that we would have never treated as journalism twenty years ago like headline news," she muses. And we treat reality TV the same way. More relevant to feminism, however, is how the reality genre has harnessed the belief in a postfeminist world and, in doing so, reframed retrograde gender dynamics as expressions of freedom and empowerment. Far more than any backlash could have predicted, the feminist rhetoric of individuality, opportunity, autonomy, and choice has been co-opted by a consumer media that has very non-ulterior motives for presenting women as willingly sexualized, hyperfeminine ciphers.

In Pozner's 2010 book *Reality Bites Back: The Troubling Truth About Guilty-Pleasure Television*, she asserts that one of the most jarring features of reality TV is the way it urges its female participants—and, often, the women and girls who watch them—toward narrower and narrower definitions of beauty, self-worth, and success, as well as a truncated sense of what kind of life is possible and desirable, all while encouraging them to see other women only in terms of competition and comparison. But "reality" functions as a magic shield against accusations of racist and sexist cliché and regressive storylines: producers and participants alike will reason that if you put twenty-five women in a room with a man they barely know, *of course* the evening will end with the women sobbing, yelling, yanking each other's hair extensions out, calling each other sluts, and drunkenly slurring, "We're meant to be together" to floor lamps. Reality TV is part of an ongoing narrative of postfeminism that, like Wonderbra billboards once did, assures women that feminism has granted them the power and the freedom to be whatever they want to be. And if what they want to be just so happens to conform to a smorgasbord of insecure, catty, vapid, and villainous stereotypes that even Walt Disney's frozen head would reject as too cartoonish, who's to say that's not empowering?

Let's take *The Bachelor*—because, since it's one of the highest-rated network shows for more than a decade, we kind of have to. Since its debut in 2002, ABC's reality flagship has drawn in advertisers' favorite cash-cow demographic, women 18–34, by the millions, and has served as a barometer of how young, heterosexual, and mostly white women are encouraged to alter their ambitions, personalities, and behaviors to compete in the dating market. The show, mused media critic Susan J. Douglas when it premiered, "offers highly normative female 'types' into which most women allegedly fall . . . urged to place themselves on a post-feminist scale of femininity to determine how far they have to go to please men without losing all shreds of their own identity and dignity. In the process, young women calibrate, for better and for worse, what kind of female traits are most likely to ensure success in a male-dominated world."[7] For twenty seasons, the series has confirmed centuries' worth of entrenched beliefs about what women want (marriage, money, the knowledge that they've beaten out masses of other women for the a man they barely know), and what men seek (a thin, deferential woman who's only as ambitious as she needs to be to bag a husband).

Season after season has proceeded according to formula, with a spray-tanned pack of interchangeable beauties in glittery pageant dresses pledging instantaneous love for an equally vague mass of square jaws and biceps, playing heavily stage-managed roles of crazy bitch, party girl, drunkity hot mess, and more. But over time, as the franchise soldiered on through doomed engagements (and expanded with *The Bachelorette* and *Bachelor In Paradise)*, something a little odd began happening: women, most of them young and, again, white, began ascribing feminism to the show and, even more frequently, pledging allegiance to it as the ultimate feminist guilty pleasure.

One 2014 blog post, headlined "*The Bachelor* Season 19 Contestants Seem Proudly Feminist," took snippets of the contestants' bios ("Alisa said she'd be a wild mustang because they're 'free to run and explore [and] they're unpredictable and beautiful.' You go, girl. Just like Miley Cyrus, you can't be tamed") to make a case that the show was committing to a stance of equality. (Never mind that that season's Bachelor was a farmer who took as a given that any future wife would give up her career to move to his Iowa hometown.) An exploration titled "The Feminist Bachelorette" gave props to reality TV for allowing women the same promiscuity as men, an assessment that somehow managed to overlook the glaring double standard particular to *The Bachelor*'s sister show: when Bachelors get frisky with two dozen strangers, it's just part of the fairy tale; when Bachelorettes do the same, it's a big slutty slutfest. (The storyline for *The Bachelorette*'s 2015 season was that our girl Kaitlyn slept with one contestant "too soon"; the rest of the season was built around the fallout from her guilt and the nasty hate mail she received from viewers for being "a whore.") And listicles like "9 Reasons Strong, Intelligent Feminist Women Watch *The Bachelor*," and "7 Reasons It's Okay to Be a Feminist and Watch *The Bachelor*" worked themselves into impressive contortions to frame the show's reliable tropes—references to "feeling like Cinderella," contestants dissolving into tears because they just "have so much to give" the guy who's dating twenty-four other women—as honest and refreshing strong-women representations.

The Bachelor and its counterparts have made their contestants' desire for a full-blown princess narrative explicit, but the underlying themes of everything from *America's Next Top Model* to the *Real Housewives* franchise, *What Not to Wear* and *How Do I Look?* and the I-feel-dirty-even-mentioning-it, *Toddlers & Tiaras*, aren't all that different. Each one pushes the idea that appearance is the most important thing a woman has, and a man the most important thing she can get, and other women merely obstacles to knock down or kick over. If she's still unhappy or alone, well, she just needs to try harder on all fronts.

As Pozner points out, this couldn't be better for advertisers. "It's far easier to shill cosmetics and clothing—not to mention Match.com and Bally Fitness memberships—to insecure women scared of being alone than it is to self-confident people who believe they're beautiful, lovable, and capable of being happy just as they are."[8] To this end, the most heinous premise ever committed to screen delivered a group of the former on a silver platter. A combination of *Extreme Makeover* and a beauty pageant held in a dumpster behind Satan's 7-11, *The Swan*, which ran for two seasons in 2004, introduced viewers to a group of "ugly ducklings" who shared stories of how their looks have impacted their lives, from bullying and eating disorders to agoraphobia and abusive relationships. The fix? A head-to-toe surgical overhaul that board-certified plastic surgeons (and a largely ornamental psychologist) promised them would change their entire lives. But that's not all. After they emerged from their gauze cocoons believing that they'd never be judged so harshly again, they were made to compete with one another in a beauty pageant—because even when you've literally been remolded to fit mainstream media's ridiculously narrow beauty standard, you can still come up short in relation to another woman.

No one has looked to reality TV for feel-good authenticity in a long time, but there's a case to be made that reality shows have been welcomed not just for economic reasons, but precisely because they occupy a weird sort of limbo with respect to attitudes about women. As in advertising, feminism has been taken into account, taken for granted, and neither explicitly repudiated nor overtly embraced. Every reality-show decision, from trying out for the show to undermining other women to cannily deploying sex as leverage, is an individual one that may not be considered feminist, but within a cultural discourse where "choice" is paramount, also can't be dismissed as patently *un*feminist.

A decade-plus of reality-TV acculturation has recently led to the opening of a more fascinating, if no less normative, space for satirical, and even sinister, takes on the genre. *Burning Love*, a web series–turned–cable TV offering, lampoons the sameness of both *Bachelor* contestants and male "prizes" with goofball twists on the real show's gender, race, and personality stereotypes: the "crazy bitch" character is actually homicidal, the "cougar" is an octogenarian grandmother, etc. More ethically probing is the Lifetime metadrama *UnREAL*, which arrived in 2015 to pull back the soft-focus bead curtain on the business of reality-TV romance and reveal the power puppeteering and mind games that go into creating a "successful" franchise. We see the male prize coached to butter up specific women. We see that, deprived of any outside contact and plied with booze, the contestants become increasingly suggestible to producers. And we see those producers competing amongst themselves for cash bonuses based on how well they craft key "characters" (the queen bitch, the ghetto princess, the basket case, the MILF) and fluff their charges toward ratings-boosting emotional money shots. The best of these producers at manipulation is Rachel Goldberg, a hollow-eyed dark wizard with a dead soul who sleeps in a prop truck; when we meet her, she's wearing a grimy gray t-shirt that proclaims "This is What a Feminist Looks Like." The joke is that women like Rachel and her co-producers believe themselves to be feminists, but they earn their living by shepherding other women through a self-esteem–destroying black hole of princess fantasy, horror movie, and softcore porn. They're not just the emissaries of this retrograde version of reality; they're also the architects.

UnREAL was created by Sarah Gertrude Shapiro, who was herself a producer for nine seasons on *The Bachelor*, an experience she's described as not unlike being "a vegan in a slaughterhouse."[9] And indeed, the most notable part of *UnREAL* is its critique of the larger illusion of equality and choice that defines marketplace feminism. Rachel's life is a microcosm of the show-within-a-show, in which she's as trapped as any of her charges in a disempowering game. She even has a mentor more heartless than her—the show's executive producer, Quinn—expertly manipulating her emotions and actions. The close of the first season found Quinn and Rachel sprawled on lawn chairs at the set's mansion, assuring each other with well-meaning lies that things would be different in the next go-round. It was a perfect illustration of how the reality-TV marketplace defines "freedom"—and, by extension, feminist autonomy—as freedom within a circumscribed fantasy realm where women hold only a small handful of the puppet strings.

Radicalizing the Antiheroine

By the mid-2000s, with scripted offerings less and less of a priority for major networks, premium cable became the place to watch a new paradigm of television in the public interest take shape: topical, well-written shows about complex, not-always-likable, often straight-up immoral people. This time is now fondly recalled as the beginning of TV's "new Golden Age," and the writers, producers, and actors on the shows that ushered it in—*The Sopranos*, *The Wire*, *Six Feet Under*—are these days held up as pop culture kingmakers. Except, notably, for one HBO show that was there at the same time as the others, but has since been relegated to a gaudy footnote: *Sex and the City*.

When the series debuted in 1999 in the guise of a sexually sociological comedy (it was based on Candace Bushnell's 1997 nonfiction book of the same title), it was kind of a big deal. Though HBO already boasted a number of prurient documentary series like *Real Sex* and *G-String Divas*, most viewers didn't openly admit to watching them; *Sex and the City* was bona fide watercooler material. The NYC–centered series fell short of reality on a number of levels—the diversity of the characters, the profusion of stiletto heels as streetwear, the fact that one column in a weekly newspaper supported Carrie Bradshaw's lavish lifestyle—but in terms of reshaping conventional wisdom about women and sex, it was a weighty cultural coming-out that mirrored conversations all kinds of women were already having. But as time went on, the characters became caricatures, and once-serious dialogue about feminism's place in sexual mores and negotiations became flip one-liners. As the *New Yorker*'s television critic, Emily Nussbaum, mourned in a 2013 consideration on the occasion of *SATC*'s fifteenth anniversary, once cable networks began crafting more and more prestige TV, the groundbreaking series was swiftly reduced to "a set of empty, static cartoons, an embarrassment to womankind" that former viewers were relieved to no longer have to contend with as a constant pop culture touchstone.

I agree with Nussbaum that *Sex and the City*'s rise and fall in pop culture estimation can be explained in part by "the assumption that anything stylized (or formulaic, or pleasurable, or funny, or feminine, or explicit about sex rather than about violence, or made collaboratively) must be inferior." Against its Manhattan backdrop, *SATC*'s lack of engagement with race as a force that shapes and impacts sexual mores became increasingly indefensible, especially compared to its often pointed takes on class. And, certainly, the two cartoonishly bad feature films based on the series didn't do anything to shore up its cultural legacy. But as someone who watched the show from the beginning, the show's implicit feminism also became less and less credible as it shifted from an ostensibly collective view of women's desire to be authentic sexual agents to one that was all tunnel-vision egotism and individual quirks.

Consider the first season, which, watching it now, seems almost indie-movie spartan in its aesthetic. The unifying theme was an anthropology whose signature "I couldn't help but wonder . . . " queries addressed the ways feminism (as well as capitalism, AIDS, and urban gentrification) had and had not changed the stakes of dating and sex. Women could have sex "like men," for instance—without attachment or expectation—but what if their partner doesn't know that? Is fidelity a realistic expectation when casual sex has become a sport? What counts as "weird" or a fetish when everything is pretty much on the table? The four women represented four different responses to feminism "taken into account," understood as a thing of the past whose "spent force," as Angela McRobbie theorized, has given rise to a range of at-will meanings untethered from political significance.

Charlotte, as the most traditional of the foursome, symbolized the outright rejection of feminist social politics and the embrace of the idea that, despite all this equality talk, what women really craved was the stability of heterosexual marriage. Miranda was the frustrated embodiment of second-wave feminism: career-focused, beauty standard–rejecting, occasionally even emasculating ("Sometimes it's like you're the *guy*," raged her on/off lover Steve in one episode); her outrage on behalf of women as a category was funny to everyone but her. Samantha was postfeminism, leveraging her occasionally aggressive sexuality against men because it was the most expedient route to getting what she wanted from life, and confused when she realized that it didn't always translate into actual parity. And Carrie represented marketplace feminism, blithely picking and choosing from a buffet of various ideological and material stances as they suited her, and discarding them when they didn't.

But though it's been tarnished by time, hindsight, and memories of giant flower brooches, *Sex and the City* remains a turning point in feminist television because its characters were so polarizing, flawed, even unlikable. The show was the realization of what Bella Abzug had characterized in 1977 as the measure of true equality: "Our struggle today is not to have a female Einstein get appointed as an assistant professor. It is for a woman schlemiel to get as quickly promoted as a male schlemiel." Equality is not simply elevating women, but also allowing them to fail as spectacularly and often as anyone else, and these four women were the female schlemiels that television had never quite created for fear of driving audiences away from women who were as challenging and unlikeable as any other kind of human.

It would be inaccurate to say that we're now swimming in female schlemiels—but we have definitely entered the age of female antiheroes. This isn't only because more channels, more web series, and more streaming services have brought us more television in general, but also due to a cultural re-envisioning of television as a writer's medium, populated by a more diverse range of writers than ever before; as well as those writers' understanding that audiences don't want everything packed neatly up and tied with a bow at the end of each episode.

Putting Up the Numbers

Twenty years ago, the main front in what onlookers described as a "culture war" was in the country's living rooms. When Pat Buchanan campaigned for the Republican presidential nomination at 1992's national convention, his doomy conjuring of a godless America included not just the specters of abortion, homosexuality, women in combat, and other right-wing faves, but also pop culture in particular. Vice President Dan Quayle invoked TV's Murphy Brown in a now-famous speech positioning "family values" as America's bedrock, suggesting that she was making single parenthood acceptable, contributing to a nationwide poverty crisis, and "mocking the importance of fathers by bearing a child alone and calling it just another lifestyle choice."[10] Groups like the American Family Association and Christian Leaders for Responsible Television galvanized crusades against TV shows like *Roseanne*, *Saturday Night Live*, and *Ellen* by targeting sponsors like Clorox and Burger King until they pulled their financial support from the offending shows.

I sometimes like to think about Buchanan turning on his television any given night in 2015 and promptly bursting into flames at the sight of homosexuals, transgender parents, women in combat, single mothers, and even the odd abortion—but also of drug dealers, extravagantly corrupt government officials, amoral religious leaders, ass-kicking spies, and heartless crime bosses. Oh, and those are just the women. Buchanan and his culture crusaders have continued to try to influence the moral fiber of our small-screen content, but the combination of a new generation of writers, directors, and showrunners; as well as the evolution of TV industry economics, has turned down the volume on their outrage. TV has prevailed, and many of its fictions have far surpassed real life in political intellect, social and legal justice, gender equality, and more. On episodes of police procedurals like *Law and Order* and *CSI*, the killer, rapist, kidnapper, or criminal mastermind is just as likely to be a doctor, lawyer, stockbroker, or clergy member as a mental patient or drug addict or punk teenager. The drug addicts, mental patients, and punk teenagers, in fact, might be the sympathetic leads in their own shows. In the past decade, four TV presidents have been women. In culture-war terms, the "immoral" have triumphed—and they've made for some great viewing.

Meanwhile, the increasing number of female creators who have ushered in what *Huffington Post* TV critic Zeba Blay calls "The Golden Age of Feminist TV"—among them Mara Brock Akil, Tina Fey, Jenji Kohan, Liz Meriwether, Shonda Rhimes, and Jill Soloway—have been both heralded and complemented by feminist coverage in blogs, magazines, and social media. And a critical lens on feminism, antiracism, and LGBTQ representation has become almost commonplace in mainstream television criticism, from *Entertainment Weekly* to *Rolling Stone* to the *Wall Street Journal*. But while what's on TV right now offers pop culture's closest reflection of real life—with almost 42 percent of characters that are women, including transgender women—a look behind the scenes reveals that television is neither a feminist industry nor a particularly female one.

The Directors' Guild of America report on diversity for the 2014-15 TV season revealed that while 16 percent of all episodes that year were directed by women, 84 percent of first-time directors were men—suggesting that, much like with movies, the men tend to end up with a disproportionate vote of confidence from above. The Center for the Study of Film and Television numbers for the same season noted that women created 20 percent of all shows and comprised 23 percent of all executive producers; meanwhile, they accounted for 13 percent of directors and 17 percent of editors, with a whole 2 percent working as directors of photography.

In other words, the Golden Age of Feminist Television is thrilling to watch and gratifying to hear its creators discuss, but, as with TV itself, things are often much better looking on the surface. It's absolutely crucial for people—young people, in particular—to see that the creators of shows that they love are people who look like their parents and teachers and friends, to be able to see themselves in the position to construct their own stories and worlds for TV. But the flip side is that too much emphasis on all the good stuff can lead us to gloss over how many intractable barriers remain. "It's still not *enough* women creators, not enough women writers," emphasizes Women in Hollywood's Melissa Silverstein. And, she adds, the dialogue that exists around these numbers is evidence enough that core attitudes that have informed the industry still run deep. "You don't hear people say to the showrunner, 'Listen, you have enough male writers on this TV show.' But I've had showrunners regularly tell me stories about being told, 'You have enough female writers now.'" The fear of a conference room in which men hear the voices of more than one woman and imagine dozens is a perception fallacy that exists in many spaces, but it's so endemic to film and television production it's even been studied.

Geena Davis left a celebrated career of roles in films, like 1991's *Thelma & Louise*, that were supposed to change everything for women in Hollywood. They didn't, of course, and she founded the Geena Davis Institute for Media Studies in 2004 to research and quantify gender imbalance and find ways to rectify it. More often than not, she found that male producers and studio heads with whom she spoke were shocked—shocked!—to hear how few women appeared in their movies. They scratched their heads over the Institute's finding that in family-rated movies, women and girls comprise only 17 percent of any given crowd. "If there's 17 percent women, the men in the group think it's 50-50," Davis revealed on an episode of NPR's *The Frame*. And if there's more than that, well, it may as well be a full-blown matriarchy; Davis found that in a group that was 33 percent women, men perceived themselves outnumbered.[11]

That said, money seems to talk at least slightly louder in television studios than in those that make movies, perhaps because the sums tend to be less bloated, and this goes some way toward explaining why television seems light-years ahead of film, if not behind the scenes than in front of them. When I interviewed Blay in July of 2015, she'd just been to the "upfronts," the events where TV networks preview the next season's offerings for advertisers and industry media. At ABC's, she reported, "suddenly we're seeing all these shows with black leads and female leads, and we're all very excited. And I think we should be, ultimately." But she also notes that it may be less a true measure of institutional change than one of big-money potential. "[Diversity] is not a decision that an executive has made because"—she shifts to a blissed-out voice—"'Oh, diversity is so important and we need more powerful women onscreen.' No! They're doing it because they realize that we're in a moment right now where people are more and more concerned with these things. They're not doing it out of a moral or ethical obligation; they're doing it to make money. And that's the sort of insidious part of this."

The Social (TV) Network

Television is a prime vehicle for marketplace feminism because its features and values are primarily subjective: ask fifty people what feminist television looks like, and you may well get fifty different answers. For Blay, *Orange Is the New Black* is the new standard, a show that "is a blueprint for how to do women on television the right way."[12] For some viewers, a feminist TV show or series is one that, regardless of the subject, is made by a staff that is diverse in race and sex and gender presentation; for others, it's a never-before-told story that creates an entire world from scratch. And part of what seems exciting in this new

Golden Age is that fans, once entirely at the mercy of the least objectionable content, now have a sense that their own voices might be a critical part of shaping TV's trajectory, particularly in realms that have been erased, sidelined, and marginalized throughout the medium's lifespan.

TV has a colorful history of audience-fueled activism. A vocal fandom saved *Star Trek* from cancellation after only two seasons, via a 1967 letter-writing campaign organized by a couple named Bjo and John Trimble. ("All the news at that time was about Women's Lib and 'the little housewife speaking up,'" Bjo recalled of her sudden media notoriety.) In the 1980s and early '90s, the advocacy group Viewers for Quality Television convinced networks to save shows like *Designing Women* and *Cagney & Lacey* that weren't commercial blockbusters but did attract a prized advertising demographic of middle-class, college-educated viewers. The cancellation of cult sci-fi series *Firefly* in 2003 provoked such an injured response from fans (and a subsequent run on DVDs of the series) that director Joss Whedon had a chance to offer closure with a stand-alone movie. And the Internet pioneered a new way to engage both audiences and creators, often at the same time.

At *Television Without Pity*, one of the first—and definitely the best—TV fan sites, viewers could read witty, analytical recaps of their favorite shows (often a necessity in the years before digital video recorders and instant-streaming technology made the scene) and discuss them in fan forums where writers and producers might also be lurking. As fan sites multiplied and social media enabled even more rapid response, the relationship between viewers and creators began an ineluctable shift. Everyone—literally, *everyone*—was a critic. But while paid, professional critics were charged with keeping an objective distance from the shows they reviewed, fan-critics had no such responsibility, and began loudly contesting plot points they hated, characters they felt were half-baked, and motivations they didn't buy. For viewers, says Zeba Blay, "we're at a place now where we almost can't consume pop culture without breaking it down, even as we are entertained by it; even as we're watching *Orange Is the New Black,* we're not just watching it as this really great, funny show, we're thinking about, 'What does this scene say about rape?' and 'What does this scene say about relationships between white and black women?' It makes me wonder what it means for us to, you know, not just gobble them up but constantly be analyzing them. Does the analyzing come to anything? Or are we just doing it because that's just how we experience entertainment now?" The constant buzzing of social media makes it hard for creators to filter out criticism, feminist and otherwise, a fact that can be both exhilarating and discomfiting.

Feminist critics in particular have been vocal in pushing back on themes and tropes that are both frustratingly common and undoubtedly popular. In the spring of 2015, for instance, *The Mary Sue,* an omnivorous geek-culture Web site geared toward female readers, announced that it would no longer be promoting the HBO series *Game of Thrones.* Its reasons were understandable: over five seasons, the fantasy epic based on George R.R. Martin's best-selling series *A Song of Ice and Fire* didn't scrimp on showing terrible people committing horrible acts, but there was something especially unsettling about the show's reliance on the rape of female characters as the driver of their stories. (As Maris Kriezman put it in one consideration, "*Game of Thrones* is a show for *Star Wars* fans who thought Princess Leia should have been raped."[13]) *The Mary Sue* didn't throw in the towel because its writers wanted *GoT*'s producers to see the error of their ways and change; rather, it was making explicit the terms of a marketplace transaction: the return on our investment in this show is diminishing. Thus, as Mary Sue editor Jill Pantozzi wrote, "There will no longer be recaps, photo galleries, trailers, or otherwise promotional items about *Game of Thrones* on *The Mary Sue.*" Blay recalls a similar incident with the FOX show *Sleepy Hollow,* a racially diverse revisiting of the tale of the Headless Horseman. Fans loved its black female lead, Abbie Mills, and revolted when she was shunted to the sidelines after the first season so more time could be spent with white characters. Viewers tuned out, ratings plummeted, a hashtag campaign (#abbiemillsdeservesbetter) mourned the show's bait-and-switch—and the show's creators heard them loud and clear.

In a buyer's market, amid the constant hum of social media, people who create television can't wholly ignore the grumbles, complaints, or reasoned arguments of viewers. Simultaneously, our stake in the honesty and authenticity of pop culture shouldn't overrule creative freedom. But when viewers ask questions like "How many pointless rapes are too many pointless rapes?" (hopefully Ryan Murphy, whose anthology series *American Horror Story* has featured violent rapes of both men and women in each of its five seasons, can answer), it's not an ultimatum, but a way to point out the failure of imagination that remains apparent in a still-gendered medium.

Some creators have actually addressed their critics via plot points in their shows, with mixed results. In 2011, an episode of *30 Rock* went more meta than usual in its show within a show, with a plot that nodded to a discussion that was percolating in the feminist blogosphere, about women and sex appeal in male-dominated comedy spaces. The episode featured a new hire on the fictional *TGS*: Abby, a standup comedian with a "sexy baby voice," that Liz Lemon, the showrunner played by Tina Fey, argues is a self-defeating sop to the patriarchy. Liz believes that the *TGS* "fem-o-lution" she hopes to foment will be hampered by Abby's braless, smut-talking, bubblehead schtick, so she tries to prove that Abby is just as funny as a non-sexy, non-baby-voiced comic by dredging up old video footage and sending it to Jezebel manqué JoanofSnark.com ("this really cool feminist Web site where women talk about how far we've come and which celebrities have the worst beach bodies"). But it turns out that Abby's ditzy-smutty charade is an attempt to conceal her identity from an abusive ex. Liz, in trying to be what she thinks is a "good" feminist, has done the exact opposite.

The episode was an attempt to confront the ouroboros of contemporary discourse around choice, agency, and judgments, and resolved itself by, ultimately, not resolving anything. As Fey explained in a *Fresh Air* interview shortly after the show aired, "It's just such a tangled-up issue, the way women present themselves—whether or not they choose to put their thumbs in their panties on the cover of *Maxim* and judge each other back and forth on it. It's a complicated issue, and we didn't go much further on saying anything other than to say, 'Yeah, it's a complicated issue and we're all kind of figuring it out as we go.'"

Criticism of other female-created pop culture, including Mindy Kaling's *The Mindy Project* and Lena Dunham's *GIRLS*, have similarly wrestled with the heightened expectations that come with viewing pop culture through a feminist lens. The critical reception greeting both shows—*GIRLS* as the latest in a long history of narratives about four somewhat unlikely female friends, *Mindy* as a classic workplace-as-family sitcom—has been disproportionate to the aims of the shows themselves. Both Dunham and Kaling were hustled under the hot lights of feminist-media interrogation as soon as their respective shows debuted, called upon to answer for the shows' racial diversity, attitudes toward and representations of sex and romance, and portrayal of female friendships. Instead of being acknowledged as young creatives in an industry where the playing field is not yet level, they have been forced to defend their visions in ways that male creators are rarely asked to. Dunham, for instance, was promptly swarmed with criticism about the fact that her show, set in modern-day Brooklyn, featured no people of color in either leading or secondary roles. It was definitely an important criticism for a show whose selling point was its verisimilitude—but it also brought up the question of why a young, female creator was being taken to task for something that had never been publicly voiced to male creators of *How I Met Your Mother*, *Bored to Death*, *True Detective*, and many other contemporary shows with the same level of whiteness.

Scandal, the first network drama since 1974's *Get Christie Love!* to feature a black female lead, faced a similarly overwhelming set of expectations when it premiered, and has become TV's version of Beyoncé in the way it is alternately worshipped and contested for its feminist readings. Can Olivia Pope be feminist given her emotionally abusive relationship with the white, Republican President of the United States who jealously keeps her under secret surveillance? Like *UnREAL*'s Rachel, Pope's career success depends on her facility with lying, cheating, and head-gaming others—can that ever be truly progressive? *Scandal* can be read as showrunner Shonda Rhimes's retort to the much-loved male antiheroes of prestige dramas, pointing out that the latitude afforded portrayals of white male (and female) foibles is categorically different when applied to a drama centered on a black woman. Now that Olivia Pope has been joined by a small number of other black female lead characters in dramatic TV—Annalise Keating of *How to Get Away with Murder*, Mary Jane Paul of *Being Mary Jane*, and the mighty Cookie Lyon of *Empire*—the pressure on her has lessened somewhat, but the fact that all antiheroines are not received the same still remains.

The rise of marketplace feminism makes discussing television—or movies, or fashion, or celebrities—an often frustratingly binary affair. One of my most frequent experiences at social gatherings involves people sidling up to admit their love for a particular TV show and how guilty they feel because they know they "shouldn't." In a time of feminism taken into account, there's a sense that if one's choices—even in something as minor as a favorite chill-out show—can't be rationalized, they should probably be kept quiet. As with most-feminist movies and most-feminist underpants, this suggests that feminism is a unvarying entity, a stamp of approval or gold star, rather than a living ethic at the foundation of a larger system. It suggests that feminism is something that either is or is not okay to consume, rather than a lens through which creators and audiences see stories, characters, and communication. Rejecting or embracing it based on static values isn't the goal; the goal is to value the vision and perspective of an increasingly larger, varied group of creators, writers, directors, editors, and DPs as much as we've always valued the industry status quo of white boy wonders.

I don't believe in guilty pleasures when it comes to television. But I understand the impulse to disclose those shameful favorites. For TV-loving feminists, the stakes are high because television is one area of pop culture where we've seen demonstrable change in a fairly short time. It's kind of a chicken-or-egg situation: Has TV come to seem more potentially progressive because viewers engage more with it than ever before, or have we started to engage more because we see new faces and more fascinating and inclusive narratives? Regardless, that change is all the more reason to keep watching; after all, we already know that even a small amount of female-driven content looks to the powers that be like a small screen crawling with women. The Golden Age of Feminist TV is a descriptor that implies it might someday be a cherished memory, but if feminism can change the industry itself, we might be happy to see it go.

CHAPTER 5

Our Beyoncés, Ourselves: Celebrity Feminism

"You're a feminist if you go to a Jay Z and Beyoncé concert and you're not, like, 'I feel like Beyoncé should get 23 percent less money than Jay Z. Also, I don't think Beyoncé should have the right to vote and why is Beyoncé singing and dancing?'" —Aziz Ansari

Over the past eight years, as I've spent time on various college and university campuses around the country, I have seen the emergence of a phenomenon I now think of as Yoncé's Law. Basically, it's this: get a group of mostly white women between the ages of eighteen and fifty together for a panel discussion or seminar or discussion group that's broadly about young women, feminism, and American culture, and within the space of an hour, whatever the initial topic, you will find yourself in the midst of a heated discussion about Beyoncé. There are many, many questions to parse, and you will hear them over and over: Is she good for feminism? Is she bad for feminism? Do *you* think she's a feminist? But if she is a feminist, why did she call her 2013 world tour "The Mrs. Carter Show"? If she's so feminist, what's with all those crazy-skimpy stage costumes? What about her adoption of a seemingly Caucasian beauty standard with those blonde weaves?

What about that "Eat the cake, Anna Mae" line in "Drunk in Love" that references Ike Turner's abuse of Tina? What about Jay Z's misogynistic lyrics? Is she *really* a feminist? And if she's not, is it okay that I love her?

And so on. The questions themselves echo more than a decade's worth of headlines parsing Beyoncé's lyrics, marriage, clothing, and hairstyles, and revealing profound anxiety among (again, mostly white) feminists about a world-famous black woman as an icon of modern liberation. "Beyoncé: Being Photographed in Your Underwear Doesn't Help Feminism," tsked a 2013 *Guardian* headline. "Don't Call Beyoncé's Sexual Empowerment Feminism," warned another. There was musical icon-on-icon sniping from Annie Lennox, who name-checked Beyoncé in a 2014 NPR interview when proclaiming that "twerking is not feminism." And even bell hooks, who literally wrote a book called *Feminism is for Everybody*, recently reconsidered whether "everybody" means, well, *everybody*. As part of a 2014 panel discussion about how black women's bodies are represented in media, hooks had damning words for Mrs. Carter, saying, "I see a part of Beyoncé that is, in fact, anti-feminist—that is a terrorist—especially in terms of the impact on young girls," and noting that when the megastar agrees to things like posing in her underwear on magazine covers, she is "colluding in the construction of herself as a slave." The condemnation of Bey's bona fides, though by that time a predictable media talking point, seemed especially harsh precisely because it came from someone who believes in feminism's populist potential.

Of course, the number of self-described feminists who have appointed themselves to an unofficial Beyoncé feminist-approval task force is easily balanced by the number who have long observed feminism in the singer's lyrics, interviews, and persona, and were just waiting for her to confirm it: the Destiny's Child fans who threw their hands up at Bey as they sang along to "Independent Women Part 1," the ones who noted key passages from her 2014 contribution to *The Shriver Report* on their Tumblrs, the ones who cited the entirety of her

2013 solo album as the sound of a fully grown, sexually confident woman. (There's also a third group, one that would worship Beyoncé even if she came out as a Juggalo, which arguably could still happen.)

The fascination with Beyoncé's feminism, the urge to either claim her in sisterhood or discount her eligibility for it, speaks to the way that a focus on individuals and their choices quickly obscures the larger role that systems of sexism, racism, and capitalism play in defining and constraining those choices. The columnists who wrung their hands over what Beyoncé wore to perform at the Super Bowl or on the cover of *GQ*, after all, didn't also take those institutions themselves to task for aesthetic traditions whereby women in general are treated as little more than eye candy. The people who pursed their lips over Beyoncé taking her husband's name may not have considered a larger context wherein black families—and black single mothers in particular—have long been held responsible for a host of social problems rooted in systemic racism. ("A tangle of pathology," was how then–Assistant Labor Secretary Daniel Patrick Moynihan described often default urban matriarchies in his 1965 report "The Negro Family: A Case for National Action.") If these circumstances were taken into account, it definitely wasn't evident in stories like "Beyoncé's New Album Is Not as Feminist as the Media Is Making It Out to Be."

Tamara Winfrey Harris, author of 2015's *The Sisters Are Alright: Changing the Broken Narrative of Black Women in America*, has noted that many self-described feminists, usually careful to look under surfaces to systems and contexts, seemed willfully sloppy when it came to Beyoncé—"hating the player and ignoring the game."[1] Whatever Beyoncé is or isn't, she's not acting (or singing, or dancing) in a vacuum, but as both a product and a symptom of ongoing inequalities that she had no part in creating.

In making the writing of Chimimanda Ngozi Adichie and the word "feminist" the final statement of her 2014 MTV Video Music Awards performance, Beyoncé acquainted young girls around the world with the concept of feminism completely free from more than a century of baggage. It's hard to overstate how important that is when you consider how many of us learned about feminism through media and pop culture stereotypes of angry, sexless harpies. What does the dictionary definition of feminism look like when it's loosed from all its sour history and negative associations? Well, it looks like Beyoncé herself: confident, compelling, powerful, beautiful, loud. It looks like something you want to be. What Bey staked her claim to that night, for better or worse, was feminism as part of a host of other aspirational products already associated with the Beyoncé brand.

Friends in High Places

In 1978, an eight-year-old girl named Melissa Rich noticed that the many kinds of trading cards she collected featured no women. She brought this to the attention of her mother, Lois, who in turn discussed it with her sister, Barbara Egerman. The sisters realized just how invisible successful women were when they asked Melissa and her friends to each list five women they admired and everyone came up short: according to Lois Rich, girls and boys in her daughter's peer group were unaware of any woman who wasn't either a First Lady or a television personality. So the women came up with their own list of five hundred accomplished women, wrote five hundred letters asking the women for a small favor, and the following year Supersisters became the first trading card set to highlight women's achievements in sports, politics, science, the arts, and more. The initial run, produced with a grant from the New York State Education Department, was distributed to local schools; teachers seemed thrilled to have examples of contemporary heroines to share with their students, and the ten thousand sets that were printed sold fast.

Supersisters were great (and still are: they're archived in the Drawings and Prints department of New York's Metropolitan Museum of Art, and the full set my husband scored on eBay is one of my prized possessions) in that they not only introduced kids to an array of women—from Margaret Mead and Shirley Chisholm to Ntozake Shange and Rosie Casals—but they showed how easy it was to make feminism visible by putting recognizable faces on it.

Celebrities have always been crucial to raising the profile of social movements: Harry Belafonte and Josephine Baker stood for Martin Luther King, Jr. at the March on Washington. Marlon Brando had Sacheen Littlefeather decline his *Godfather* Oscar and use the broadcast platform to decry Hollywood's treatment of Native Americans. Elizabeth Taylor, Madonna, and Elton John ramped up AIDS awareness with fundraisers and danceathons. You might not have known that Tibet needed freeing until the Beastie Boys threw a concert for it. Sad but true: it's much easier to pay attention to a famous person talking about a current event or social issue than it is to listen to someone who may have far more knowledge and experience in the area, but might also have the charisma of dry toast. Feminism, as a political movement that has never been widely popular, has in some ways been needier than most, and the celebrities who have offered their voices, images, and pocketbooks over the years have done so less as spokespeople or heads-for-hire than as strategic partners. The classic children's album *Free to Be You and Me,* conceived by TV actress Marlo Thomas, wouldn't have been half as beloved had it not featured the voices and personalities of TV and movie stars of the era. Thomas's husband, talk-show host Phil Donahue, used his platform to showcase activists and experts to translate the political tenets of the movement into everyday language. The movie, TV, and pop icons who have been cover stars for magazines like *Ms.* and *BUST* may be fascinating in themselves, but they also serve to reassure newer readers that feminism is not the fringe identity they've heard about.

Ms., in its early years, courted Hollywood types as ambassadors for what was in the magazine's first decade a key issue: ratification of the Equal Rights Amendment. The provision drafted to ensure that "Equality of rights under the law shall not be denied or abridged by the United States or by any state on account of sex" was first introduced in Congress in 1923, but failed to pass both houses of Congress again and again, even with bipartisan support. By 1972, it looked like the ERA's time had come, despite the organized efforts of Phyllis Schlafly and her STOP ERA crusade.[2] But though it passed Congress, it still required ratification by three-quarters of state legislatures. By 1979, with the deadline looming, and three states short of ratification, passing the ERA was mainstream liberal feminism's most tangible goal—and a logical rallying point with which to garner celebrity support. A 1978 issue of *Ms.* featured Mary Tyler Moore, *M*A*S*H*'s Alan Alda, *Good Times*'s Esther Rolle, and thirty-four other TV, film, and music personalities in what the cover line promised was "Hollywood's new act"—stumping for the ERA. Robert Redford, Shirley MacLaine, Warren Beatty, and others were publicly on record as supporters; Alda became an official feminist heartthrob when he stated that "Feminism is not just women's business." (The ERA was still three states shy by the extended deadline of 1982; as of 2016, the U.S. Constitution does not prohibit discrimination on the basis of sex.)

Celebrity participation in politics and culture has changed as politics itself has shifted to be more and more about celebrity, as presidential debates turn into clown-car clusterfucks, and "Would you have a beer with this candidate?" is considered as crucial a factor as policy positions. Politicians today have to be entertainers, on top of everything else, because unless we know whether our future leader can crack wise on *The Tonight Show* or gamely dance alongside Ellen DeGeneres, dammit, we just won't know whether they're personable or friendly or not-uppity enough to lead the country. This, too, is less about the players than it is about the game; conglomeration of media creation and an increased focus on the bottom line functionally privilege soundbites over substance and virality over rigor. (I would definitely vote for Hillary Clinton, but that doesn't mean I want to see her attempt to do the Whip with Ellen or stumble over dialogue on *Saturday Night Live.*)

When actual entertainers get political, things often seem just as ungenuine. In the churn of Web sites, podcasts, talk radio shows, social media platforms, and gossip forums competing for fickle eyeballs, the difference between a bombshell scoop and a dud retread rests on the name of the celebrity involved. Fashion magazines regularly include pages documenting the celebrity attendees of charity events for nonprofits you'll never hear about again. Marches and boycotts are out, replaced by art-directed "brand ambassadorships" on behalf of socially-minded corporations. Hollywood's PR ecosystem includes firms that exist solely to match celebrities with humanitarian causes, and though plenty of stars are low-pro about buffing up their brands, they still have to tread lightly lest their names get mixed up with partisanship, moral or religious judgment, or hot-button controversy. (AIDS activism in South Africa? Too political. Children's aid in South Africa? Perfect—the adorable photo ops alone are money in the bank.)

But as a social issue that celebrities get behind, feminism is categorically different than fighting against tiger extinction or hosting fundraisers for the World Food Programme or Heifer International, and more complicated as well. Rather than simply pushing awareness of gender-equality issues beyond a strictly activist arena, we still need celebs for the far more basic task of proving feminism's legitimacy as a movement to begin with. If we can't get an action-movie star with gazillions of impressionable young fans to understand, for the *millionth goddamn time*, that feminism isn't about hating men or not wearing deodorant, what chance do we have of convincing anyone else? This is why the wave of celebrity feminism that began cresting in 2014—in which a number of famous actors, comedians, and pop stars jostled to claim the term like a free tennis bracelet in an awards-show gifting suite—has seemed so full of potential. And so consequently disappointing, but we'll get to that shortly.

Starting in 2014, headlines that used to invoke feminist refusal began glowing with admiration for those who nodded to its importance.

"We Heart: Terry Crews, Fierce Feminist" cooed *Ms.* about the burly *Brooklyn 99* actor and author of *Manhood* (who does seem like a total badass). "Kiera Knightley Deserves a High Five for These Feminist Truth Bombs," insisted MTV News, while "Benedict Cumberbatch Just Became Everybody's Favorite Feminist," offered *Elite Daily*. Reading Twitter feeds and headlines on any given day has begun to feel like watching election-night results roll in on one of CNN's giant interactive maps: We've got Swift! We're getting close to winning Portman ... closer ... we've got Portman! Aziz Ansari and John Legend are in! We lost Kelly Clarkson, well, but ... Joseph Gordon-Levitt, he's good too! What's that? We've got Ruffalo? HIGH FIVE FOR RUFFALO!

Add to this those who have been on Team Gender Equality for even longer—Jane Fonda, Geena Davis, Rosie Perez, Lily Tomlin, Amy Poehler, and, whether you like it or not, Beyoncé—and there is something approaching a critical mass among big-marquee names. Many of them are even walking the walk, though even pointing that out reveals the puny standards of expectation for celebrity activists. Davis, Lena Dunham, Kerry Washington, Gabrielle Union, and Scarlett Johansson are among the celebrities who have appeared in ads or informational videos for Planned Parenthood in the face of its proposed federal defunding. Poehler launched the online girls-empowerment community *Smart Girls at the Party* in 2008. Natalie Portman, who in 2015 signed on to play a young Ruth Bader Ginsberg in the biopic *On the Basis of Sex*, made clear that she wouldn't do the movie unless a female director was hired.

Ironically, part of the catalyst for the celebrity-feminism boom of the last few years was not that so many stars were identifying as feminists, but that in many cases, they weren't. Though "Are you a feminist?" was a question long asked of high-profile women and men interviewed by magazines like *BUST* and *Ms.* and *Bitch*, it's a bit unclear how the question became a red-carpet staple wedged between "Was it hard to change your hair color for this role?" and "Who are you wearing?" Maybe the query's popularity was tied to the increased presence of young women as leads in blockbuster action franchises like *The Hunger Games* and *Insurgent*. Perhaps it was just a result of stiff competition for celebrity scoops in an increasingly crowded field of monetized celebrity gossip, where one grabby headline can yield a whole lot of ad dollars. Actually, it's probably both of those, but I'd argue that the growing awareness has also just reflected the more general tenor of conversation on reproductive choice, sexual harassment, high-profile rape and domestic-violence cases, and more spilling out from feminist news and social media spheres.

It's undeniable that, for a time, asking young female celebrities a question about feminism almost always rang up an embarrassment of triple cherries. There were the young kittens who didn't understand the term, like former *Teen Mom*–turned–porn star Farrah Abraham ("What does that mean, you're a lesbian or something?") and actress Evangeline Lilly ("I'm very proud of being a woman, and as a woman, I don't even like the word feminism because when I hear that word, I associate it with women trying to pretend to be men, and I'm not interested in trying to pretend to be a man"). There were a few who had absorbed the man-hater rumors, like Taylor Swift ("I don't really think about things as guys versus girls") and Lady Gaga ("I'm not a feminist. I love men. I hail men. I celebrate American male culture, and beer, and bars, and muscle cars . . ."). Katy Perry was among the stars who made it clear that it was the word, rather than the entire concept, that she rejected ("I am not a feminist, but I do believe in the strength of women"). Perhaps the most confounding was *Insurgent* star Shailene Woodley, who somehow combined all these things, plus a dash of zero-sum fallacy, into her free-associative answer: "No, because I love men, and I think the idea of 'raise women to power, take the men away from the power' is never going to work out because you need balance. With myself, I'm very in touch with my masculine side. And I'm 50 percent feminine and 50 percent masculine, same as I think a lot of us are. And I think that is important to note. And also, I think that if men went down and women rose to power, that wouldn't work either. We have to have a fine balance."

From these answers and others like them, a media cycle was born: A celebrity, usually young, white, and female, says something dopey that becomes fodder for barbed headlines (e.g., "Don't Go Calling Taylor Swift A Feminist, Says Taylor Swift"). The celeb gets dinged for it in tweets and shares and Tumblr quotes, which causes the original clickbait to expand into a flurry of "write-around" stories—meaning ones that construct a narrative based on previous coverage—about the Fucked-up Thing She Said About Feminism. Those, in turn, spawn an attendant series of think pieces that insist said celebrity is a feminist whether she knows it or not ("Country Music Has Always Been Feminist, Even If Taylor Swift Isn't"), followed by another string of articles that use the celebrity as a news peg to take a broader look at Why Young Women Are Rejecting Feminism. Then comes the backlash to the backlash, which involves a handful of contrary takes defending the celebrity from feminist attack ("Stop Shitting on Taylor Swift's Feminism"). And finally, there's the feminist-redemption arc, in which the celebrity makes headlines once again, this time for announcing that she's rethought this whole feminism thing and, turns out, she is one ("Taylor Swift Changes Her Mind About Feminism"). Is everyone happy now?

More vexing are the famous folks who embrace the label but then became "problematic," to use a now-shopworn catchall of the social justice sphere. In the fall of 2013, for instance, British pop star Lily Allen released her video for "Hard Out Here," a snarky tune that pulled few punches in excoriating pop music's double standards ("If I told you 'bout my sex life, you'd call me a slut/ When boys be talking about their bitches, no one's making a fuss"). The video, which opened with Allen on a gurney, undergoing liposuction (a dig at UK tabloids that constantly monitored her weight gains and losses) would "make feminists proud," gushed one blog. Instead, it made many of them cringe when they saw that Allen, like so many male artists before her, had populated the video with a group of black and Latina female dancers. Or, to be more specific, with their asses. Where Allen stood tall, they crouched; where she preened, they twerked. The vision of a fully clothed white artist accessorizing with the scantily clad tushes of women of color while sneering "Don't need to shake my ass for you/ 'cause I've got a brain" was especially badly timed. Only a month before, at 2013's MTV Video Music Awards, Miley Cyrus had committed the Twerk Seen 'Round the World alongside her own hired crew of black booties that Cyrus interacted with as though they were only incidentally attached to actual women. If Allen's video was meant to be a parody of Cyrus, it didn't land—it wasn't clear whether she was critiquing the way nonwhite bodies are aggressively sexualized in pop culture, or just replicating the insult. Though Allen had plenty of defenders to argue the former angle, and addressed the criticism herself with a public statement, the video's tacit assertion that brains were for white artists and butts for black ones sparked some well-deserved ire from feminists of all shades. It may have been a catchy song, but the most salient part of the "Hard Out Here" video was that it inadvertently highlighted the way celebrity-feminist high-fives are delivered almost exclusively to white celebrities. It's no accident that Cyrus's twerky-jerky sexual pantomimes and frequently-naked appearances in videos and magazines have been deemed to be the work of a "feminist icon," while Rihanna and Nicki Minaj, both known for equally risqué presentations, continue to have onlookers shaking their heads and clutching their pearls.

Cyrus's journey from wholesomely perky preteen fame to hedonistic, tongue-wagging notoriety is a good example of how labeling celebrities as anything, really, is a losing game. In a time of 24-7 celebrity surveillance, corporate media has a habit of anointing famous women—especially young, white ones—as role models for the Youth of America, and then slavering over their eventual downfalls and snatching back their crowns. We've seen it with Britney Spears, with Lindsay Lohan, with Amanda Bynes, and with Miley. And yet it's entirely likely that the actual parents wringing their hands over these reversals of fortune are far outnumbered by media outlets like *The Huffington Post* and *TMZ*, which leverage faux concern into scads of money by milking the incident for two solid weeks of content. Every time one of these stars crashes a car or goes to rehab is a new chance to resurrect ghosts of fallen role models past in online slideshows like "Top 10 Celebrity Girls Gone Bad."

And as with so much related to famous women, the boundless desire to drum up female competition makes role model–seeking into a kind of two-feminists-enter-one-feminist-leaves cage match. Emma Watson became an overnight sensation in November 2014 in the immediate wake of her speech to the United Nations, which was widely shared online. As the ambassador for the U.N. initiative HeForShe—"a solidarity movement for gender equality," according to its Web site—Watson's message, like Alan Alda's before her, was a simple one: gender equality is not simply a woman's fight. ("It is time that we all see gender as a spectrum instead of two sets of opposing ideals.") Within hours of the video's Web debut, media outlets were tripping over each other to find synonyms for "savior of feminism." "Watch Emma Watson Deliver a Game-Changing Speech on Feminism For the U.N." urged *Vanity Fair*'s Web site. "Emma Watson Gives Feminism New Life," raved a CNN editorial.

Watson's speech was heartfelt, eloquent, and far more accessible to what she termed "unintentional feminists"—that is, people who basically believe in the idea but don't self-apply the term—than a theory-heavy text or a 202-level blog post. And the media response was a perfect example of the volatile chemistry of celebrity, branding, race, and politics. The bulk of the news coverage was about Watson herself and the impact that her identification as feminist would surely have on feminism. Within that was a subcategory of missing-the-point stories like "Emma Watson Hits a High Note with Gender Equality Speech—and Wardrobe Choices" and "She Means Business! Emma Watson is Smart and Sophisticated in a Belted White Coat Dress at

UN Event in Role as Goodwill Ambassador for Women"; and another subcategory of listicles reliving the groundbreaking speech itself ("The 5 Most Magical Moments from Emma Watson's HeForShe Speech"). Amid all this, finding out exactly what HeForShe is about was not particularly easy.

Then there was the immediate rush to hold other feminist-identifying celebrities up to Watson's example to see who was more deserving of the title of top celebrity feminist role model. *Vanity Fair* promptly noted that Watson's signature role as Hermione Granger placed her in pole position, with an influence on impressionable youth that's "even stronger than other high-profile defenders of the F-word like Beyoncé." Not to be outdone, the Ms. Foundation actually ranked celebrity feminists in an end-of-year list, its undisclosed criteria putting Watson at the top and Bey at #4, which led to headlines like *Billboard*'s "Beyoncé Loses Feminist of the Year Title to Emma Watson." In a competition that no one had asked for, corporate media outlets seemed to breathe a collective sigh of relief, as though finally, *finally*, there was a straightforwardly appropriate celebrity vessel to express exactly the right amount of feminism in exactly the right way, with no complicating factors like scanty stagewear and Jay Z (Beyoncé), being outspokenly sexual (Rihanna, Nicki Minaj) and insufficiently angular (Lena Dunham), or doing whatever it is Taylor Swift does that precludes a wholehearted feminist embrace of her.

The run of media Watsonmania was less about what Watson planned to accomplish in the name of feminism than it was about the "bravery" of her identity. Ditto for the cascade of fellow Hollywood types whose own declarations of feminism followed hers. Judging from the language that outlets used when reporting on this hot new phenomenon—"9 Celebrity Women Who Aren't Afraid to Call Themselves Feminist," "10 Celebs Who Are Proud of the Feminist Label," "10 Celebs Who Aren't Afraid to Use the F-Word"— the big story wasn't what feminist issues these stars cared about, but their revelatory lack of fear and disgust about aligning themselves with the word.

In the celebrities-with-social-causes realm, this isn't really the norm. Sure, when Elizabeth Taylor began the AIDS awareness activism that defined her post-movie life, helping to found the American Foundation for AIDS Research (amfAR), she shocked more than a few moralists; the combination of a relatively new, largely misunderstood disease and a fearfully closeted industry could have harpooned the profile of a less revered figure, and Taylor was certainly lauded as brave. But it was still the tangible content of her activism that was most often the focus. Contrast that with the list of "9 Male Celebrity Feminists Who Will Make You Swoon," in which one marginally positive interview response, even a jumbled one (per Watson's *Harry Potter* castmate Daniel Radcliffe: "I mean, yes, of course I'm a feminist inasmuch as I'm an egalitarian about everything and I believe in meritocracy") is recycled in listicle after listicle. I'm not questioning Radcliffe's beliefs about equality; for all I know, he has single-handedly constructed a school for girls in a remote village somewhere using cast-off scraps of Gucci tuxedos. And if young, male *Harry Potter* fans happen to read "6 Times Daniel Radcliffe Was Loud & Proud About Being a Feminist" while they're, you know, perusing the women's blogosphere, that's great. But as with many aspects of celebrity feminism, this is setting a low bar and getting excited that it's not actually touching the ground.

Listicle feminism isn't all pointless fluff; an important part of social change is shifting public perceptions with images, language, and a general subtext of *This is no big deal, you guys*. Representations of divorce, interracial relationships, homosexuality, and transgender identity are some of the formerly taboo subjects that have been normalized in large part because of pop culture and media representations. (Remember how weird it was when we had to pretend that Ellen DeGeneres just hadn't found the right guy?) But there's a fine line between transforming the controversial into the mundane and simply refashioning it into a hollow trend, and celebrity feminism is too often falling ass-first on the wrong side of it.

In all movements for social justice, there's been an off-key refrain from outside that goes like this: If only you could be just a little bit less combative, maybe your cause would be more attractive. If only your demands for equality were less *strident*, then people might really get on board—in fact, do you have to *call* them demands? There are few activists who haven't heard some variation on this theme, and though history confirms that social justice just doesn't work that way, feminism in particular has been prone to internalizing the criticism. Those semi-regular calls to "rebrand" feminism over the decades are based on the idea that feminism has alienated so many people that the only way to get it back on track is with a makeover so hypnotically alluring that people will forget what it is they thought was so distasteful about it in the first place.

Such was the outcome of Watson's HeForShe moment. The central focus on working toward gender equality in the world was quickly eclipsed by an emphasis on convincing men that feminism's image isn't as scary as they think—as if they can only be expected to care about equality if it doesn't pose any challenge to their own personal comfort. Mia McKenzie, author and creator of the *Black Girl Dangerous* blog, neatly summed this up, writing: "[Watson] seems to suggest that the reason men aren't involved in the fight for gender equality is that women simply haven't invited them and, in fact, have been *unwelcoming*. Women haven't given men a formal invitation, so they haven't joined in. It's not because, you know, men benefit HUGELY (socially, economically, politically, etc. ad infinitum) from gender inequality, and therefore have much less incentive to support its dismantling. It's not because of the prevalence of misogyny the entire world over. It's just that *no one's asked*."[3]

The feminist movement's dependence on celebrities to legitimize it is frustrating because it's both so seemingly necessary and so self-defeating, and I say this as someone who cofounded a magazine based on the potential of pop culture—including celebrities—to demystify feminism. The reasons that feminists are often anxious to get celebrities on our side are the same ones that have undermined feminism's public image to begin with: we want the inherent value, the *rightness* of the movement to be acknowledged by people who have the megaphone that most of us don't. Celebrities are taken seriously in a way that regular feminists aren't because, ironically enough, they are perceived to have less skin in the game, and therefore less bias. A lot of people would probably assume that Emma Watson, rich and educated and beautiful and famous since she was a child, doesn't *have* to care about gender equality as much as, say, the single mother who keeps getting passed over for promotions in favor of less encumbered male colleagues; the fact that she *does* care must mean maybe it's a legitimate cause. I'm not saying this is any kind of logical train of thought, but it is part of a group of long-extant fallacies that most feminist-identified people will recognize. (See also: "You're too pretty/funny/nice to be a feminist.")

The downside is the way these celebrity engagements with feminism are filtered through media channels: too often, what's emphasized is not the right to be equal and autonomous, but simply the right to have the existence of feminism itself acknowledged as legitimate. Corporate media doesn't want to focus on the numerous systemic issues that keep gender inequality alive and kicking—particularly since that could involve acknowledging its own complicity in some of those systems. Framing a new, cool feminist image solely in terms of how it departs from an older and much less cool feminist image is a safe way to pat celebrities on the back without putting them on the spot. (This is also why in many cases the discussion begins with a question like "How do *you* define feminism, Famous Person?" which informs everyone that a celebrity's definition is just as good as the very clear definition of feminism that already exists.)

This has made for some pretty shallow analyses of celebrity feminist coming-out moments. *Fortune* magazine's 2014 article titled "Will

Young Celebrities Make Feminism 'Cool'?" kicked off with the following all-too-familiar assessment: "Bra-burning. Man-hating. Angry and unattractive. Such stereotypes have shadowed the women's movement over the past few decades—and a slew of young, fashionable celebs are working to clarify feminism's true definition." Similarly, the main takeaway from Beyoncé's VMA performance, judging from the excited responses in tweets and op-eds, seemed to be that she's now proven definitively that feminists don't have to be: a) morally opposed to marriage and children; b) unfashionable; and c) (once more with feeling!) a man-hater. When you consider that, in previous decades, media made the same points about Gloria Steinem, Rebecca Walker, Naomi Wolf, and others, this doesn't exactly count as a groundbreaking revelation. As well-meaning as individual feminist celebrities might be, this mediated response to them just serves to reinvent a wheel that didn't get us very far to begin with.

The Enemy of the Good

The combination of fame and feminism has always been an uneasy one; intra-movement criticism of both ideals and icons was a theme long before second-wave feminism made "trash" a verb. A 1948 consideration of the women's-suffrage movement published in *The Nation* by feminist organizer Ramona Barth prodded readers to "consider the hitherto unanalyzed weaknesses as well as the obvious strengths of the movement which was begun at Seneca Falls; it is healthy to unveil not only marble statues to their memory but the inner motives of the first feminists."[4] Barth's minor shade was majorly echoed in 1970s women's liberation when many members initially shunned the term "feminist": as Alice Echols notes in her second-wave chronicle, *Daring to Be Bad*, they associated it with the "bourgeois and reformist"—as well as racially exclusionary—stripe of Elizabeth Cady Stanton, Susan B. Anthony, and others, seeing their own movement as having more in common with revolutionary women's movements in Cuba and China.

The third wave of the 1990s, in turn, loudly defined itself against the second wave's ostensible sex-negativity, racism, classism, and separatism, the generational equivalent of an emo teenager slamming a bedroom door in her mother's face. And the fourth wave is more of a tsunami, sweeping up fragments of feminisms past and deploying them in everything from focused grassroots organizing to cynical commercial product pitches.

But though feminism is arguably less monolithic than it's ever been, there is one thing that hasn't changed and likely never will, and that's the fierce internal conflict that ensues when individual figures, intentionally or not, come to symbolize the movement through media and pop culture representations. There have always been "famous feminists" who, via best-selling books, viral videos, or hit songs, become the face of feminism, if only temporarily. The skepticism that accompanies their rise is connected to an anxiety about how they will "sell"— and more to the point, perhaps, sell out—an ideology that has largely been defined by people hostile to it.

"Women rise to [feminist] fame not because they are lauded as leaders by other feminists . . . but because the mainstream media sees in them a marketable image—a newsworthy persona upon whom can be projected all sorts of anxieties, hopes, and responsibilities," wrote Rachel Fudge in a 2003 essay on the struggle to reconcile activism and renown. This is important, both as it relates to feminism's past and to its improbable embrace by mainstream American pop culture. On one hand, social movements need the diplomacy and charisma of people who can speak and agitate on behalf of them. On the other, the need to distill complex ideas and goals down to their most simple and quotable talking points has unquestionably done harm to those movements, feminism included. Mainstream attention has oversimplified complex issues—the wage gap, the beauty myth, the debate over decriminalizing sex work—and misrepresented goals. It has attributed collective successes to one person and minimized the plurality of feminist movements themselves. And it has turned countless would-be colleagues and compatriots into foes scrapping over crumbs of access and affirmation.

Jo Freeman's *Ms.* article "Trashing: The Dark Side of Sisterhood" still regularly makes its way from inbox to inbox because the anguish with which it articulates the process of being sidelined, gaslighted, and shunned—all in the name of sisterhood—is still so relevant. Freeman defined trashing as something that often masquerades as critique but is wholly different: "a particularly vicious form of character assassination" that "is not done to expose disagreements or resolve differences" but "to disparage and destroy." After its publication in 1976, the piece garnered more letters than any previous piece in *Ms.*—"all but a few," notes the essay's current preface, "relating [the writers'] own experience of being trashed." Formerly a member of the Chicago branch of radical feminists, Freeman left the movement completely after her deflating experiences. But two of her essays, "Trashing" and "The Tyranny of Structurelessness"—the latter an outline of the idealistic, leaderless context in which trashing often occurs—still put words to ongoing phenomena.

Individual feminists are used to being insulted and bullied by people who bear an inventory of beefs with feminists in general, especially these days, and inevitably online. Trashing—or its contemporary cousin, "calling out," is different and usually a lot more painful because it comes from fellow feminists. Thanks in part to social media, trashings have become more public and more frequent—with participants, as feminist sociologist Katherine Cross put it, "hyper-vigilant against sin, great or small, past or present."[5] It's possible for trashings to start out with a core of completely valid critique but spiral outward into chaos as more people pile on and context is diffused. Some are way pettier: I was once informed that I was being trashed on an online bulletin board because I hadn't posed an apparently crucial question to a screenwriter I'd profiled. Trashings might be focused on an ideal of ideological purity: "careerist," for instance, is a sneer aimed at feminists who have the temerity to want to be known (or at least paid) for their work. Other trashings might result from an opinion that's unforgivably at odds with current feminist orthodoxy.

The competitiveness that leads to trashing obviously isn't unique to feminist movements, but as many people have pointed out over the years, it's likely to thrive within them because so many women, across ages and races and classes, are socialized to see themselves as connectors and uniters rather than experts and leaders; it's even more likely to fester because of the unmended rifts of past feminist movements. The incendiary tone of trashing is also heightened because the line between one's activism and identity is often as substantive as a vapor trail; trashing someone's work becomes indistinguishable from trashing the person themselves.

A joke among academic professionals is that "the politics are so vicious because the stakes are so low." Rerouted to describe feminist movements, it's just as true. Take a movement that continually battles to justify its very existence, made up of millions of individuals with attendant millions of personalities, politics, and priorities. Throw in the multitude of causes and projects intrinsic to that movement, as well as the structural issues that too often make addressing them an exercise in wheel-spinning: lack of interest, lack of funding, and lack of time, to name just three. Add to those a history in which "feminism" has been broadly defined and disproportionately led by middle-class, educated, able-bodied white women. And finally, drizzle in the contemporary mainstream- and social-media climate that prizes conflict over nuance and shock over substance.

Navigating the half-finished project of feminism amid all this is a staggering task, so it's not surprising that so much frustration isn't channeled outward to the larger world of inequality but inward, at the microcosm of it that exists among fellow feminists. There are hundreds of ways that people are understood to be "doing feminism wrong"—I might be doing it right now!—particularly in online spaces where seasoned thinkers and activists find themselves engaging with people freshly enrolled in their first Women's Studies class. There's a

Sisyphean slog through the same sets of arguments, over and over: feminists of color are taxed by having to explain and defend the concept of intersectionality; feminists engaged in sex work are frustrated by others who presume to know their lives better than they do. Within these virtual and actual spaces, such issues feel urgent, and personal, and crucial. But from outside, it can look very much like a movement that's eating its own.

This makes celebrities adopting feminism as their brands an especially complicated prospect. Feminism may be something that individual celebs honestly care about, but often their knowledge of actual feminist issues is inversely proportional to the reach of their voices. When Patricia Arquette won the Best Actress Oscar in 2015, for instance, she turned her acceptance speech into a chance to talk about wage equality—on its face, an excellent use of a momentary worldwide platform. But Arquette got in the way of her own well-meaning comments later, in the backstage press room, when she said, "It's time for all the women in America, and all the men that love women and all the gay people and all the people of color that we've all fought for to fight for us now." The oddly-worded statement seemed to suggest that struggles for LGBT individuals and people of color were a settled matter that white women had ingeniously fixed as we patiently waited for "our" turn; the reaction to it was as angry as it was swift.

Later in 2015, as Amnesty International prepared to vote on a policy to decriminalize the sex trade, a cluster of Hollywood feminists—including Lena Dunham, Meryl Streep, Emma Thompson, and Kate Winslet—signed on to a petition opposing the new policy. The issue of decriminalization is thorny and regularly misunderstood (especially with regard to where it differs from legalization); and debating its complexities is generally best left to those with the most experiential knowledge of the issues, e.g., sex workers themselves. The fact that famous actresses for whom the realities of the sex trade are almost wholly abstract were unwittingly putting sex workers' livelihoods and safety in the balance offered a great illustration of how celebrity feminism can be as much a hindrance as a help. As one anonymous sex worker told *The Daily Beast*, "The fact that celebrities who have no stake in this and will not be impacted by it are getting the largest voice is frustrating and, frankly, dehumanizing."

Meanwhile, as public figures in increasingly crowded fields, celebs' work as actors or pop stars or viral sensations necessitates keeping themselves relevant. It all adds up to an unavoidable skepticism about what stake celebrities really have in feminism, and an understandable frustration when even their best intentions are badly executed. As happened in the wake of Arquette's Oscar-night words, there's a chance that the baby gets thrown out with the bathwater, with people disregarding the root content of her wage-gap activism due to her careless phrasing. It's valid to critique such statements when they're made: the problem is, those critiques can easily be construed as just another form of trashing.

Reasonably or not, we tend to treat celebrities as authorities, which means they can validate the legitimacy of feminist ideas and politics in a way that feminist movements themselves may never be able to do. The one thing they can't be is perfect: not even Beyoncé can be everything to every feminist, though please don't tell her I wrote that. Celebrities should be able to be as fallible as the rest of us, but unfortunately we never quite let them, and it's this that most likely dooms celebrity feminism's potential for real change-making. They embody the danger of making the perfect the enemy of the good, but in adopting feminism as part of their individual brands, they also risk reducing it to a buzzword that will be out of style by the time next year's awards season rolls around.

Brand-name Feminism

At its simplest, the difference between a celebrity-branded feminism and a feminist movement as a social and political force is that one is about individuals and the other about systems. Individual celebrities are great at putting an appealing face on social issues. But the celebrity machine is one that runs on neither complexity nor nuance, but on cold, hard cash. How much can celebrity feminists do if their prominent voices emanate from within systems—the film, TV, and music industries, for starters—in which gender inequality is a generally unquestioned m.o.? Emphasizing the personal empowerment of individual actors, comedians, and pop stars, whether for itself or in relation to others, only serves to pull focus from the ways in which their industries make money from stereotyping and devaluing women. Is it celebrities' responsibility to fix those industries single-handedly? Of course not. But it's also not ridiculous to suggest that publicly taking on feminism as a pet cause should ideally be about more than just basking in the media attention you get for taking that stance. Again, paragon-hood is not the goal, but at the very least, boning up on current feminist issues and perspectives will prevent more unfortunate incidents like Arquette's wage-gap fiasco.

In continuing the dialogues about equality and representation, small shots of honesty and transparency go a long way. Actor and comedian Amy Schumer is among the celebrity feminists who have been tagged as problematic (like many a stand-up comedian, her work has leaned heavily on casual racism), but she's also been refreshingly unwilling to buy into the women-are-on-top-now! media spin that's been amplified by her own speedy ascent to Emmy-winning fame. In the fall of 2015, as Madonna's "Rebel Heart" tour took over Madison Square Garden, Schumer served as Madge's opening act and promptly took aim at the idea that it's a new, exciting day for women in Hollywood. "Why would it be exciting?" she retorted. "In an industry that judges you solely based on your appearance, when you know that every day you're just decomposing, barreling toward death while smaller, younger starlets are popping out and you know you're just six months away from having to wear a long white button-down and trying to fuck Michael Douglas at a Thanksgiving party? No. It's not an exciting time for women in

Hollywood. Are you serious?" The bit echoed her instantly-viral 2015 video sketch "Last Fuckable Day," in which Schumer discovers Julia Louis-Dreyfus, Tina Fey, and Patricia Arquette lunching in the woods to commemorate Louis-Dreyfus's passage from, in casting terms, "believably fuckable" female roles to ones "where you go to the wardrobe department and all they have for you to wear are long sweaters."

Schumer's cutting honesty is an exception that she's able to get away with in part because her medium is comedy—but, more important, because with her own successful movie and Comedy Central show, she has more control over her career than many of her Hollywood peers. Former romantic-comedy mainstay Katherine Heigl is an example of a woman whose honesty about the treatment of female characters hasn't gone nearly as well: After her breakout role in 2007's *Knocked Up*, Heigl made the mistake of telling *Vanity Fair* that she found the film's plot "a little sexist" in its portrayal of "the women as shrews, as humorless and uptight" while the men are "lovable, goofy, fun-loving guys." She was promptly branded "difficult," with even ostensibly feminist Web sites like Jezebel frowning on her bad form, and her career foundered. Who knows whether Heigl's relatively tactful criticism would go over better in the brave new slightly-more-woman-friendly film environs of today, but at that time her treatment in the media served as an effective warning to other women to keep a lid on their opinions.

Several years later, the spotlight was on another woman who was deemed insufficiently grateful: though she didn't call out the film's content, *Precious* star Mo'Nique was pilloried for her diffident approach to promoting the film and campaigning for the Best Supporting Actress Oscar that she eventually won. In an interview with the *Hollywood Reporter*, the actress recalled *Precious* director Lee Daniels telling her that she'd been "blackballed" in Hollywood because of her unwillingness to "play the game"—you know, the game of cuddling up to an industry that regularly erases or sidelines women of color.[6]

Cautionary tales like these might help explain why celebrity feminists (and the media that flocks to them) seem more comfortable with feminism as an identity than with its substance. Then again, there aren't many media outlets pressing them to talk specifics. "If you're a celebrity, you're able to capitalize on the zeitgeisty moment that feminism is having in popular culture," notes J. Maureen Henderson, a writer and self-described "millennial expert," when I call to get her take on the new power of the feminist brand among young luminaries. "You can say 'I'm a feminist' and we're not really going to ask you to put your money where your mouth is, to look for that in practice in the roles that you choose or the collaborators that you work with or the songs that you write. It's enough that you've self-identified—that gets the headline, and living the practice is much less interesting to us, it seems."

Furthermore, there's no real incentive for celebrities to back up their identities with action. Sure, some corners of the feminist blogosphere might *want* to hold their feet to the fire, but the feminist blogosphere isn't paying their bills or casting their next project. Shortly after her HeForShe speech at the U.N., Emma Watson announced that her next film was a live-action remake of *Beauty and the Beast*, the most heartwarming Disney tale ever to be based around Stockholm Syndrome. What a great opportunity for the newly crowned Top Feminist of 2014 to make connections between her global cause and a story about a woman who falls in love with a man who overpowers her and locks her in a castle! Can't wait to hear what she has to say!

<Crickets.>

Okay, so Emma Watson's individual belief in feminism isn't compromised by taking on the role of a kidnapped princess, just as, say, George Clooney's activism on behalf of political and journalistic ethics didn't preclude him from voicing *The Fantastic Mr. Fox*'s very unethical title animal. With feminism as both a Hollywood buzzword and an identity she's publicly taken on, it's not illogical to think Watson would *want* to speak to how it informs the roles she chooses. But, again, the media outlets that have made her feminism a focal point of coverage aren't asking. It's a pretty good illustration of the fact that while most celebrity feminism is no doubt individually well-meaning, it often has no tangible connection to the images and fantasies we pay those celebrities to construct.

In writing about the celebrity-feminist phenomenon for the UK's *Guardian*, writer and cultural critic Roxane Gay, who authored 2014's *Bad Feminist*, put it plainly: "So long as we continue to stare into the glittery light of the latest celebrity feminist, we avoid looking at the very real inequities that women throughout the world continue to face. We avoid having the difficult conversations about the pay gap and the all-too-often sexist music we listen to and the movies we watch that tell women's stories horribly (if at all) and the limited reproductive freedom women are allowed to exercise and the pervasive sexual harassment and violence too many women face. We avoid having the conversations about the hard work changing this culture will require."[7] It's as though feminists are becoming part of a celebrity movement, rather than celebrities joining up with a feminist one.

As with branding, celebrity isn't about complexity, but about offering up an enticing package that the largest number of people can understand with the smallest amount of effort. Which is why it seems important to approach and query celebrities in a way that corporate media will never do. Instead of asking celebrities how they "define" feminism, we should ask how they enact it in their work and their communities. Rather than focusing on the clothes they wear when agitating for causes, we can find ways to amplify their messages. These are not unreasonable requests, but we've been conditioned to think they are via a mediated celebrity culture that can withstand politics only until they begin to reflect poorly on the industry itself. If celebrities truly have a stake in feminism, it can no longer be about who is "bravely" embracing a maligned word. We've spent enough time patting actresses and pop stars on the back for "redefining" feminism with their beauty and appeal, or "changing the game" simply by showing up and agreeing that, yes, totally, we *should* all be equal. Media and pop culture have to help change the narrative whereby simply claiming an identity that's feminist stands in for actually doing work in the service of equality. It can no longer be about who says they stand for feminism, but about *how* they stand for it. Like past Hollywood stances on AIDS awareness, environmentalism, antiwar activism, and more, celebrity feminism may well fade out to make way for the next big thing, but while it's here, we have a small chance to refocus the spotlight.

PART TWO

The Same Old Normal

CHAPTER 6

Killer Waves

If the backlash against feminism that began in the 1980s had a theme song, it would be the ominous musical score to *Fatal Attraction*, the 1987 thriller that packed all the fear and loathing of women's liberation into 119 minutes of running time and became the backlash's filmic standard-bearer. We probably all know the story by now: Married man meets single woman for a one-night stand. He peaces out, she becomes obsessed. Suicide is attempted, a tranquil suburban home is invaded, a pet bunny is boiled. Order is restored when the wronged wife kills the imposter who has dared to sully her marriage (not to mention her bathtub). The moral of this cautionary tale? Single career ladies are fucking scary, man.

I would submit, though, that 1987's John Updike adaptation, *The Witches of Eastwick*, is at least as emblematic of 1980s big-screen backlash as *Fatal Attraction*. As Updike originally wrote them in his novel of the same name, the witches Alexandra, Jane, and Sukie are formerly partnered but now happily single women who are aware and in control of their supernatural powers, and deploy them occasionally and shrewdly. In the movie, by contrast, the women are widowed, divorced, and deserted ciphers (played respectively by Cher, Susan Sarandon, and Michelle Pfeiffer) who only become attuned to their flair for witchery once the rich, mysterious, and bizarre Daryl Van Horn moves to town to seduce them and turn their boring lives upside down with sexual chaos. Jack Nicholson's Van Horn mesmerizes each women in turn with windy monologues about the nurturing, elemental power of the female sex, as well as denigrations of the average dick-swinging male. "Men are such cocksuckers, aren't they?" he coos to Sarandon's Jane, the town's prim orchestra conductress. "You don't have to answer that. It's true. They're scared. Their dicks get limp when confronted by a woman of obvious power and what do they do about it? Call them witches, burn them, torture them, until every woman is afraid. Afraid of herself... afraid of men... and all for what? Fear of losing their hard-on."

The film (whose director, George Miller, is the man behind 2015's most-feminist-movie-of-the-year, *Mad Max: Fury Road*) revels in superficial ideas of female power and potency, but tempers them at every turn by punishing the characters who dare to believe that their power offers them independence. When small-town gossip about the women threatens to derail their livelihoods and they pull away from Van Horn, he wastes no time punishing them: calling them witches and torturing them until . . . well, he said it himself. Finally, in desperation, the ladies pool their powers to fight back, and Van Horn's true feelings about women are revealed in the spectacular set piece that results. As he stumbles, vomits, and pratfalls (did I mention this is a comedy?) into the town church under the women's spell, Van Horn rants about the evil that women inflict on any poor soul willing to love them, and appeals to God to explain these infernal creatures: "Women: A mistake, or *did he do it to us on purpose?*"

In Updike's novel, as Margaret Atwood pointed out in her 1984 *New York Times* review of it, the source of the witches' power was simple: "They became husbandless . . . embodiments of what American small-town society tends to think about divorcees." At novel's end, all three are remarried. And in the film, Van Horn gets the last laugh the old-fashioned way, foreclosing on the women's independence from him by knocking each of them up. The film's final scene shows that while the women managed to vanquish Van Horn's physical form, they're saddled with three literal spawns of Satan, all boys, who are summoned by the disembodied devil through a giant bank of television sets. It's a final warning to not just the witches, but to any women uppity enough to think that they can dare to be autonomous from or change the essential man: *Don't get too comfortable, ladies.*

As a confluence of movements that, taken together, posed a burgeoning threat to the status quo, the women's liberation efforts of the 1960s and '70s were promptly and ungenerously mediated. The activists who demonstrated and marched in the streets were deemed "a small band of braless bubbleheads"; reporter Marilyn Goldstein of *Newsday* was instructed by her editor to "Get out there and find an authority who'll say this is all a crock of shit." Some of the earliest examples of what Jennifer L. Pozner has dubbed False Feminist Death Syndrome (a "pernicious, media-borne virus" that "contaminat[es] our collective understanding of the history, ideology, and goals of the women's movement,"[1]) were presented in the "No Comment" section of a 1982 issue of *Ms.* The page, known mostly for collecting egregiously sexist and racist ads, this time comprised newspaper and magazine headlines that crowed over the apparent downfall and obsolescence of the fight for gender equality. "Requiem For the Women's Movement: Empty Voices in Crowded Rooms" (*Harper's*, 1976), "Women's Lib is Dead" (*Educational Digest*, 1973), and "Is Feminism Finished? (*Mademoiselle*, 1981) were among the declarations and bad-faith queries that were symptoms of the media's chronic condition.

The backlash that Susan Faludi described, in her 1990 book of the same name, as a "relentless whittling-down process . . . that has served to stir women's private anxieties and break their political wills" was effective because it had an ace disguise: postfeminism. Though the term's origin is sometimes contested, before 1980 it was found chiefly in academic writing alongside a host of other "post"-prefixed theories (postmodernism, postcolonialism, poststructuralism); the "post" postulated what came next to build on the foundation of feminist theory.

But as the term seeped out of the academy into a new, conservative era, mainstream media seemed unnervingly pleased to embrace the "post" in postfeminism to mean "against." As in, pack it up, go away, you're done. The books had been written, the marchers had marched, nothing more to see here.

The first mainstream use of the term was in a 1981 *New York Times* piece titled "Voices From the Post-Feminist Generation," in which writer Susan Bolotin found that young, middle-class women were actively retreating from the concept of feminism. Bolotin's subjects spoke of feminism and the women's movement with barely disguised pity. "It's all right to be independent and strong, but a lot of those women are alone," said one. Another offered, "Sure, there's discrimination out there, but you just can't sit there feeling sorry for yourself. It's the individual woman's responsibility to prove her worth. Then she can demand equal pay." It was a striking bit of cognitive dissonance, and even the author didn't bother to draw connections between second-wave feminists' work on behalf of equality and her interviewees' freedom to disparage it.

The rejection identified by the *Times* article centered on a very specific demographic—mostly college-educated, career-minded young white women whose thoughts and experiences would become invaluable to media coverage of "the death of feminism." In fact, feminism flowered in the 1980s; it just happened to be in places that mainstream media wasn't inclined to look. Black and Latina women, in particular, whose involvement in second-wave activism was mostly eclipsed by the movement's focus on the concerns of white and middle-class ones, spent the decade shaping a feminism that better acknowledged how race and class identities intersect with gender to inform and impact women's lives. The groundbreaking texts of womanism and intersectional feminism published during the 1980s—Angela Davis's *Women, Race, and Class*; Cherrie Moraga and Gloria Anzaldua's *This Bridge Called My Back*; Gloria Hill, Patricia Bell Scott, and Barbara Smith's *All the Women are White, All the Blacks are Men, but Some of Us are*

Brave; Paula Giddings's *When and Where I Enter*; Audre Lorde's *Sister Outsider*; and bell hooks's *Feminist Theory: From Margin to Center*—simply didn't fit the mainstream media's narrative of feminism as a finite movement whose time had come and gone. As a media story, women of color broadening the scope of feminist theory in the academy and beyond wasn't nearly sexy enough for column inches. White women cruelly brushing off the efforts of their predecessors while greedily enjoying the fruits of their labors? *That* could sell.

Media postfeminism didn't happen in a vacuum, but in an enormously changed national climate. President Ronald Reagan swept into office in 1980 on a wave of increasing conservatism and neoliberalism, and his platform—anti-abortion, anti-civil rights, anti-social services, anti-affirmative action—was, among other things, the start of decades of policy that pointedly targeted women's autonomy. Reagan struck the Equal Rights Amendment from the Republican platform, backed the anti-abortion Human Life Amendment, buddied up to the Religious Right, and set the tone for rising enmity toward families in poverty with his florid image of the government-draining "welfare queen." The GOP veered rightward with shocking speed, becoming a bizarro mix of cowboy fantasy and cartoon villainy in its attitudes toward women, ethnic minorities, immigrants, the mentally ill, and more. ("We have tried for two years to meet with him, but he will not see women's groups," noted the leader of the National Women's Political Caucus, herself a Republican, in 1983. "I don't think there is any woman within shouting distance of the President."[2])

Against this backdrop, the concrete successes of second-wave feminism—including no-fault divorce, criminalizing of domestic violence, hiring equality, equal access to education, and more—were recast as failures by much of the mainstream media. Such freedom, their stories and op-eds charged, had created monsters in the form of ultra-independent women who realized too late that they were childless, lonely, and starved for love. Newspapers and magazines were only too happy to cherry-pick statistics and warp study findings into fainting-couch stories about equality run rampant. As Faludi pointed out, the media's adoption of postfeminism wasn't an accident, but a crusade built on faulty logic, lack of nuance, and a fundamental discomfort with actual feminist gains. "The press," she wrote, "was the first to set forth and solve for a mainstream audience the paradox in women's lives . . . women have achieved so much yet feel so dissatisfied; it must be feminism's achievements, not society's response to those partial achievements, that is causing women all this pain."[3]

The news story that most famously anchored the backlash was *Newsweek*'s 1986 report on "The Marriage Crunch." On the magazine's cover was a graph that looked like the world's worst single-drop roller coaster, and next to it, the headline "If You're a Single Woman, Here Are Your Chances of Getting Married." Inside was the now-notorious assertion that heterosexual, college-educated women who had not married by age forty had a better chance of being killed by a terrorist than of nabbing a husband: that asserstion alone launched a thousand trend stories, dating services, man-catching seminars, and advice columns. But as Faludi noted, the story extrapolated from a study, "Marriage Patterns in the United States," whose actual findings, when broken down, were not nearly as dire as *Newsweek*'s interpretation (and said nothing about terrorism). But in an increasingly conservative time, as "family values" became coded language for hetero, male-breadwinner/female-homemaker marriage, the mainstream media was hungry for any news that might help to discredit or undermine feminism, and *Newsweek*'s bombshell accomplished both. Not only did it point the finger at feminism for making women delay marriage at their peril, the panic it sowed intimated that, for all this talk about liberation and independence, what women really wanted was a traditional, normative love story. This narrative not only had legs, it had control-top hose and running shoes. Fifty-three feature articles bemoaning the lonely state of career woman (and feminism's role in their unhappiness) ran between 1983 and 1986, as compared with five during the previous three years.

A Passion for Bashin'

As the film version of *The Witches of Eastwick* illustrated, the specter of uppity white women hoisted by their own petard of liberation was Hollywood gold. Anxiety about what the women's movement would mean for the nuclear family and for heterosexual love had been a theme in a handful of the movies produced as the second wave unfolded. Films like *Up the Sandbox*, *Alice Doesn't Live Here Anymore*, and *Sheila Levine is Dead and Living in New York* offered a window into women's frustration with traditional gender roles, as well as their well-socialized instinct to resist rebellion. Others, like *The Stepford Wives* and *Looking for Mr. Goodbar*, directly linked freedom and danger. But postfeminist popular culture was unequivocal in portraying liberated woman as either manipulative shrews upending men's lives with their unholy mix of sexual independence and emotional neediness, or unhinged victims of their own ambition. In *Kramer vs. Kramer*, for instance, selfish career woman Joanna needs to "find herself," leaving her hapless husband to raise a child he's barely interacted with. Jane Craig, *Broadcast News*'s neurotic star producer, can't move up the career ladder without plummeting down the romantic one. And Jill Davis, the ex-wife to Woody Allen's Isaac in *Manhattan*, is portrayed as an ice queen who publishes a warts-and-more-warts account of their marriage, and an emasculating lesbian. (Both Jill and Joanna were played by Meryl Streep; make of that what you will.)

On the small screen, the stories were often similar: some of TV's most prominent female characters were the conniving, backbiting matriarchs of prime-time soaps like *Dynasty*, *Falcon Crest*, and *Knots Landing*, who undercut the idea that sisterhood is powerful with copious hair pulling and bitch slapping. This was feminism as individual power struggle, and the women involved ruthlessly sacrificed anything that stood in the way of their ascent to wealth and control.[4] In the relatively new genre of workplace procedural dramas like *L.A. Law*, *St. Elsewhere*, and *Hill Street Blues*, female characters who chose work over family paid dearly (and dramatically) for it with nervous breakdowns, drug addictions, and vengeful husbands. Adding to TV's generally retrogressive vibe was the popular rise of televangelism, which, though it existed before the 1980s, assumed its place in cultural dialogue as Ronald Reagan aligned his presidency with fundamentalist Christianity. Ministries like Jim and Tammy Bakker's PTL (Praise the Lord) Club, Jerry Falwell's Moral Majority, and Jimmy Swaggart's Assemblies of God attracted monster audiences to their small-screen sermons. Though you could argue that they were most often preaching to the converted, it wasn't long before their theatrical denunciations of divorce, homosexuality, the ERA, and women working outside the home oozed into the sightline of secular audiences.

And then there's our friend *Fatal Attraction*. The blockbuster was initially conceived and made by its British writer, James Dearden, as a short film called *Diversion* that focused on the moral consequences of a man's affair. As its original champion, Hollywood producer Sherry Lansing recalled, "What I liked in the short film is that the man is made responsible. That there are consequences for him . . . And that's what I wanted to convey in our film. I wanted the audience to feel great empathy for the woman."[5] But after Lansing brought the script to Paramount, Dearden was pressured to rewrite the story so that it no longer lingered on the moral grays of imperfect people, instead casting the man as utterly innocent and the woman as an unhinged neurotic whose sexual freedom and great career can't make up for the family she really wanted. Director Adrian Lyne was blunt in his scorn for liberated women—"Sure, you got your career and your success, but you are not fulfilled as a woman"—and star Michael Douglas was equally disparaging, saying, "If you want to know, I'm really tired of feminists, sick of them. . . . Guys are going through a terrible crisis right now because of women's unreasonable demands." Such vehement ire left no room for nuance. The film's original ending—in which homewrecker Alex commits suicide, in the process framing innocent, pentitent Dan for murder—was vetoed in favor of having Dan and his wife defend themselves against the homicidal Alex. (Twenty-five years after *Fatal Attraction* was released, Dearden finally got to produce the story he'd originally written, as a stage play in London.)

The era's onscreen image of a sexually independent black woman was just as controversial, if somewhat less melodramatic. In Spike Lee's debut feature, 1986's *She's Gotta Have It*, the "she" of the title is Nola Darling, an artist with three lovers who hate each other on principle, but hate Nola even more for daring to be unapologetic about her desires. Her blithe attitude toward sex, in their eyes, makes her a "freak" and a "nympho"—there are simply no neutral terms for a woman who enjoys sex but doesn't link it to love or long-term relationships. The dramatic peak of the film comes toward its end, when Nola's lover Jamie hurls her down on a mattress and rapes her while demanding to know "Whose pussy is this?" It's not meant to be horrifying; instead, it's depicted as the only way Nola can be "tamed" into a proper woman and partner. Reviewing the film at the time it was released, black feminist Cora Harris lamented that the rape seemed meant to be read as an action provoked by Nola's autonomy, rather than by Jamie's macho possessiveness: "In Spike Lee's own words," Harris wrote, "Nola is 'acting like a man'—a pseudo male. And in thus stepping outside [the] 'women's role,' Nola is fair game for depression, nightmares, and rape."[6] Lee, who is currently rebooting *She's Gotta Have It* as a series for the Showtime network, told *Deadline Hollywood* in a 2014 interview that the one regret of his career was the rape scene: "If I was able to have any do-overs, that would be it."

When most people consider the source of feminism's bad reputation, the images are of loud, marching women agitating for their rights while wearing unflattering slacks—an army of Andrea Dworkins. But the media and pop culture images that accompanied the backlash were at least as destructive. As someone who came to feminism as a teenager in the '80s, my ability to articulate ideas and opinions—even to friends and family—was absolutely tempered by the animosity that was baked into so much of the decade's pop products. There was a dissonance between what women and girls were told we had—equality, full stop—and what we often experienced, but the language to talk about it was, for most of us, still out of reach.

Waving, Not Drowning

Among the fearsome stereotypes constructed in 1980s political, economic, and social culture—the money-grubbing yuppie birthed by Wall Street, the Cadillac-driving welfare queen conjured up by Reaganomics—the Feminist was both abstract and deeply potent. In her 1991 book *Feminist Fatale*, journalist Paula Kamen surveyed the toll of the backlash on her generation, finding overwhelmingly that the young, diverse women and men she interviewed supported the *goals* of feminism but shunned the word itself; only about 16 percent were willing to use it to describe themselves. That jibes with attitudes I encountered in my initial forays into college feminism in the early 1990s; I can recall one meeting of a burgeoning student feminist club at which three-quarters of the allotted time was spent debating whether putting the word itself on banners in the student center would be "too much." The stereotypes that haunted us were legion, as Kamen wrote: "bra-burning, hairy-legged, amazon, castrating, militant-almost-antifeminine, communist, Marxist, separatist, female skinheads, female supremacists, he-woman types, bunch-a-lesbian, you-know-dykes, man-haters, man-bashers, wanting-men's-jobs, want-to-dominate-men, want-to-be-men, wear-short-hair-to-look-unattractive, bizarre-chicks-running-around-doing-kooky-things, I-am-woman-hear-me-roar, uptight, angry, white-middle-class radicals."

But in 1991, there was a crucial moment, a portent that galvanized many young people like those Kamen interviewed into realizing that, hairy-legged or not, feminism was a far-from-finished project. It came in the form of the congressional hearings that confirmed Clarence Thomas as a U.S. Supreme Court justice and made law professor

Anita Hill a household name. If there was one event that was poised to refute the lie of postfeminism, it was the televised hearings that found Hill recalling her treatment by Thomas, her former boss at the Equal Employment Opportunity Commission. It's hard to overstate how groundbreaking the hearings were in the understanding of sexual harassment: they marked the first time many viewers—myself included—realized that there was a name for behavior that we were expected to laugh off or be flattered by in our school and work environments. For the young women who had grown up being assured that they were equal in potential to boys, that they had unheard-of choice and opportunity, the hearings were an unsettling revelation about what it meant to be a woman in public life still defined by men. And for women of color, many of whom already felt erased by the tacit whiteness of both feminism and postfeminism, it was a reminder of what Frances Beal called the "double jeopardy" of race and gender in her 1969 essay of the same name. (In *Anita*, the 2014 documentary about the hearings, Hill acknowledged, "I couldn't be a black woman *and* a woman.")

My college suitemates and I rushed back from the dining hall to watch the hearings with the same urgency we brought to weekly viewings of *Beverly Hills, 90210*. Seeing the cloud of disdain that enveloped Hill both inside and well beyond the hearings was terrifying. On Capitol Hill, on news reports, on talk shows, and in newspapers, there was a widespread reluctance to accept Hill's accounts—and, by extension, to accept the idea that sexual harassment was a thing that existed. As she faced down the row of skeptical, pale males that made up the Senate Judiciary Committee, Hill's very right to exist seemed in question. ("Are you a *scorned woman?*" demanded square-jawed senator Howell Heflin, trying to find a reason why Hill would agree to speak against Thomas; the entire panel seemed largely to forget that it was they who subpoenaed her in the first place.)

Many black men and women resented Hill for betraying a putative brother who, even if they didn't care for his conservative politics, stood positioned to be a landmark addition to America's highest court. More than a few well-meaning women (including, I'm sad to say, my mother) wondered whether Hill had done something to "lead him on." And a hum of media chatter about "oversensitivity" and "boys will be boys" permeated the atmosphere of the hearings, a sense that Hill's objection to talk of pubic hair and penis size in the offices of the EEOC was a case of feminism run amok. In the often surreal circus of the hearings, even Senate Judiciary members who seemed somewhat sympathetic to Hill managed to undermine her at every turn. It's hard to forget, for instance, that our now-lovable VP Joe Biden, as chairman of the committee, not only refused to call on Hill's key witnesses, but basically rolled out a red carpet for Thomas, assuring him that he had "the benefit of the doubt" and failing to query Senator Alan Simpson about letters and faxes that Simpson claimed had been sent warning him to "watch out for this woman" about "this sexual harassment crap."[7]

The hearings may have been an unwanted catalyst for a national conversation about sexual harassment, but they did force a mainstream media that for more than a decade had been content to declare feminism dormant or dead to take notice. Shortly after Thomas was confirmed, a full-page statement appeared in the *New York Times*, stating that "many have erroneously portrayed the allegations against Clarence Thomas as an issue of either gender or race. As women of African descent, we understand sexual harassment as both. . . . This country, which has a long legacy of racism and sexism, has never taken the sexual abuse of black women seriously." It ended with a declaration: "We pledge ourselves to continue to speak out in defense of one another, in defense of the African American community and against those who are hostile to social justice, no matter what color they are. No one will speak for us but ourselves." The signatories, 1,603 in number, had pooled their money to purchase the $50,000 ad—as critical-race theory scholar Kimberlé Williams Crenshaw later noted, "buy[ing] themselves into the discourse"[8]—and declared themselves

African American Women in Defense of Ourselves. The fact that the women paid for their voices to be heard underscored that feminist identity was more complex and more necessary than most media was willing to acknowledge.

The Hill/Thomas hearings are widely credited with prompting a resurgence of vocal feminism and prodding young women in particular toward the realization that, unlike Susan Bolotin's "post-feminist generation" refuseniks, they couldn't take for granted the efforts of those who had fought on their behalf. Rebecca Walker, daughter of the eminent second-wave author, poet, and womanist Alice Walker, was one of them. The younger Walker's debut as an activist came in the special issue of *Ms.* published several months after the hearings, in which she revisited the rage the televised character assassination had brewed up in her. "I am ready to decide, as my mother decided before me, to devote much of my energy to the history, health, and healing of women. Each of my choices will have to hold to my feminist standard of justice," she wrote. But the essay's last line—"I am not a postfeminism feminist. I am the Third Wave"—was its knockout punch: a stand-up-and-cheer rebuttal to the backlash. The response to the essay was overwhelming, and shortly after its publication, Walker, along with Shannon Liss, founded Third Wave Direct Action Corporation with the aim of translating the passion of young feminists into social and political change.

The early articulations of what was promptly dubbed "third-wave feminism" came not from single-author polemics or manifestos, but from compendiums of writing about activism, identity, and social-change potential by a racially and politically mixed group of mostly young, mostly female writers. The first of these, both published in 1995, were *To Be Real: Telling the Truth and Changing the Face of Feminism*, edited by Walker, and *Listen Up: Voices from the New Feminist Generation*, edited by *Ms.* executive editor Barbara Findlen. The essays in both books spanned a range of subject matter: ethnicity and beauty standards, subverting familial expectations, sexism and hip-hop, navigating sexualities, and more. But what both had in common was a sense that their contributors were grappling not just with the entrenched, still-extant limitations imposed by gender, but with the limitations of the feminist label itself. They struggled under the inherited baggage of previous feminisms, wondering aloud how to honor the toil, the successes, and the failures that came before while doing things a bit differently. And they acknowledged that what they knew as monolithic, big-F feminism had bred an unconscious guilt in them: they had new tools, but so much unfinished labor.[9]

Straw Feminist, Meet Loophole Women

Chronologically speaking, American third-wave feminists (I include myself in this group) were the symbolic children—if not, like Walker, the actual children—of a generation that in large part was politicized during the 1960s and 70s. Between national water and oil shortages, an overseas hostage crisis, "stagflation," drug epidemics, an ever-looming threat of nuclear war, Son of Sam, and a vogue in unnatural fibers, the world in which we grew up was not exactly utopia. But pop culture with a social conscience: that we had. We were the beneficiaries of Title IX who watched Billie Jean King thump Bobby Riggs in the "Battle of the Sexes." We knew every word of *Free to Be You and Me*, the soundtrack of a liberal-leaning childhood on which burly football star/needlepoint enthusiast Rosey Grier assured us that "It's Alright To Cry" and Carol Channing's "Housework" dismantled the advertising industry. We had the TV empire of Norman Lear, whose slate of topical, race- and class-conscious sitcoms lobbed issues like abortion, racism, white flight, and rape directly toward the nation's Barcaloungers. Even toys were sort of enlightened: Elizabeth Sweet, a doctoral candidate at University of California–Davis, recently studied changes in Sears-catalogue toy ads, and found that 1975 was the peak of gender-neutral toy marketing, with 70 percent of such ads making no overtures to gender at all and a good number of them consciously "def[ying] gender stereotypes by showing girls building and playing airplane captain, and boys cooking in the kitchen."[10]

We didn't necessarily talk about social justice movements in elementary school, but almost every part of our lives was shaped in some way by feminist and civil rights activism, and plenty of us were lucky enough not to know just how lucky we were. Regardless of whether the mothers, fathers, grandparents, and guardians of America aligned themselves with women's liberation as a political movement, a social consciousness had been established in the mainstream, solidified with legislation, and disseminated by media and pop culture. But as we grew, so did a creeping sense that maybe this equality stuff had been overpromised. The elementary-school teachers who scolded girls for playing "too rough" with boys in schoolyard kickball or tag became the high-school teachers who expressed doubt that girls could "really understand" physics. And all the while, the double standards for dating and sex remained unyielding.

Susan Sturm, a professor at Columbia University's law school, uses the term "second-generation bias" to describe the sexism and racism tucked unassumingly away in schools, corporations, and other institutions that have supposedly been "fixed" by the gains of women's and civil rights movements. If "first-generation" bias took the form of explicit barriers to autonomy and achievement—college departments that refused to admit women and racial minorities, illegal contraception, gender- and race-segregated want ads—the second-generation form was far more subtle and likely to be explained and internalized as an individual matter. The insidiousness of second-generation gender bias—informal exclusion, lack of mentors and role models, fear of conforming to stereotypes—colluded with the ideological spread of neoliberalism to recast institutional inequity as mere personal challenges. If women now had the right to do most everything a man could do, went the logic, then any obstacles or failures weren't systemic, they were individual and could be remedied by simply being better, faster, stronger, wealthier. This was the fertile environment in which a new iteration of postfeminism—call it "I'm-not-a-feminist-but" feminism—was taking root in opposition to the third wave, and, not coincidentally, catching the attention of mainstream media and pop culture.

By the early 1990s, the political landscape was pocked with a bitter conventional wisdom that feminism had, if not outlived its usefulness, then certainly aided the creation of a culture of victimhood that infantilized girls and women, demonized men, and made sexual dynamics a minefield. Neoliberalism was curdling into an I've-got-mine-so-fuck-you attitude toward social responsibility, and there was a whole new corner of American media intent on mourning a time when nobody was forced to acknowledge things like inequality, institutional bias, or offensive language. "Political correctness" was referenced with barely hidden derision, as though it was just too exhausting for people to have to think about what they said or how they said it. "THOUGHT POLICE" boomed a 1990 cover story in *Newsweek* magazine, adding in its subtitle, "There's a 'politically correct' way to talk about race, sex, and ideas. Is this the New Enlightenment—or the New McCarthyism?" (Cue the portentous music.) The article itself detailed efforts on college campuses around the United States to broaden curriculums and increase tolerance, but the ostentatious quotation marks around terms like "diversity" and "multiculturalism" made clear that the reporters saw those things as pointless, oversensitive claptrap.

It was here that the terms of postfeminism began to shift a bit, from exaggerated reports of feminism's demise to the realm of what Ariel Levy would describe in her 2005 book *Female Chauvinist Pigs* as "loophole women"—those who believed themselves so evolved they had no need for the feminist fun police and their starchy ideology. Their leader was the grandstanding theorist Camille Paglia, whose early-'90s trio of books—*Sexual Personae*; *Sex, Art, and American Culture*; and *Vamps and Tramps*—needled movement feminist gospel with all the glee of a teenager mooning a church picnic. For Paglia, the feminist movement's fatal misstep was that it wanted to block off the male vitality that she claimed was naturally expressed in rape: "Feminism with its solemn Carrie Nation repressiveness cannot see what is for men the eroticism or fun element in rape, especially the wild, infectious delirium of gang rape." (Yes, well, our bad, I guess.) She found women in general to be lacking, in part because they just don't *pee* with as much élan as men: "Male urination really is kind of an accomplishment, an arc of transcendence. A woman merely waters the ground she stands on." Though Paglia proclaimed herself (along with Madonna) to be culture's staunchest feminist, she discredited any feminism other than her own as out-of-date victimology, sneering that the movement "has become a catch-all vegetable drawer where bunches of clingy sob sisters can store their moldy neuroses."

As the decade went on, the Paglia school grew to include a handful of fellow loophole women who made the mainstream media's job of trash-talking feminism a lot easier. Katie Roiphe, daughter of second-wave feminist author Anne Roiphe, made a media splash in 1993, when *The Morning After: Sex, Fear, and Feminism on Campus* was published. Roiphe had been covering what she skeptically called "date rape hysteria" for a year or so before the book was published; in it, she asserted that the rise of acquaintance-rape cases was the result of women primed by feminism to see themselves as victims. (Rather than, say, the outcome of no longer referring to a sexual assault as a "bad date," as mothers like hers and mine did.) Though her thesis was little more than "I don't know anyone who's been raped, so it's probably not a thing," the twenty-five-year-old Roiphe, like Paglia, fancied herself to be offering a brave corrective to doctrinaire second-wave ideas of women as perpetual prey.

Elsewhere in 1993, Naomi Wolf's *Fire With Fire: The New Female Power and How It Will Define the 21ˢᵗ Century* defined hard-charging "power feminism" as an alternative to—you guessed it—"victim feminism." And though Rene Denfield's 1995 book *The New Victorians: A Young Woman's Challenge to the Old Feminist Order* contained some important challenges to liberal feminism's erasure of nonwhite, non-middle-class women, it mostly focused on caricaturing feminists as emasculating, goddess-worshipping wingnuts. What all these authors had in common, both with each other and with the cultural climate, was the belief that no real value remained in collective action, that having the ability to transcend gender inequality was a project not of feminism, but of individual women who simply willed themselves to do so.

As with postfeminism, glomming onto the irresistible image of the new guard flipping off the old allowed mainstream media to sidestep the challenge of actually understanding what third-wave feminism was up to, and instead reduce it to a catfight between fusty second-wavers and headstrong upstarts. *The Morning After*, *Fire With Fire*, and *The New Victorians* weren't, for the most part, engaging with the flesh-and-blood young activists and thinkers who penned essays in foundational third-wave anthologies like *Listen Up* and *To Be Real*. They didn't acknowledge the hip-hop feminism defined by Lisa Jones and Joan Morgan in *Bulletproof Diva* and *When Chickenheads Come Home to Roost*, or the transnational feminisms of Chandra Mohanty and Gayatri Spivak. It was more accurate to describe the trio of books, as Astrid Henry did in *Not My Mother's Sister: Generational Conflict and Third-Wave Feminism*, as the work of women who simply "create[ed] a monolithic, irrelevant, and misguided second wave against which to posit their own brand of feminism."

This wasn't just an intergenerational slap fight: it was also a narrowing of the lens through which media and pop culture would consequently view complicated social realities and changes. In the case of *The Morning After* and date rape, hugely influential media outlets like the *New York Times* took what Roiphe herself had termed an "impressionistic" survey of elite campus life and served it up as fact. In making her a spokesperson for feminism, such outlets used pushback against the book's central failure of logic (date rape doesn't exist, but if it happens it's the victim's fault) to buttress Roiphe's caricature of whinging feminist indignation. And what Jennifer Gonnerman wrote in the

1994 *Baffler* article "The Selling of Katie Roiphe"— "Ultimately, Roiphe's personal impressions defined the terms—and, more significantly, the limits—of the date rape debate"[11]—has turned out to be all too true. More than twenty years later, there's undoubtedly a far more sophisticated dialogue about campus sexual assault (for starters, we don't call it "date rape" as much), and a wealth of writing, advocacy, and policy to address it. And yet there remains a substantial number of people with big media mouthpieces who blame rape on everything but rapists; and debates about how best to address and combat campus rape are still stymied by the belief that women are either outright liars or simply unreliable witnesses to their own experiences.

Postfeminist Fatigue

The socially aware pop culture of the 1990s, not unlike that in the '70s, was meaningful in part because it suggested that feminism could exist without being in-your-face political—or, if it was political, exist in a form where the fun parts outweighed the heavy ones. And most of it was pretty fun: the feminist hip-hop from Queen Latifah and MC Lyte, Monie Love and Digable Planets was a great alternative to the other women on MTV, most of whom were grinding behind lite-metal hair farmers like Warrant and Poison. Liz Phair and Garbage's Shirley Manson offered up frank, saccharine-free songs about love, sex, and longing. Even the Beastie Boys pulled a notable progressive U-turn after several years of girl-disparaging lyrics and inflatable-penis stage props. *Sassy* magazine chronicled—indeed, fueled—the rise of youth-driven scenes like Riot Grrrl and encouraged their readers to resist and respond to sexism; *Sassy*'s short-lived brother publication, *Dirt*, hyped conscious hardcore and hip hop artists and prodded its teen-boy readers into considering girls as people, rather than as body parts to be conquered. *HUES* magazine, founded by three University of Michigan undergrads, was the first national magazine for multicultural women, just as serious about fomenting feminist dialogue as it was about showing models of all sizes, shapes, and colors. The rise of what was termed "lipstick feminism"—a reaction to the perceived feminist norm of shunning all cosmetics—reflected the third-wave idea that wearing makeup and caring about fashion could be as much about expressing individuality as about capitulating to beauty imperatives. These were early manifestations of marketplace feminism: *Sassy* packaged feminism as a way for image-conscious teenagers to nonconform, and even independent cosmetics lines quietly reflected feminist sensibilities, from Urban Decay's purposely unlovely color names ("Roach," "Oil Slick") to the quotes from Elizabeth Cady Stanton on Stila's eco-friendly cardboard packaging.

Still, caricatures of old-style sledgehammer dude-bashing made for much better copy. In 1991, Ohio's small, liberal, and now-shuttered Antioch College became nationally famous when it took steps to adopt a comprehensive policy on sexual conduct. Among other things, the policy foregrounded enthusiastic verbal consent for each ascending level of contact ("Is it okay if I remove your shirt?"), and for that reason alone it was roundly mocked in most outlets. Never mind that the policy's emphasis on transparency, communication, and active participation in sex ("a person cannot give consent while sleeping," for instance) was eminently sane. The sheer amount of *talking* required by the policy, and the irresistible fact that it was drafted by a campus group called Womyn of Antioch, was a source of both outrage and amusement in media and popular culture. By 1993, the policy was a cultural punch line: *Saturday Night Live* mocked it with a faux game show called "Is it Date Rape?" that featured *Beverly Hills 90210* star Shannen Doherty as a "Victimization Studies" major; the *New York Times* fretted that "legislating kisses" would take the spontaneity and excitement out of sexual exploration. Even those who agreed with the general aims of the policy weren't exactly jumping up to support it. "Media coverage framed the Antioch policy in a way that divided men and women into groups with conflicting and competing interests, instead of portraying a policy that created a cohesive community devoted to eliminating the frequency with which sexual violence is perpetuated on college campuses," recalled Kristine Herman, one of the students who helped draft the document.[12]

As the 1990s continued, feminism began to assert itself with increasing enthusiasm, not only via multifaceted Third Wave theory and activism, but in the uncharted region of what was then called cyberspace, where a profusion of webrings, newsletters, and online bulletin boards were buzzing with feminists finding ways to utilize the new medium for theory, criticism, and activism. But in mass media, the Paglia-Roiphe brand of postfeminism offered convenient distance from past feminisms both real and imagined. *BUST* magazine, in a quiz called "Are You a Card-Carrying Feminist?" defined the postfeminist woman as one who "take[s] real responsibility for the shit they're in, without blaming 'the patriarchy'—a self-limiting, apologists' concept that denies women the self-respect they'd otherwise gain from knowing that all their problems are of their own damn making. All feminists are accused of being humorless, but post-feminists really are."[13] Though *BUST*'s assessment was emphatically tongue-in-cheek, self-proclaimed postfeminists like the authors of the Web site Postfeminist Playground proved its point with screeds against what they saw as the hopelessly dull project of working toward gender equality, writing in the site's introduction, "Postfeminists want to move on from feminism . . . the time for crabbing and bitching is over." Though Susannah Breslin and Lily James, the site's authors, delighted in offending those who weren't advantaged enough to be able to "move on" from feminism, it was never clear what they did want in the way of ideological evolution. Breslin, in another *BUST* article titled "I Hate Feminism," joined Paglia and Roiphe in painting all feminists as starchy condemners of sex and sex work. Yet all she had to do was look around her—or flip through the rest of *BUST*, for that matter—to see a spectrum of avidly pro-sex feminism that included author Susie Bright, the women of *On Our Backs* and the stripping chronicle *Danzine*, the rowdy spoken-word roadshow

Sister Spit, the anthology *Whores and Other Feminists*, feminist cyber-sex pioneer Lisa Palac, and female-gaze pornographers like Nina Hartley and Candida Royalle.

Mostly, these postfeminists wanted you to know that they were *cool*—you know, like men. The postfeminist didn't mind when her male coworkers go to a strip club and don't invite her. The postfeminist didn't sweat being harassed on the street, because catcalling, per Paglia, honors men's essential nature—and who doesn't love a compliment? The postfeminist was tired of hearing about women not being paid equally or promoted proportionally, because complaining about anything was definitely not cool. Cris Mazza, an author who edited two anthologies of postfeminist fiction—1995's *Chick Lit: Postfeminist Fiction* and 1996's *Chick Lit 2: No Chick Vics*—introduced the concept of postfeminist writing in the books' introductions primarily by stating what it wasn't. Postfeminism was

> Not anti-feminist at all, but also not: my body, myself/ my lover left me and I am so sad/ all my problems are caused by men/ . . . but watch me roar/ what's happened to me is deadly serious/ society has given me an eating disorder/ a poor self-esteem/ a victim's perpetual fear/ . . . therefore I'm not responsible for my actions.

In other words, postfeminism wasn't antifeminism so much as it was a mockery of feminism as just too earnest. Mazza has since acknowledged that she had no familiarity with the term "postfeminism" before editing these anthologies, and allowed that her introduction of the term was decidedly "clumsy."[14] But at the time, the need to distance women's writing—and women's attitudes more broadly—from the sober realm of consciousness-raising groups and swath it in ironic, knowing distance was a very real phenomenon in which Mazza was far from alone. (As for the Postfeminist Playground women, for all their pro-sex chill, they weren't too thrilled to find that a porn site poached their domain after they failed to renew it.)

In 2006, *Newsweek* issued a mea culpa for the panic it sowed twenty years earlier with the single women/death-by-terrorist story, admitting to having incorrectly interpreted the study findings and invoking the story's panicky framing as "a cautionary tale of what can happen when the media simplify complicated academic work." Points for admitting it, but day late, dollar short, etc.: the media's tendency to amplify even modest trends or events to declare a referendum on what feminism got wrong has, if anything, gotten even stronger since the 1980s.

2009, for instance, sounded a new feminist death toll. Apparently, women just weren't as happy as they once were. The linchpin of this narrative was an academic paper published that year ("The Paradox of Declining Female Happiness," by economists Betsey Stevenson and Justin Wolfers), but the general time period also saw the publication of similar studies based in the United States and abroad. Stevenson and Wolfers' research revealed that women were both less happy than they were forty years ago and less happy relative to men, a finding that jibed with results from the other surveys to suggest a steady downward trend of aging women with declining joy levels. Stevenson and Wolfers didn't press any specific takeaways from their conclusion that "a new gender gap" had opened up, but mainstream reporting on the study was thrilled to supply one: feminism strikes again.

The headlines came fast and frenzied: "Women Are More Unhappy Despite 40 Years of Feminism," "Liberated Women are Unhappy. Are You Surprised?" "Women Are Unhappy—Blame Feminism." *New York Times* columnist Maureen Dowd quipped that "Blue is the New Black." ("It doesn't matter what their marital status is, how much money they make, whether or not they have children, their ethnic background, or the country they live in. Women around the world are in a funk.") And though Dowd's colleague Ross Douthat suggested in his own op-ed that the study invited readings from both pro- and anti- sides (feminists "will see evidence of a revolution interrupted, in which rising expectations are bumping against glass ceilings, breeding entirely justified resentments. The traditionalist will see evidence of a revolution gone awry, in which women have been pressured into lifestyles that run counter to their biological imperatives, and men have been liberated to embrace a piggish irresponsibility"), the title of his column—"Liberated and Unhappy"—offered resounding editorial judgment on the source of women's bummer attitudes.

Twenty years after the original media backlash, blaming feminism was still a slam-dunk story simply because people remained eager to believe it. Even the most intelligent and well-reasoned rebuttals usually didn't register. Investigative reporter Barbara Ehrenreich, for instance, was thorough in her assessment of the critical blind spots in Stevenson and Wolfers' study and the way it was reported: she pointed out that despite the supposed happiness gender gap, rates of suicide for women were falling, while men's remained "roughly constant" during a research period of thirty-four years. Ehrenreich also pointed out that Stevenson and Wolfers ignored the data point in which the happiness of black women and men was actually trending *upward*.[15] And finally, she highlighted the study's most striking inference: contrary to what most of them had been told via social, religious, and cultural channels, marriage and children were absolutely no guarantee of happiness for women. But whatever study finding didn't fit the narrative that outlets wanted to publish—*Feminism has failed women! In your face, Gloria Steinem!*—was absent from their sad-ladies analysis.

As with the story about single women and terrorists, the suggestion that women's unhappiness is due to feminism itself still reverberates loudly as a media and pop culture trope, falling somewhere between "ladies be shopping" and "casual sex will definitely kill you" in frequency. It doesn't help, of course, that individual women occasionally validate this narrative by suggesting that the tenets of women's liberation "duped" them into thinking that life was going to be, I don't know, free ponies and ice cream. It doesn't seem to register that it wasn't feminists themselves who sold that fantasy, but a media culture that toggles between soft-pedaling and weaponizing feminist imagery and rhetoric.

This version of postfeminism still asserts itself regularly, popping up to remind us that the *real* problem isn't a world bogged down in gender imperatives and systemic inequality, it's the fact that some people just won't stop pointing it out. In December 2014, *Time* magazine listed "feminist" on a list of words that should be struck from the nation's lexicon in the coming year—one of the only definite words amid meme-born slang ("om nom nom"), appropriated teen talk ("obvi"), and African American Vernacular English ("bae"). A short while later, a Facebook page and Tumblr called "Women Against Feminism" appeared, featuring photos of young women holding up hand-lettered signs bearing declarations like "I don't need feminism because I like men looking at me when I look good," and "I don't need feminism because I believe in love, not condemnation and hate." This wasn't an organized movement as much as it was an illustration of just how much exclusively individual-minded rhetoric has warped both history and logic. The Women Against Feminism were young (mostly college-aged), almost all white, and armed with rainbow markers and dubious statistics. ("I'm against feminism because feminists are guilty of virgin shaming.") Their assertions propped up the same straw women utilized by postfeminists of yore, dressed up with dashes of Rush Limbaugh and Disney princesses.

Needless to say, the phenomenon was media catnip—not just for the delighted and overly credulous conservative and libertarian crowd, but also for media outlets who have come to depend on the word "feminist" to draw eyeballs. Some outlets offered thorough castigations of Women Against Feminism, reminding them that, among other things, they might not have all the individual freedoms they enjoy if not for feminist movements. Others, like the BBC, presented a neutral point-counterpoint format, in which women against feminism and women against Women Against Feminism faced off to, well, mostly talk past one another. Cathy Young, a writer affiliated with the libertarian Independent Women's Forum, argued for the WAF in a *Boston Globe* op-ed, stating that "these arguments need to be engaged, not dismissed and ridiculed"—pretty hopeful talk, considering how many of the "arguments" seemed to understand feminism as a singular, Rapture-like event, in which every male person in the world vanishes. ("I don't need feminism because who will open the jars if there are no men?") Finally, the inevitable Tumblr called Cats Against Feminism was a fittingly absurdist rejoinder. ("I don't need feminism because it's not food. Is it food?")

Treating feminism like it's a personal accessory that just isn't appropriate anymore obscures the places where feminism hasn't made strides for people who still need it. The fearsome coven of straw feminists that's conjured wherever such discussions pop up is now familiar enough to be its own online meme and source of satire (the comic artist Kate Beaton is especially gifted at tweaking straw-feminist fear), but it's also a force people believe has disproportionate power against the status quo. Like the loophole women of the '90s, these folks suggest that feminism is so pervasive, so successful, that traditional gendered stereotypes will become endangered if they're not boldly resurrected by a brave few. "Women are rediscovering the joy of being loved for their bodies, not just their minds," wrote the columnist Kate Taylor in a 2006 *Guardian* op-ed that suggested sexual objectification was not only vintage enough to be cool again, but an actual political statement. ("The ultimate feminists are the chicks in the crop tops.") "Instead of desperately longing for the right to be seen as human beings," she added, "today's girls are playing with the old-fashioned notion of being seen as sex objects." You can't be both, is the message—you can be the boring, sexless blob of brains that straw feminists want you to be, or the super-fun sex objects that they hate. There's no middle ground. It's an idea that was even more recently essayed by the book *Hot Feminist*, written by another British columnist, Polly Vernon. *Hot Feminist's* premise is that feminists, mean old humorless feminists (she doesn't specify who), have deprived feminism of the age-old feminine joys of wearing pink and getting catcalled on the street. As Vernon tells it, a gal can't even get her nostrils waxed without a Greek chorus of feminist disapproval! It's downright oppressive.

We've heard this all before, and we'll hear it again before too long. The cycles of media backlash and "postfeminism" roll on, not because the arguments have changed all that much, but because they still encompass a broader social anxiety about women, men, sex, power, achievement, and more. When it comes to women's and gender equality, backlash will probably always sell better than consensus, individual exceptionalism better than collective effort, and choice better than almost anything else.

CHAPTER 7

Empowering Down

"Feminism to me is following whatever makes you happy—whether it means banning 'bossy' or 'bitch' from your vocab, or binge-watching *The Bachelorette* or fighting superhero battles versus the evil Patriarchy, do what makes you happy." —*BUST* article

I have a bad case of empowerment fatigue. The causes are legion: PR emails that begin with the phrase, "I represent a brand whose sole purpose is to empower women, particularly around that time of the month." Women's-magazine articles that promise "empowering beauty tips!" followed by celebrity interviews in which Jennifer Aniston exclaims that not wearing makeup for a role was "so empowering."

As a catchall phrase that can be understood to mean anything from "self-esteem–building" to "sexy and feminine," to "awesome," empowerment has become a way to signify a particularly female way of being that's both gender-essentialist—when was the last time you heard, say, a strip-aerobics class for men described as "empowering"?—and commercially motivated. Over the past two decades, a partial list of everything that has been deemed empowering by advertising campaigns, pop culture products, and feminist rhetoric includes the following: High heels. Flats. Cosmetic surgery. Embracing your wrinkles. Having children. Not having children. Natural childbirth. Having an epidural. **169**

Embracing fat positivity. Embracing anorexia. Housework. Living like a slob. Being butch. Being femme. Learning self-defense. Buying a gun. Driving a truck. Riding a motorcycle. Riding a bike. Walking. Running. Yoga. Pole dancing classes. Being a Pussycat Doll. Growing your own food. Butchering your own meat. Doing drugs. Getting sober. Having casual sex. Embracing celibacy. Finding religion. Rejecting born faith. Being a good friend. Being an asshole. By the time satirical newspaper *The Onion* announced "Women Now Empowered By Everything a Woman Does" in a 2003 article, it really did seem that "Today's woman lives in a near-constant state of empowerment."

More than ten years after that article, empowerment's association with women, power, activism, and success seems to be its most robust legacy. And in media and popular culture, it's still very much in earnest and unquestioning use by younger generations who have never known the term as anything other than a way to say, "This is a thing that I, as a woman, like to do." Shortly after her performance at the 2013 MTV Video Music Awards, for instance, Miley Cyrus told British *Cosmopolitan* that she is "a feminist in the way that I'm really empowering to women. . . . I'm loud and funny, and not typically beautiful." Duly informed, the celebrity tabloid *OK!* used the quote as the hook for a whole piece on "empowerment" as "the ability to do what you want to do."

> Many celebrities today are earning empowerment over their careers by embracing their unique styles. Miley Cyrus enjoys controversy and isn't shy about it as she makes twerking an everyday dance move. Emma Stone gets her empowerment by landing roles as the stable go-to girlfriend of the world's most loved superhero. Taylor Swift has become a music mega-mogul by building her reputation as a clean teen regardless of who she does or doesn't date. They've all found what's worked for them and built their brands off of it.

The article ends by asking, "Now, how can you be empowered like a Hollywood celebrity?"

Empowerment is both a facet of choice feminism—anything can be a feminist choice if a feminist makes that choice—and a way to circumvent the use of the word "feminist" itself. But what is empowerment, and who does it benefit? In most of these cases, the answers are, respectively, "whatever I decide it is," and "pretty much just me."

Empower to the (Girl) People

"Empowerment" wasn't widely used in general, let alone to denote women's self-esteem/achievements/purchasing power, until the late 1970s and early '80s. The term was first used in the realm of social services, community development, and public health, particularly among minority communities: Barbara Bryant Solomon's *Black Empowerment: Social Work in Oppressed Communities*, a 1976 book that outlined strategies for social workers, appears to be the first American book to use the word in its title. As the philosophy of helping underserved, socially sidelined populations access tools for both individual and collective success gained popularity in applied social research, the term began to be associated with those demographics and their movements. "Empowerment" denoted an intra-community effort to work toward both financial stability and power, an alternative to a top-down model that depended on the benevolence of those already possessed of such things, like foundations, missionaries, NGOs, and more.

The phenomenon of empowerment as a social-change framework for feminism, meanwhile, came to popularity through activism in the Global South—especially Southeast Asia and Latin America, where activists had become frustrated with paternalistic, charity-focused efforts like those undertaken by the United Nations. Leading global woman's advocate Srilatha Batliwala's 1994 book *Women's Empowerment in South Asia: Concepts and Practices* distilled the new approach as a radical revisioning of power structures themselves, what she would later describe as a "political and transformatory idea for struggles that challenged not only patriarchy, but the mediating structures of class, race, ethnicity—and, in India, caste and religion—which determined the nature of women's position and condition in developing societies."[1] Empowerment wasn't defined as a static concept or standalone occurrence, but as an evolving way to rethink entire power structures and value systems, draw on shared skills and knowledge, and endow marginalized communities with tools for economic sustainability. By the time the fourth United Nations Conference on Women convened in Beijing in 1995, the word ("an agenda for the empowerment of women") was an official talking point.

As "empowerment" ambled off the pages of research journals and international-development agendas, it found a home within burgeoning third-wave feminism, whose expansive goals it fit perfectly. (I first heard it in a women's studies class in college and thought it was just a fancier way to say "power," kind of like when people say "upon" because it sounds grander than "on.") A young martial arts instructor named Rosalind Wiseman founded the nonprofit Empower program in 1992 after listening to her preteen female students discuss girl-on-girl bullying; within a short time, Empower was among an in-demand group of organizations devoted to helping young people, girls in particular, negotiate what Wiseman and her social science colleagues called "relational aggression." (Tina Fey later adapted Wiseman's 2002 book, *Queen Bees and Wannabes: Helping Your Daughter Survive Cliques, Gossip, Boyfriends & Other Realities of Adolescence* into the film *Mean Girls*.) Giving young people the means to understand and talk about the insecurities and pressures that lead to bullying and ostracizing offered them control beyond appealing to adults for help. Empowerment was also, notably, a softer way to talk about actual power—something that girls in particular are traditionally socialized away from. It might seem like semantics, but the difference between urging girls to empower themselves and urging them to *be powerful* mirrored the gendered social anxiety that often leads to bullying itself. "When women are uncomfortable with the word 'power,' muses third-wave activist and *Manifesta* coauthor Jennifer Baumgardner, "they say 'empower.'"

Or, alternately, they say "Girl Power." A hat tip to both power and empowerment that became a hallmark of '90s-era marketing to women, girl power was a direct product of feminist media and pop culture that converged that decade on the strength of three key cultural phenomena—1992's so-called Year of the Woman, the radically unpretty Riot Grrrl movement, and the prefab musical sensation the Spice Girls.

The Year of the Woman described a spike in female elected officials that was widely considered to be a direct result of the Clarence Thomas-Anita Hill debacle: the hearings snapped enough Americans out of complacency and into voting booths to propel Bill Clinton's victory over Republican candidate Bob Dole and account for a challenge to the sausage-party House and Senate. The number of congresswomen almost doubled, going from twenty-eight members to forty-seven; the number of women in the Senate tripled from a pitiful two to a more respectable six. Used in political reporting as well as in movies and TV, "Year of the Woman" was media hyperbole that often came off as more patronizing than celebratory; one of the new class of senators, Maryland's Barbara Mikulski, noted that "[c]alling 1992 the Year of the Woman makes it sound like the Year of the Caribou or the Year of the Asparagus." But the handle also encompassed the National Organization for Women's 1992 March for Women's Lives in Washington, D.C., an event timed to coincide with the Supreme Court's consideration of Pennsylvania's *Planned Parenthood v. Casey* ruling on abortion access. At the time, it was the largest explicitly feminist march in history, but the fact that it was held because women were still fighting for control of their own bodies made that a Pyrrhic victory.

Further underground brewed a music subculture-turned-ideological revolution that too was galvanized by how much hadn't changed for women. Riot Grrrl filtered punk culture of the 1980s and early 1990s through a declaratively female, politicized gaze. Part of the focus of

Riot Grrrl's loose coalition of nationwide chapters was on creating an entire culture of girl-produced, DIY media—hand-scrawled paste-up zines and posters, radio shows, guerrilla theater, and, of course, chaotic guitar-driven outbursts with titles like "Suck My Left One" and "Don't Need You." What made Riot Grrrl resonate with many women was that it said out loud something that no mainstream media or pop culture seemed to be saying: postfeminism was a lie. As Sara Marcus writes in her Riot Grrrl history, *Girls to the Front: The True Story of the Riot Grrrl Revolution*, "The world was insane. Women were under attack but weren't supposed to acknowledge it, weren't supposed to resist it."

The first issue of *Riot Grrrl* zine made note of the "general lack of girl power in society as a whole, and in the punk underground specifically"; part of the active participation of Riot Grrls was drawing attention to the way punk's ostensibly progressive façade of anti-authoritarian, anticapitalist politics often concealed gender stereotypes, sexism, and even violence. Alice Bag, whose early-'80s band, The Bags, was part of the influential first wave of L.A. punk, has noted that though the scene began with an eruption of mixed-gender and mixed-race bands in close-knit chaos, the attendant rise of hardcore, with its hypermasculine performers and violent mosh pits ("a bunch of white guys slamming into each other," as Bag put it) came to define the genre.[2] For the girls and women who loved the punk ethos but were tired of being treated like appendages to hardcore guys, the revolution of Riot Grrrl was the act of simply taking up space—on stages, in mosh pits, on paper, in public. The cry of "Girls to the front!" was about more than demanding an expansion of the mosh pit; it was about foregrounding female experience. That didn't always happen with sophistication, and it quite often ignored race and class analysis, a fact that has been a chief focus of contemporary Riot Grrrl revisionism. But for a generation that had been brought up believing that feminism had come and gone, the permission to question the culture's default-male settings was seismic.

The subjects Riot Grrrls addressed in zines and songs (rote gender stereotyping, devaluing of intelligence and musicianship, sexual
objectification and abuse, mental health) and the institutional issues
with which the movement itself grappled, for better and worse (classism, racism, sex work, power dynamics) mirrored the efforts of second-wave consciousness-raising groups in the microcosm of punk
music. In carving out space where girls were both the creators and
the primary audience, bands like Bikini Kill, Heavens to Betsy, and
Bratmobile directly mirrored the intentionally political Women's
Liberation Rock Bands of the 1970s, whose statement-making
ruckus was all about upending the equation of "rock" and "cock." The
fact that rock and punk purists, most of them male, sneered at the
largely unschooled sounds that resulted was beside the point—"We
seek to create revolution in our own lives every day by envisioning
and creating alternatives to the bullshit christian capitalist way of
doing things," read an early version of the Riot Grrrl manifesto, and
that included not giving much credence to what "real" musicians or
critics thought.

Riot Grrrl's separatist inclinations meshed with both straight-
edge punk and "homocore" scenes, whose stalwarts, including bands
like Fugazi and Pansy Division, labels like Dischord and Lookout!,
and zines like *Outpunk*, gazed somewhat warily on the major-label
ascension of musical peers like Nirvana and Sonic Youth. But for
male bands, it was arguably different: their idealism might be
mocked as rigid or overly self-righteous, but few outsiders disputed
their right to *actually exist*, or interrupted their sets yelling, "Take it
off, you cunt!" Early mainstream coverage of Riot Grrrl was sniffy—
Spin, for one, was irked that Bikini Kill frontwoman Kathleen
Hanna declined an interview and painted an unflattering portrait of
a band trading on their bodies and boyfriends.[3] So as music magazines, TV networks, and other media began poking and prodding to
see what made these Grrrls tick, an unofficial but deliberate media
blackout took shape, with access rationed out to feminist journalists

and independent-minded publications. (*Sassy* magazine, with its early and devoted Riot Grrrl boosterism, turned out to be a great recruiting tool.)

The blackout was sensible but ultimately limiting. What mainstream media outlets couldn't confirm by talking to actual participants, they simply made up, painting with cartoonishly broad strokes a picture of lemming-like teens in combat boots, ratty hair, and torn fishnets screaming into microphones and thumbing their noses at boys. There was dismissive coverage like *Spin*'s, and there was fearmongering coverage like that of Britain's *Mail on Sunday*, which spoke ominously of Riot Grrrl lyrics as "a prayer against men. . . . They call themselves feminists but theirs is a feminism of rage and, even, fear." (As opposed to the happy-go-lucky feminism the writer was used to, I guess.) In *Girls to the Front*, Marcus wrote: "The system was weighted against the issues that they cared and cried and bled about. It was stacked so that the way their lives *really were* never had any relevance at all." A 1995 episode of *Roseanne* seemed like the revolution-girl-style's death rattle: In it, Roseanne and her sister, Jackie, pick up a gum-snapping hitchhiker named Garland who foists a Bikini Kill cassette on the duo. Even though Roseanne grudgingly admits "At least they're saying something," the caricature of Riot Grrrls as trend-chasing bubbleheads was proof that the movement had been forcibly assimilated.

In the inevitable cycle by which mainstream culture sanitizes, dilutes, and repackages radicalism, by 1997 the phrase "Girl Power" was harvested from Riot Grrrl zines and re-emerged, a marketplace-feminist Frankenstein's monster, in the juggernaut of the Spice Girls. Created by Simon Fuller (later the impresario behind *American Idol*), the Spice Girls, like a *Teen Beat*'s worth of boy bands that came before, were plucked from cattle-call auditions and engineered for maximum demographic and commercial appeal, as prefab as Riot Grrrl was unpolished. With their carefully crafted personas—Sporty, Scary, Baby, Posh, and Ginger—the Spice Girls were pretty and accessible, and the girl power they espoused in profiles and interviews ("It's woman power, it's an essence, it's a tribe") was a fun, firmly apolitical departure from Riot Grrrl rhetoric. There were no sharp edges here, no anger, and no analysis—why would there be? The Spice Girls could have been any singing group that was signed and sold. Girl Power was packaging, bright bubble letters that suggested power was as simple as putting on a t-shirt proclaiming "Girls Kick Ass" and going dancing with your friends. The Spice Girls as individuals seemed genuinely excited about the young girls who were their instantly devoted listeners, but they (and their management) had no interest in taking any stand more controversial than, "Of course you can wear hot pants and still be a feminist!" In the 1997 movie *Spice World*, Sporty Spice even lampooned the emptiness of Spice rhetoric, posing as Ginger while bleating, "Blah, blah, blah. And Girl Power, feminism, d'you know what I mean?"

It's not as though ten-year-old girls would have been cranking up Bratmobile if the Spice Girls didn't exist, although they might have tuned into the slightly older-skewing angry-girl artists, like Alanis Morrissette, Fiona Apple, and Meredith Brooks, whose rise had also been finessed by Riot Grrrl. But the significant difference was that where Riot Grrrl's vision of empowerment was inherently self-sufficient—Why *not* start a band or make a zine with your friends?—girl power was centered on empowerment by way of the market. What girl power meant in a post–Riot Grrrl world was simply whatever elevated girls as consumers.

Within weeks of the Spices' top-100 ascendancy there was a wealth of Spice Girls product on offer, from t-shirts and lollipops to vinyl change purses and "Girl Power" dolls in each woman's likeness. The feisty, sisters-before-misters attitude of the Girls was all well and good, even if no one seemed exactly sure how seriously to take the line, "If you want to be my lover, you gotta get with my friends." But it was the depoliticized, kitchen-sink quality of "Girl Power" that gave the slogan, and the Spice Girls themselves, merchandising heft: their personas suggested that empowerment came in a number of flavors, all of which lined up with existing female-consumer categories and none of which had to compromise accepted notions of femininity or desirability. (The nail-polish colors associated with Baby Spice and Scary Spice, for instance, might be different, but the point—*buy this nail polish!*—was the same.) Nor did Girl Power acknowledge the structural barriers to actual empowerment for many young women; in the free market of pop music, anyone with $5 for a Spice Girls pencil case could be empowered.

"Girl Power" was anodyne enough to encompass almost any and every worldview, a point that was driven home when Geri Halliwell, aka Ginger Spice, called notoriously unprogressive former British prime minister Margaret Thatcher "the first Spice Girl." Halliwell's enthusiasm for a woman whose political glory came at the expense of Britain's poor and working classes wasn't necessarily shared by her co-Spices—but as ludicrous as the comparison was, it wasn't totally inaccurate. Along with Ronald Reagan, Thatcher was one of global neoliberalism's head cheerleaders, and in arguing for the primacy of economic markets she ignored the social barriers to participating in them. The Spice Girls' agenda obviously had none of the heartlessness of Thatcher's. But they were a handy tool of neoliberalism: Girl Power was used less in the service of reaching girls as people than in reaching them as a market on behalf of Pepsi, Polaroid, and the other corporations that helped brand the Spices and their audience as a new kind of confident, spunky female consumer.

The Girl Power marketing frenzy seemed, in theory, like a good corrective to the girl crisis identified by the likes of Carol Gilligan and Lyn Mikel Brown in the late 1980s. It allowed retailers, advertisers, and even the U.S. government to feel like they were doing something to alleviate the problem of plummeting self-confidence. (The government's Girl Power initiative, launched by the department of Health and Human Services, was formed with the somewhat fuzzy mission of helping "encourage and motivate nine- to thirteen-year-old girls to make the most of their lives.") Commercial girl power was wholly decontextualized from the social dynamics that Riot Grrrl addressed. Instead, it spotlighted a kind of elementary-school sass that fueled the mass production of t-shirts reading "Girls Rule, Boys Drool" and "Boys Are Stupid, Throw Rocks at Them."

Feminists who were preteen girls during peak Spice, who thrilled to "Wannabe" on the radio and played Spice Girls with their friends, were very much like my friends and me a generation before, playing with Wonder Woman and Bionic Woman dolls and playacting as Charlie's Angels or Christie Love: hungry for pop cultural role models, we glommed on to the few that existed. They weren't perfect, but they were there. There are thus a lot of blog posts about the Spice Girls written in the past decade with titles like "In Defense of the Spice Girls" (at *Rookie*) and "What the Spice Girls Taught Me About Feminism" (at Autostraddle), which posit that, as gateway feminism, you could do worse than a gaggle of British babes advocating friendship, trust, and safe sex. That's probably true. But the cultural legacy of the Spice Girls is as much about empowering marketplace feminism as about empowering girls. As their hits faded from the radio and MTV, their girl power became just one more element in what Peggy Orenstein calls the "gender apartheid" of retail sales, where "boy" is denoted with sports logos and robots while "girl" is encompassed in phrases like "princess" and "spoiled brat." Instead of teaching girls actual self-advocacy and confidence, a shift toward increasingly gendered capitalism turned Girl Power into little more than a cute, chauvinist retail fad.

"Choice" of a New Generation

With the Spice Girls as its most visible ambassadors, Girl Power marketing moved squarely into mass culture by the early 2000s, increasingly positioned by TV networks, movie studios, record labels, and advertising executives to sell women and girls on their own retail influence and consumer identity. Consumer empowerment dovetailed nicely with third-wave feminism, whose ideology was in part about rejecting what many young feminists perceived as inflexible dogma and embracing varied, intersecting identities instead. And this empowerment was certainly of a piece with the neoliberal ideal in which individuals operate independent of cultural and economic influence, proving that all you need to succeed—or, in liberatory terms, to achieve equality—is the desire and will to do so. It seems significant that when asked to define the word "feminism," women today are as likely to say that "It's about choice" as "It's about equality." I have occasionally had to bite my tongue around students and others who burst out with, "Feminism is all about having *choices*!" It's not that simple, and that's not the whole story; but I also don't want to be the judgmental scold who scares them away from feminism.

Equality makes way for an increased number of free, considered choices, and an increased number of people with access to them. But choice itself isn't the same as equality, even if the conflation of the two goes back at least as far as John Stuart Mill's 1869 essay, *The Subjection of Women*. In his argument for women's equality and enfranchisement, Mill evoked choice as a necessary element in both:

> I consider it presumption in anyone to pretend to decide what women are or are not, can or cannot be, by natural constitution. They have always hitherto been kept, as far as regards spontaneous development, in so unnatural a state, that their nature cannot but have been greatly distorted and disguised; and no one can safely pronounce that if women's nature were left to choose its direction as freely as men's, and if no artificial bent were attempted to be given to it except that required by the conditions of human society, and given to both sexes alike, there would be any material difference, or perhaps any difference at all, in the character and capacities which would unfold themselves.

Yet Mill presumed that even with such choices, most women would likely go with the societal flow and take up the roles of wife and mother, rather than vie for a spot in a male-dominated workplace. For Mill, it wasn't what women did with their choice that was important, but simply the fact that they had it.

"Choice" came to its modern prominence as a feminist signifier by way of one of feminism's landmark victories: the 1973 Supreme Court case *Roe v. Wade*. Though safe and legal abortion as a platform of second-wave feminism regularly used the word "rights" to refer to this act of self-determination, *Roe*'s ruling changed the frame: it decided that abortion, rather than being protected as a right of bodily autonomy, was instead a feature of the privacy guaranteed by an interpretation of the Fourteenth Amendment. The language used in the Court's majority ruling was deliberate and specific in not referring to safe and legal abortion as a *right* but rather as an *option*. In reading the opinion, Justice Harry Blackmun used "this choice" repeatedly to refer to abortion, a tactful construction that was crucial to gaining mainstream support for something that, regardless of legal status, would remain highly controversial. "Choice" worked because it was simultaneously active and passive; as historian Rickie Solinger noted, the term "evoked women shoppers selecting among options in the marketplace."[4] Similarly, second-wave feminist groups had been unambiguous in differentiating "abortion on demand" from therapeutic or medically necessary abortion—it was part of asserting that women, not doctors, were the drivers of the act. But as the issue was increasingly put before nonfeminist Americans for judgment, "demand" became too pushy, too sure of itself—too, well, *demanding*. As though to distract from the power and freedom that legal abortion represented, the language used to talk about it became increasingly polite.

That "choice" and "rights" are not the same thing had already been made abundantly clear by pre-*Roe* termination procedures. Women who could afford to access illegal abortions—which necessitated scaring up hundreds of dollars, not including travel to cities with underground providers—had already been doing so for decades. Women who couldn't access abortions had the "choice" to give their babies up for adoption to more ostensibly deserving women—again, hardly a free choice given that so many birth mothers were young women shamed and pressured by family and clergy to surrender children that in many cases they actually wanted. Both abortion and childbirth were already marketplaces that only some women could afford to enter; in the case of legal abortion, *Roe* simply transferred control of that marketplace to the government. And 1976's Hyde Amendment, which prevented federal money from being used to fund abortion (via Medicaid, for instance), effectively shut a huge percentage of low-income women out of that marketplace, making a post-*Roe* world for all practical purposes not much different than the one that had come before.

Once *Roe* shifted the language of bodily rights from demands to choices, the advent of neoliberalism did the rest, normalizing the self-focus and singularity made ever more possible by a booming free market. The parlance of the marketplace became the default way to talk about almost all choices made by women.[5]

Naomi Wolf's 1993 polemic *Fire with Fire* pitted two opposing camps against one another: "Victim feminists," she charged, were stuck in a hopelessly collectivist mindset that looked down on individualism and was mired in outdated patriarchy-bashing. "Power feminists," on the other hand, engaged with an existing status quo by grabbing it by the balls, politics be damned. The only limits, Wolf declared, were in women's own minds: "Our movement forward as individual women, as women together . . . depend[s] on what we decide to see when we look in the mirror." Women, in other words, could choose to be victims or not, regardless of any economic or social forces—poverty, abuse, political disenfranchisement—that might affect their daily lives. (Wolf's evocation of the mirror seemed notable given that her previous book, *The Beauty Myth*, so cogently indicted the image industry's complicity in the gendered wage gap, the prevalence of eating disorders, and more.)

Fire with Fire was one of the first popular texts in which neoliberalism's influence on feminism was made explicit. It skipped over the real-world systems of planned inequality that make grabbing status-quo balls almost impossible for anyone other than the people who are already in closest proximity to them. Power, in her construction, operated in a vacuum untouched by race, class, education, and access to health and child care: if you couldn't cut it, it was because you simply weren't trying hard enough.

Wolf tried her hardest to make the phrase "power feminism" happen, but it never quite happened. (Perhaps if she'd called it "empowerment feminism," it would have caught on.) But her conception of a feminism that is individualist, determined, and has no time for boring talk about structural inequality has blossomed since then. Its appeal is undeniable—you can simply claim an identity, and feminism becomes a sort of muffin basket or fruit bowl to be picked from rather than a set of living ethics and rights that must be fought for.

Writer and philosopher Linda Hirshman somewhat peevishly coined the term "choice feminism" when writing her 2005 *American Prospect* article "Homeward Bound," an analysis of the "opt-out revolution" that was trumpeted in mainstream media as a reaction against liberal, career-focused feminism. "Homeward Bound" considered how the predominance of "choice" in feminist rhetoric disguises the unchanged expectation that women are responsible for the bulk of domestic labor. "Women with enough money to quit work say they are 'choosing' to opt out," wrote Hirshman, nodding toward stories like the one on the cover of the *New York Times Magazine*, whose headline—"Q: Why Don't More Women Get to the Top? A: They Choose Not To"—was a gleeful jab at feminism. But the deliberate nods to choice reified inequality by assuming that women, whatever else they're doing, are still holding down the fort at home.[6] If the sexes had truly achieved the level of equality presumed by the glut of opt-out narratives, then there surely wouldn't only be women who were in the position of weighing domestic responsibility against paid work and choosing only one. And they certainly wouldn't have to bear the brunt of society's judgment when they chose the latter.

Trend stories like the *New York Times Magazine*'s—and they popped up like perky toadstools as "the opt-out revolution" became the media's newest backlash narrative—were based on the idea that the choices of the influential demographic written about (college-educated, heterosexually partnered, financially stable) are value-neutral, with no relationship to a larger, indelibly gendered culture. This was both a neoliberal fallacy and a big, honking mistake: yes, such women were free to make the choice to leave the workplace, but they were not free to believe that such choices have no impact on the way women are treated in society at large. (Why offer college scholarships or medical fellowships to women, after all, if there's only a 50 percent chance of a return on the investment?)

When I visit Hirshman at her New York City apartment in 2014 to revisit the arguments of "Homeward Bound" and the book she expanded it into, 2005's *Get to Work*, it's not long before we get on the subject of *Sex and the City*—and I'm a little relieved that the imposing Hirshman says she regards the show as "an enormously influential text" before I have to. The episode we discuss is the one in which Charlotte, the foursome's most conservative member, chants "I choose my choice! I choose my choice!" like a mantra when her friend Miranda questions why she would quit the art-gallery job she loves simply because she's now a wife. It was an absurd, out-of-left-field moment: Charlotte, after all, was the least ideologically radical of the *SATC* women, prone to wearing (and clutching) pearls and believing in the fairy tale of marriage and motherhood even as real life continually disappointed her. It was Charlotte who uttered the unutterable in the show's season 3 premiere, suggesting to the horror of her friends that "women just want to be rescued" by a good man. Putting the language of feminism, however watered-down, into Charlotte's perfectly glossed mouth was like putting slam poetry there—its comic impact came from its improbability. The show's sly critique of the marketplace-feminist notion that every choice can be a feminist one so long as a feminist (even a momentary one) is doing the choosing has become a meme; nearly every woman I spoke to for this book cried, "I choose my choice!" in mock outrage when the subject of choice feminism came up. What remains important about the episode is that it was likely the first pop culture moment to expose choice feminism's live wires, asking why, if no one choice can be judged as more meaningful than any other, we need to spend time defending them at all.

Choice feminism has flourished in recent decades in particular because, though corporate media and popular culture (much like the Supreme Court with *Roe*) are not particularly interested in arguing for women's equality, they are most definitely zealous about portraying women in opposition to one another. A big part of how choice feminism has finessed the project of never judging one choice as better than another involves retooling institutional norms and mores in individual terms and letting women themselves duke it out in the public sphere. There is gold in those choice-feminism hills, especially in a new-media sphere that prizes the pageviews and ad revenue yielded by a good, solid tug-of-war between, "My choice is feminist and empowering!/ No it's not, and here's why!"

"Empowerment as a function of consumer choice is not feminism," states one feminist scholar I interviewed, "because feminism is at base about equality and capitalism is completely at odds with that." But, she adds hurriedly, right before asking to be quoted anonymously, "When we have these conversations, it often becomes people saying, 'Stop judging me for liking what I like!' You can't engage without interpretation of that as judgment." Feminist consumers have a responsibility to acknowledge the limitations of the choice-plus-empowerment-equals-feminism frame—it's part of being a critical thinker, which itself is crucial in a mediated culture. The problem is, to echo the anonymous scholar, such questioning itself risks being interpreted as insufficiently feminist.

With choice established as the lens through which to view anything and everything, no one wants to come right out and suggest that one choice might, just might, be even a fractional step in the direction toward or away from an objectively more equal world. The subsequent pile-on (as Hirshman can vouch from beneath a mountain of hate mail garnered by "Homeward Bound") would be overwhelming. So most often we feint toward and then retreat from anything that might be mistaken as publicly judging another woman's choices; a conspiracy-minded onlooker might say that choice feminism has been a magical antidote to activist feminism, moving public feminism's focus from the redistribution of power and resources and winnowing it down to the narcissism of small differences.

Indeed, it's important to note that choice feminism, at least at the start, wasn't something nurtured within actual feminist movements, but rather a frame that, like "postfeminism," was built by trend stories and amplified because—also like postfeminism—it pressed the ever-dependable conclusion that feminism had hurt rather than helped women. It had convinced them they needed jobs when they'd really rather be at home with kids, pressed them to compete with men as rivals instead of turning to them as protectors, repelled their natural baby-making instincts until it was too late.

Choice feminism and its offshoot, the so-called Mommy Wars, became a talking point in the mid-2000s—a time when, as it happens, grassroots feminism was easier to find and participate in than ever. It was sprouting up in group blogs online, simmering in political action committees, and rapidly expanding into less traditionally academic areas like prison and labor reform. But as a media story, women working together to craft new legislation, share tech skills, or lobby for incarcerated women to give birth unshackled is a giant snooze—and definitely a less economically rewarding option than the cost-effective write-around or op-ed whipped up from a mass of trends and polls and celebrity flotsam. By contrast, a point-counterpoint opinion piece, where one woman's contention that high heels aren't feminist is countered by a second woman's equally vociferous defense of her choice to wear high heels, accomplishes a bunch of things at once: It fills content space cheaply, no reporting or research needed. It legitimizes the notion that women's empowerment is provided by the marketplace and makes it enticing to advertisers. And it suggests to its audience that the real roadblock to feminist progress isn't antiwoman lawmakers or greedy corporate policy or, you know, *gender inequality itself*, but women bickering amongst themselves about what does or doesn't count as empowerment.

The further into the marketplace "choice" has moved, the more it has become a nebulous designation—which is maybe ironic, since the more it's associated with women's reproductive rights, the less focus is drawn to legislative failures that also affect women's autonomy, from affordable child care to equal wages for equal work. The use of "choice" to rationalize individual choices—and, perhaps more important, to signify that criticizing those choices is *un*feminist—isn't unethical or amoral so much as it is underachieving.

We know logically that choices aren't made in a vacuum: we assign financial, aesthetic, and moral value to any number of choices in the course of each day, and most of us get that these choices mean something in the larger world. People vote, recycle, volunteer, and donate to causes that they feel deeply about. They are gentle with children and old people, and they don't kick kittens and puppies. Or they *do* kick kittens and puppies. And they embezzle, abuse family members, don't tip at restaurants, and vandalize national parks. Sociopaths aside, most of us regularly express a sense of ethics and values in our choices, and know that many of them have the potential to make the world better or make it worse. As an ideology, feminism too holds that some things—say, social and political equality and physical autonomy—are better than other things, like inequality, domestic and sexual violence, and subservience based on gender. It makes no sense to argue that all choices are equally good so long as individual women choose them. And it's equally illogical to put a neoliberal frame around that argument and suggest that a woman's choices affect that woman and only that woman. It looks like we may have empowered ourselves into a corner.

Banking on Empowerment

In 2011, Walmart launched a new initiative called the Women's Economic Empowerment Initiative. The program was announced a scant three months after the U.S. Supreme Court quashed what would have been the largest-ever class-action sex discrimination suit against a private company. Walmart, now the nation's largest private employer, has a business model in which employees earn poverty wages while reaping billions in profit for the owners, but the suit focused on the fact that female employees were paid less than male ones for the same jobs—part of a systematic devaluing of female labor fixed in the company's corporate culture. ("No position was too minor to be exempt from sex discrimination," wrote Liza Featherstone in her 2005 book *Selling Women Short: The Landmark Battle for Workers' Rights at Wal-mart*.) Though the Supreme Court eventually ruled that the 1.5 million women who were plaintiffs in the case failed to meet the requirements for a class-action suit, Walmart still had to deal with a tarnished image.

Conceived as part of an ass-covering PR campaign, the Women's Economic Empowerment Initiative combines a number of programs united under the banner of supporting women as producers and business owners. It includes the online-shopping destination Empowering Women Together, which offers products from women-owned businesses that, according to Walmart press releases, are "fueled by women with inspiring stories." The company pledged to source $20 billion worth of products from such businesses over five years, in addition to doubling its inventory from women-owned businesses internationally. Elsewhere, the initiative supports a Women in Factories Training Program concentrated in India, Bangladesh, Honduras, El Salvador, and China; Walmart boasted that it "will train 60,000 women in 150 factories and processing facilities producing for top retail suppliers in industries with high percentages of women."

Following years of public exposés of Walmart's race, gender, and labor policies, the WEEI placed a complaint-proof façade over a company-wide devaluing of women's labor. (Look at us! No, not in the actual stores—look at us over here, empowering these poor women in the Global South to make our products!) But even better, the initiative redefined women's empowerment as something that corporations could provide, burnishing their reputations as they did. (At least one entrepreneurial family who bought into Walmart's "empowering" sales pitch found that it wasn't exactly walking the walk: Michael Wooley, whose teenage daughter Christen invented a comfortable backpack/vest hybrid for Empowering Women Together, had high hopes for the program, but as he told a *Huffington Post* business writer in 2015, the retail giant over-promised and more than under-delivered, withholding both sales reports and revenue.[7])

According to Google Trends, the word "empowerment" hit a high in 2004 and 2005, as it became more deeply entrenched everywhere— feminist discourse, consumer marketing, corporate culture. "Empowering" joined "synergy," "scalable," and "drill-down" in boardroom conferences, vision statements, and business plans, and was eventually called "the most condescending transitive verb ever" by *Forbes*.[8] It's become the name of a range of businesses, a national fitness event, and an almost mind-boggling number of yoga studios. It's become a company-jargon fave at Microsoft, with former and current CEOs Steve Ballmer and Satya Nadella both using it to impressively vague effect in memos and public talks. (At Microsoft's annual Convergence event in 2015, Nadella told attendees, "We are in the empowering business," and added that the tech giant's goal was "empowering you as individuals and organizations across every vertical and every size of business, and any part of the world, to drive your agenda and do the things you want to do for your business."[9])

Elsewhere in discourses and debates around sex as both an activity and a commodity, "empowerment" has become a sort of shorthand that might mean "I'm proud of doing this thing," but also might mean "This thing is not the ideal thing, but it's a lot better than some of the alternatives." Feeling empowered by stripping, for instance, was a big theme among moonlighting academics or otherwise privileged young women in the late 1990s and early 2000s, and you can find countless memoirs about what they discovered about themselves in the world of the sexual marketplace; the same is true of prostitution, with blogs like Belle de Jour, College Call Girl, and books like Tracy Quan's *Diary of a Manhattan Call Girl*. There was a point in the mid-to-late 2000s when you couldn't swing a cat through Barnes & Noble without knocking a slew of sex-work memoirs off the shelves: Lily Burana's *Strip City*, Diablo Cody's *Candy Girl*, Jillian Lauren's *Some Girls*, Michelle Tea's *Rent Girl*, Shawna Kenney's *I Was a Teenage Dominatrix*, Melissa Febos's *Whip Smart*, and Sarah Katherine Lewis's *Indecent* among them.[10] The crucial thing these often incredibly absorbing and well-written books had in common? All were written by young, white, and no-longer-hustling sex workers.

I want to be clear that standing with sex workers on the principle that sex work is work is an issue whose importance cannot be overstated, and also clear that my complete lack of expertise on the subject makes it well beyond the scope of this book. But I am interested in the idea that "empowerment" is so often used as a reflexive defense mechanism in discussions of this kind of sex-work experience, but less so in describing the less written-about experiences of people whose time in the industry is less finite and less bookworthy—transgender women, exploited teenagers and trafficked foreigners, men and women forced into sex work by poverty, abuse, or addiction. And I'm fascinated by the fact that we see thousands of pop culture products in which women are empowered by a sex industry that does not have their empowerment in mind, but far fewer in which they are empowered to make sexual choices on their own terms, outside of a status quo in which women's bodies are commodities to be bought and sold. *Indecent* author Sarah Katherine Lewis has written that, during her time as a stripper, "I felt empowered—as a woman, as a feminist, as a human being—by the money I made, not by the work I did"; but hers is just one story. Belle de Jour and other sex workers have written about truly enjoying their work. If the market were just as welcoming of narratives in which young women were empowered by their careers as, say, electricians—if personal memoirs about a youthful, self-determining layover in the electrical trades were a thing publishers clamored for—then a handful of empowered sex workers would be no big thing. Until that's the case, it's worth questioning why the word is so often the first line of defense.

Elsewhere in pop culture, "empowerment" has become even more of a throwaway. You can find a list of "108 Women's Empowerment Films" on the yoga Web site *Awakening Women*; it includes *Seven Brides for Seven Brothers* (because, I guess, being kidnapped for marriage by a bunch of backwoods man-boys is empowering), *Sylvia* (falling in love with a philandering jerk-genius and cutting short your career as a poet by committing suicide: also empowering), *What Women Want* (having your creative ideas stolen by your boss who's been endowed with sudden mind-reading powers and who uses them to market stuff to women: empowering!). Beauty blogger and entrepreneur Michelle Phan introduced her cosmetics line in 2013 with a video titled "Empowered by You," in which Phan is shown in different guises—*Game of Thrones*'s pearl-haired Khaleesi, a platform-booted Harajuku girl—intercut with close-ups of her products. "You empower me," enthuses Pham. "What empowers you?" Advertisements for any and every product or experience aimed at women—a new style of razor, say, or a life-coaching retreat in Hawaii where you can set your intentions for the future—use the term as an all-purpose adjective, *Mad Libs*–style; pop it anywhere in that sentence, it'll make sense.

The pop cultural framing of empowerment is basically the one defined by the fluffmongering *OK* magazine article—"the ability to do what you want to do"—a meaning that isn't about change or action or demands or even community. The term is apolitical, vague, and so non-confrontational that it's pretty much impossible to argue against it. Embracing your makeup-face free one day, being empowered by cosmetics the next? Sure! A detour into sex work? Why not? Convening in

Hawaii for life-coaching and intention-setting? Don't mind if I do! In only a few decades, "empowerment" has gone from a radical social-change strategy to a buzzword of globalization to just another ingredient in a consumer word salad.

"Empowerment," like "feminism," was once a word with a definition. Both have become diluted, in part because of the fears about what their definitions stood to change, and in part by the market that's embraced (some) of their goals. Both have been, and continue to be, successful and unsuccessful, and both continue to be eminently worthwhile projects. But it's hard to think about "empowerment" in a way that's not indelibly gendered (even on HBO's *Hung*, a series about a male teacher who turns to prostitution, all the paeans to empowerment come from the dotty woman who pimps him out), and entirely overused. We can like what we like, and feel good about things that maybe society thinks we shouldn't. But continuing to hitch empowerment exclusively to women and to feminist movements has started to blur the way forward: after all, if everything is empowering, nothing is.

CHAPTER 8

The Rise of Big Woman

"Onward, Upward, and Inward" —tote-bag slogan at the 2014
Thrive Third Metric conference

It seems almost impossible to imagine now, but thirty-nine years
ago, the U.S. government funded a national conference on woman's
issues, convened with the goal of making recommendations on issues,
platforms, and needs to prioritize in the coming years. The brainchild
of congresswomen Bella Abzug and Patsy Mink, the conference was
proposed in 1975 as part of President Gerald Ford's National Commission on the Observance of International Women's Decade (back
then, women didn't just get a year every now and then) and funded to
the tune of $5 million. The conference was held in Houston over four
days in November 1977, drawing between fifteen and twenty thousand
attendees, two thousand of whom were official delegates representing
all fifty states and six territories. With Texas congresswoman Barbara
Jordan delivering a keynote address and Abzug presiding over the official business, the delegates got down to cases, eventually drawing up
an action plan for twenty-six "planks" to be submitted to Congress and
President Jimmy Carter. Among them were sex discrimination, wage
inequality, education, the rights of minority women, disability rights,
abortion, child care, the Equal Rights Amendment, and the Equal

Credit Opportunity Act. In the 2005 documentary about the conference, *Sisters of '77*, many of the women there mused about the impact of the historic, never-to-be-repeated event. There were arguments (over abortion, most prominently), there was hostility (from Phyllis Schlafly and her STOP ERA cohort, predictably), but there was also a sense that there could be no turning back to an earlier time, a time when women were simply absent from the nation's agenda. "It caused a spark in so many women," remembered Texas governor Ann Richards in the documentary, "to know that the fight was worth it and that they were not alone in their efforts, and that there were thousands of women out there who agreed with them, and who were going to be there to help."

Let's imagine a similar conference were to happen today. I'd like to think it could have that same galvanizing spirit, but I'm also 99.9 percent sure it wouldn't be funded by the government, but by a slate of multinational corporate sponsors: Verizon, Estée Lauder, Gucci. It would be held not at a convention center but at an extremely posh spa, all the better to pop out for a quick seaweed detox wrap if needed. Paparazzi would be camped out to get snaps of celebrity attendees Salma Hayek, Angelina Jolie, and Amal Clooney; there might, in fact, be a red carpet. There would be sessions on Embracing Leadership and Mindful Branding. The action planning wouldn't be the focus of the conference, but rather an optional breakout session between a panel discussion on financial empowerment and a special conversation between Hayek and Jolie that adds $175 to the conference ticket price but does include a gift bag containing chia-seed energy bars, a luxury skin mask, and a coupon for Activia yogurt.

It might look a lot like the MAKERS Conference, a two-day, invitation-only event sponsored by AOL and American Express that took place in February of 2014 at a beachside hotel in Rancho Palos Verdes, California. MAKERS, the digital storytelling platform that showcases women's stories and achievements, promoted the event as a landmark gathering that would "reset the agenda for women in the workplace in the 21ˢᵗ century." When it was noted that this seemed like a slightly presumptuous goal given that the event's guest list was heavy on celebrities and CEOs but empty of, say, labor-union leaders, the copy was hastily amended to herald the conference as one that would "gather and spotlight the prominent leaders and innovators from corporations, not-for-profits, and government organizations that are committed to women's and working-family issues."[1]

The conference was certainly about women's issues, in the broadest, most uplifting sense: speakers included Martha Stewart, astronaut Mae Jemison, and congresswoman Gabrielle Giffords. Work issues were addressed in sessions titled "Brand Maker: Living IN Your Brand," and "Fear Means Go: Learning to Embrace Change and Challenges." Though the word "feminism" was absent from MAKERS' press materials for the conference, a few of the event's featured speakers didn't shy away from using it—Sheryl Sandberg, in conversation with PBS anchor Gwen Ifill, urged the audience to "ban the word 'bossy' and bring back the word 'feminism,'" and Geena Davis spoke passionately about the need to counter unconscious gender bias in film and television. But ultimately, this was a conference about very elite women patting other very elite women on the back for their individual achievements in highly rarefied fields, and, not incidentally, about helping position the conference's corporate sponsors to better market products to a female audience.

"I was really grossed out by it," confesses writer Anna Holmes, the founding editor of Jezebel and a columnist for the *New York Review of Books*, who was one of the invitees. Holmes and I are at an outpost of a New York bakery chain trading thoughts on the rapid ascent of feminism as a decontextualized style statement. "There was not any sustained discussion," she continues. "It was all platitudes and generalities. It was, like, Jennifer Aniston interviewing Gloria Steinem. I mean, what?" (Another writer who was there, Megan Koester, noted in *Vice* that "when Steinem lamented the fact that female actresses still had to be much younger than their male costars, Aniston responded,

'What do you mean?' in a manner that suggested she had never seen a film which did not star herself.") When I ask Holmes to elaborate, she pauses before stating, "There just wasn't talk about things like women's health and the ways that access to services are undermined and compromised by the political system. There was very little about the real, actual things that affect quote-unquote real-world women. I'm not saying that one-percent women shouldn't talk about things that affect them. [But] it was a very unsophisticated portrayal of the state of the world, and gender politics within it."

Holmes allows that the positive, up-with-ladies spirit of the conference was probably inspirational and empowering for some of the other women who were able to attend. But after talking with her, my mind was definitely on the millions of women who don't even get to entertain the thought of "reset[ting] the agenda for women in the workplace in the 21st century." Like Nike's "If You Let Me Play" sneakers (made by sweatshop workers) and the trickle-down feminism of Sheryl Sandberg and Marissa Mayer (enabled by squads of nannies and maids), these conferences seem like ways to access and sell a certain kind of female power at a comfortable distance from the less individualistic and far less glamorous reality of the majority of women.

The MAKERS conference is part of an emerging marketplace-feminism trend—a high-dollar "ideas" circuit that prizes networking, knowledge sharing, and cheerleading, and that defines "women" as women in corporate, often high-profile industries in urban areas. A growing number of conferences and convenings have made news in the past few years as barometers of a new female ascendancy: The Women in the World Summit, hosted by former *Vanity Fair* and *New Yorker* editor Tina Brown, is a three-day gathering at New York City's Lincoln Center that brings together "CEOs, industry icons, and world leaders, as well as artists, grassroots activists, and firebrand dissidents . . . mak[ing] vivid the stories of the courageous and intelligent women who are taking on the status quo in their native countries, leading peace movements in the face of war and conflict, and shattering glass ceilings in every sector."

Thrive, an event presented in New York City by *Huffington Post* founder Ariana Huffington and *Morning Joe* cohost Mika Brzezinski in 2014 to coincide with Huffington's new book of the same name, emphasized that women have been so busy killing it in our careers and personal lives that we're all going to burn out unless we incorporate the "third metric"—"a combination of well-being, wisdom, wonder, and giving." The three-day event offered attendees a chance to implement this metric and create "sustainable, fuller, more impactful" lives by way of speakers like Katie Couric and fashion designer Tory Burch and sponsors like Kenneth Cole, JP Morgan Chase, and Westin Hotels and Resorts. (As Thrive's Web site notes, "Throughout the day, sponsors are integrated into key customized segments to position their brand among attendees as an integral part of The Third Metric way of life.") There's Time Inc. and *Real Simple* magazine's yearly "Women & Success" event in New York City, and *Fortune*'s Most Powerful Women conference, held most recently at the Ritz-Carlton in Orange County. The conference founded by *Forbes* magazine—Forbes Women's Summit: Power Redefined—is held yearly in both the United States and Asia. And the S.H.E. Summit, a New York–based event now in its fourth year, is an "unforgettable, once-a-year experience designed to: Propel your next phase of personal and professional success; shift you into your MOST EMPOWERED state of self; re-align you with authentic goals and values; add significant relationships to your network; and provide a supportive community for your goals!"

Such conferences celebrate the experience of being an exceptional female individual among other exceptional female individuals by way of an exclusive experience that honors individuality and power as uniquely female experiences. Exclusive and expensive: tickets for Women in the World cost $500, Thrive $300, and S.H.E. $250 (if you nab the early-bird rate); *Cosmopolitan*'s Fun Fearless Life conference is a bargain at $199, even more so when compared to the $3,500 and $8,500 ponied up by attendees of the MAKERS and *Fortune* conference.

They're not technically separatist gatherings, especially given that many of the corporate CEOs who speak at them are inevitably male—MAKERS calls them "manbassadors." But a considerable part of their raison d'être is showcasing that educated, deep-pocketed women are an economic and branding force that has arrived. Make no mistake, these are not events to empower women, but to sell them to advertisers in a time when traditional magazine revenues have been hit hard by the changing economics of media. It's a vision of empowerment that, in many ways, erases the presence of anyone who isn't empowered in the most crucial sense of the word—financially so—by suggesting that their voices aren't part of resetting agendas or creating fulfilling lives. The dissonance is more pronounced when you consider that the sponsors of some of these events are hotel chains (like Hyatt, the hotel for both the Forbes Women's Summit and Time Inc./Real Simple's Women and Success events) that have been at the center of labor-union disputes over the pay, hours, and working conditions of a largely female workforce. It would be one thing if such events acknowledged their narrowly defined demographic, but suggesting they empower women as a whole class is unavoidably tone-deaf.

In a 2014 *New York Times* article on the phenomenon of elite women's conferences, one habitual attendee, a marketing consultant, asserted that "it's the formation of a new girls' club. . . . I mean, no offense, but men have been doing this kind of conference networking for years."[2] It's true; they have. That's one reason it's easy to see the suddenly omnipresent women's-conference sphere as less about the successful project of equality and more about the same gold mine of marketing to women that got cigarette and cornstarch companies so starry-eyed a century ago. Were I at a Third Metric or S.H.E. event, this kind of talk would probably get me bounced from the room, but it seems worth questioning whether this is feminism, or just a new twist on the age-old concept of selling products and ideas with gender essentialism.

Gender essentialism, simply defined, is the belief in binary, fixed differences between men and women that account for "natural" behavior and characteristics. Gender essentialism holds that men are aggressive, individualist, and rational rather than emotional; and that women are passive, community-minded, emotional rather than rational. Gender essentialism is the force that has justified centuries of unequal treatment and undergirded everything from fundamentalist religious beliefs (women as moral guardians of purity) to formulaic pop culture images of women (women as loyal wives and girlfriends) to workplace roles (women don't rise as fast as men because they're uncomfortable with power).

The father of essentialism was Aristotle, who got the party started back when he referred to the female as a "disabled male," but while the couple thousand years since then have managed to disprove that particular characterization, remarkably little has been successful in dismantling gender essentialism as a whole. Its language, themes, and images have always been the bedrock of media and pop culture, endemic to jobs across all levels in all industries, encoded by sports culture, and enforced by religious tenets and texts. But even as gender has become something that more and more people understand as an unfixed, fluid category, recent decades have seen a cultural and political insistence on biology-as-destiny, one in which the marketplace plays a more-than-meaningful role.

The Difference Industry

Aristotle would have been proud of psychologist and "father of adolescence" G. Stanley Hall, who was among many medical professionals of the early twentieth century who believed that women were best left uneducated, lest "over-activity of the brain" disrupt their chief function of bearing and raising children. And Edward Clarke, whose 1873 text had the seemingly promising title "Sex in Education, or, a Fair Chance for the Girls," held that young ladies who studied "in a boy's way" were likely to suffer atrophy of the uterus and ovaries, insanity, and death. Though such studies were debunked by plenty of researchers—some of whom were women who'd been educated and lived to tell the tale—their theories were adopted by opponents of women's equality with no small amount of relish. In 1879, Gustave Le Bon, one of the "craniometrists" whose work Stephen Jay Gould analyzed in the 1980 essay "Women's Brains," wrote perhaps the signature entry in the don't-educate-the-ladies canon: "[A]mong the most intelligent races, there are a large number of women whose brains are closer in size to those of gorillas than to the most developed male brains. This inferiority is so obvious that no one can contest it for a moment. . . . A desire to give them the same education, and to propose the same goals for them, is a dangerous chimera." (Le Bon, as you might imagine, also had some very specific beliefs about the brains of other races, ethnicities, and cultures, which can probably be summed up by noting that Adolf Hitler was a fan of his work.)

It's easy to laugh at what seems like comically outdated thinking, until you realize that often violent opposition to the education of girls and women continues to be a hallmark of many cultures, despite a sustained rise in global awareness and advocacy. Even in the United States, there's an inability to acknowledge the residue of our own culture's resistance to girls' and women's education—as though because we're not actually throwing acid in the face of schoolgirls or shooting them in the head, all traces of past inequality have been banished from the halls of learning. We can all have a knowing chuckle at, say, the fundamentalist Christian "stay-at-home daughter" movement wherein megachurch pastors warn their flocks against sending girls to colleges where they'll be corrupted by rogue bits of knowledge and led astray from their core domestic purpose. But corporate media's coverage of education often reveals a curiously similar set of worries.

There's palpable anxiety, for instance, in the language used to report stories about patterns in school performance and college attendance. Across all races, there are more women than men enrolling in colleges and universities, but the percentage of men enrolling has remained steady. In other words, it's not that men are declining to enroll; it's simply that women are doing so in greater numbers. But the articles written about this phenomenon have presented it as a titanic crisis: A 2012 *Forbes* article about the college enrollment patterns of men and women used the phrase "female domination" to describe the gap. A year earlier, *NBC Nightly News* story blared the question, "Where are the male college students?" as though they'd all vanished in a puff of smoke. A 2014 post at Pew Research Center's FactTank was headlined "Women's College Enrollment Gains Leave Men Behind." Girls are described as "leapfrogging" over boys in the "race" to college. And if you didn't get the message that women are cheerfully flipping the bird at men as they barrel over them onto our nation's college quadrangles, much-hyped books like *The War on Boys*, *Are Men Obsolete?*, *The Second Sexism*, and *The End of Men* are more than happy to offer fevered predictions of an America in which feminism has created masses of education-crazed interlopers.

One of the reliably essentialist refrains in much of the college-man crisis is, "Pray tell, who will all these overeducated girls marry?!?" The media hype around the phenomenon of educated black women who supposedly can't find husbands, for one, is a subject that's been ominously covered everywhere from *Essence* to CNN to the oeuvre of comedian–turned–relationship-expert Steve Harvey. The discussion almost never includes black women themselves, as political TV host Melissa Harris-Perry pointed out, but instead "frame[s] the issue as a black female problem rather than a community issue, offering advice that encourages women to mold themselves into a more sanitized definition of femininity that doesn't compete with socially sanctioned definitions of masculinity."[3] Likewise, books like Harvey's *Act Like a Lady, Think Like a Man* don't hang on sincere concern for the happiness or fulfillment of black women, but on the notion that too many of them being successful and uppity and single is a societal problem that requires immediate fixing. "That black women are single in large numbers, that they are advancing in education and careers, that they head so many households, that they are independent is deemed proof of their deficiency as women," wrote Tamara Winfrey Harris in a 2012 *Ms.* article. "In a nutshell: women are transgressing the boundaries we understand as 'natural,' and that is terrifying."

When it intersects with capitalism, meanwhile, there's no limit to how far biological determination can reach. Assimilation into a vast marketplace of needlessly gendered products now begins at birth, with diapers printed with cars or princesses and crib sheets that feature either pirates or flowers, but never both at once. Humorous onesies for male neonates read "Future superhero" or, worse, "Hung like a two-year-old," while those for girls denote "Princess in Training" or, still worse, ask, "Does this make my thighs look fat?" Shopping for a Halloween costume for my son several years back, I was baffled to see that superhero costumes, which once came in the form of screenprinted plastic sacks, now look like tiny, headless facsimiles of Jean-Claude Van Damme, bulked out with inches of foam-rubber musculature in case you didn't get the message that they're meant to be worn by boys. (Meanwhile, for girls on Halloween, the question is not whether she's going to be a Disney princess, but *which* princess.)

It goes without saying that a trip to a big-box toy store involves voluntary immersion in a pink-and-blue sea of product essentialism, but even in what you might expect to be more neutral consumer spaces—say, the vitamin section at the supermarket—there's no escaping it. (In case you're wondering, the Disney-princess vitamins and the Avengers vitamins are identical blobs of gelatin and glucose syrup.) At the bookstore, *The Big Book of Boys' Stuff* and *The Big Book of Girls' Stuff* both cover vital kid subjects like boogers and crushes, but have covers suggesting that boys want to know about science and girls want to know how much they should charge for babysitting; Scholastic's *How to Survive Anything* books were peddled in "Boys Only" and "Girls Only" versions, with some pretty specific ideas of what each sex needs to withstand. (For boys: shark and polar-bear attacks, zombie invasions, and whitewater rapids; for girls: fashion disasters, "BFF fights," breakouts, and embarrassment.)

This is a major shift from the more gender-neutral kid-specific marketing of the 1970s and '80s. Sure, Barbie and G.I. Joe still lived in different aisles in the store back then, but there were also action figures based on Steve Austin, the Six Million Dollar Man, and his ladyfriend Jaime Sommers, The Bionic Woman. Legos were primary-colored building blocks, not pre-made sets consisting of Star Wars scenarios and pastel beauty salons. When the Atari home videogame console made the scene, it wasn't "for boys" or "for girls," but for kids. (Or, if you were my dad, for hogging on the couch, with a drink and a smoke, after a long day at work.)

The paradox of the gendered product marketing that has intensified since the 1990s is that even as younger generations have a larger slate of powerful role models and a wider spectrum of gender identities than ever before, most of the retailers who court them have doubled down on dictating what "boys" and "girls" do and are. It's no longer enough for Toys 'R' Us to advertise its unisex Big Wheel to any child ready to pedal its sturdy plastic chassis down the driveway; instead, it sells the Big Dog Truck and the bright-pink Lil' Rider Princess Mini Quad. From Old Navy to Target to Pottery Barn Kids, inherently unisex kids' products are divided into pink and blue silos. This complicates things for everyone: the boys who feel sheepish about loving "girl" movies like *Brave* or *Frozen*; the girls who are policed for their playthings even by female peers; the transgender children whose struggles are underscored by having to define themselves through everything from pencil cases to fruit snacks; and the parents and relatives whose concerns about such commercial rigidity get brushed off with statements like "He/she's too young to care whether toys are pink or blue."

Is this really a big deal? Well, yes. It's easy to see the backlash inherent in kids' toys, room décor, and media that's so explicitly gendered. The generations of youngsters to whom these products are aimed are growing up with the fruits of feminism, gay liberation, antiracism, and growing transgender acceptance in evidence around them. Many of these kids take for granted that they will be afforded equal educational and extracurricular opportunities. They likely have two working parents, whether or not those parents are still together. And yet the world around them is ever more divided by sex, insisting that they see themselves as one of two discrete categories with attendant aesthetics and interests. Advertising and marketing philosophies that thrive on emphasizing "natural" differences don't stay in the realm of advertising and marketing—they spill into how we justify sexism and racism at every life stage.

Keep Your Chick Beer Away from my Bronuts

A marketplace that pushes Scotch tape and pink-labeled "Chick Beer" to women, or sunscreen for men and "bronuts"—that's doughnuts for men, in case regular doughnuts are too girly for you—is not just harmless free-market fun. There's a big difference between acknowledging that boys and girls and men and women are different by virtue of both nature and nurture, and encouraging them to conform to binary, sex-specific stereotypes with products that suggest such stereotypes are universally applicable. Let's say you're a woman-born-woman over the age of twelve and you like pink; maybe it's not your favorite color, but it's fine. Is it reasonable to assume that you want your pens, tissue packets, power tools, earplugs, beer bottles, ice cube trays, and freaking *glue sticks* to be pink *because* you're a woman? Unless your name is Barbie and you already live in a pink plastic townhouse with a pink plastic hot tub and a pink Corvette in your pink-gravel driveway, probably not. Meanwhile, all Brogurt does is reify the idea that being female is a bad thing. (My own slogan,

"Yogurt is a Gender-Neutral Food, Dummies" has not yet caught on, but here's hoping.)

The past three decades have generated something of an eruption in research that justifies gender essentialism as something that has a sound scientific basis and, in fact, is the key to happiness and understanding between the sexes (or, at least, the two sexes that are acknowledged in this binary construction). The big daddy of gender-essentialist media is John Gray, whose book *Men Are From Mars, Women Are From Venus* whizzed to the top of bestseller lists in 1992, and soon afterward begat a multimillion-dollar empire of follow-up books (*Mars and Venus in the Bedroom*, *Mars and Venus in the Workplace*, *Truly Mars and Venus*), workshops, games, relationship-counseling retreats, a short-lived talk show, and more. The crux of Gray's theory was the unsourced claim that "men's and women's values are inherently different"; he went on to paint a picture of Why Those Crazy Kids Just Can't Get Along using examples that even a beginning stand-up comic would reject as too cliché. *What's with men not asking for directions, am I right, ladies?* ("Mary had no idea that when Tom became lost and started circling the same block, it was a very special opportunity to love and support him"); *Guys, don't you hate it when your wife won't stop talking? I mean blah, blah blah* ("Just as a man is fulfilled though working out the intricate details of solving a problem, a woman is fulfilled through talking about the details of her problems"). With no real gender analysis to offer context, Gray didn't acknowledge that fixed-gender mindsets might, more than actual communication differences, be the thing gumming up the works. All Gray's binary constructions, as well as similar ones laid out by Deborah Tannen in *her* bestselling ladies-vs.-gents guides, were ones that complemented already-existing beliefs in What Men Do and What Women Do. They've been echoed in the rash of scare-tactic tomes pushed on black women; in addition to Steve Harvey's, there are Jimi Izreal's *The Denzel Principle: Why Black Women Can't Find Good Black Men*, Hill Harper's *The Conversation: How Black Men and Women Can Build Loving, Trusting*

Relationships, and advice books from serial-dating musicians Ray J and Musiq. As journalist Joshunda Sanders points out, these are books written by *unmarried*, famous black men—a phenomenon that suggests "that everyone but all the single black ladies knows how to be in a committed relationship."[4]

Elsewhere, as new technologies began broadening the possibilities for understanding the structures and workings of the human brain, the topic of biologically-based sex differences moved from the realm of pop psychology to the more dignified sphere of hard science, with a rash of high-minded tomes that put the imprimaturs of numerous eggheads on Gray's Mars-Venus dualism. *A Natural History of Rape*, published in 2000, echoed Camille Paglia in suggesting that male sexual violence toward women is an evolutionary legacy that's not a crime of power, as feminist theorists would have it, but one of sexual desire. Simon Baron-Cohen's 2003 book *The Essential Difference: Men, Women, and the Extreme Male Brain* mainstreamed the concept of "hard-wired" sex differences, explaining that women's brains are wired for empathy and connection while men's are wired to explore and build systems— autism, he concluded, is more prevalent in boys as an "extreme" version of this biological wiring. Two thousand six's *The Mommy Brain: How Motherhood Makes Us Smarter*, by investigative journalist Katherine Ellison, made the case that though a woman's post-baby mind often feels like a sieve, the stress and compulsory multitasking actually yields a healthy brain loaded with synapses firing like lawn darts. (No word on how fatherhood affects men's brains—parenting is a woman's job, silly!) Authored by neurobiologist Louann Brizendine, 2007's *The Female Brain* also leaned on hard-wiring as an explanation for supposedly inherent female traits like nurturance and emotional sensitivity, arguing that "girls arrive already wired as girls, and boys arrive already wired as boys." Susan Pinker, author of the 2008 tome *The Sexual Paradox: Men, Women, and the Real Gender Gap*, explained gender gaps in workplace achievement with the assertion that women are—say it with me—"wired for empathy," rather than ambition. Her brother

Steven's 2002 book, *The Blank Slate: The Modern Denial of Human Nature*, had similarly argued that biological difference, rather than socialization or acculturation, explained why early in life, girls play with kitchens and boys favor more physical games. Later, he lofted the weirdly specific assertion that women "are more likely [than men] to choose administrative support jobs that offer lower pay in air-conditioned offices."

The often common thread of these books was their authors' contention that they were taking a bold, even heroic stance in challenging a radical-feminist orthodoxy that was leading kids and adults astray, making them sadder, harder to educate, and stuck with toys they had no interest in. Naturally, this narrative of taboo-smashing scientific crusading was instant media crack. Occasionally, reviews of the books would note offhandedly that some evidence for the claims anchoring them was iffy or unsupported, but that was ultimately beside the point. The corporate media outlets that covered the books weren't too interested in the nuances of their findings or the flawed methodology that often undergirded them, though more skeptical and science-driven publications were. *Nature*, for one, fact-checked *The Female Brain* and reported that the book was "riddled with errors" and "fails to meet even the most basic standards of scientific accuracy"; others noted that, much like John Gray and Deborah Tannen before her, Brizendine conveniently ignored the existence of both transgender and intersex people, given that acknowledging them would decimate her strict binary.

Baron-Cohen's widely embraced theory of hard-wired sex differences, meanwhile, was based on a study of day-old babies that found boys fixated on a mobile, girls more focused on nearby faces. Day-old babies, don't forget, can barely keep their eyes open to begin with, and also can't hold their heads up by themselves; as media critics Caryl Rivers and Rosalind C. Barnett noted, the fact that the infants were not acting independently but physically influenced by the parents who were holding them was a crucial complicating factor that Baron-Cohen glossed over.[5] The study was never replicated, and was subsequently debunked by several fellow scientists: one, neuroscientist Lise Eliot, emphasized that "kids rise or fall according to what we believe about them, and the more we dwell on the differences between boys and girls, the likelier such stereotypes are to crystallize into children's self-perceptions and self-fulfilling prophecies."[6]

But corporate media still regularly invokes studies like these, and the conclusions they reach, when considering gender difference as an essential, objective measure of what people are "naturally" inclined to do in relationships, workplaces, and families. It's not the quality of the science that makes them resonate, but the fact that their authors' broad claims can be used to justify long-held viewpoints on sex, gender, power, and potential—all of which inform how our culture and institutions value women's and men's participation. (To say nothing of how we sideline people who identify as neither.) Gray, for one, made his bias apparent when he stated—with the extremely rational reasoning he ascribes to Martians/men—"The reason why there's so much divorce is that feminism promotes independence in women." Pinker's contention that women flock to administrative jobs and lack the mettle to work without the benefit of proper air conditioning contributes to the conservative party line that what all those testy feminists call a wage gap is really just the result of women's personal choices. It also, notably, ignores the fact that "choice" in jobs is actually not an option for large numbers of women who certainly might *want* administrative jobs in climate-cooled cubicles, but work instead in factories or fast-food restaurants so they can feed their families and keep the lights on.

None of this is to say that intrinsic brain differences between born sexes don't exist; Rivers and Barnett note that, with more sophisticated brain-research methods than ever before now available, there's considerable evidence that there are. But let's return for a moment to women's teeny-tiny gorilla brains, as Gustave LeBon characterized them. Despite a resounding lack of evidence to support his theories and those of his ideological brethren, women were kept out of higher and even secondary education for decades because such theories were in line with what was already an approved narrative about women. In less extreme forms, that tail still wags the dog. When Harvard president Larry Summers asserted to a 2005 meeting at the National Bureau of Economic Research that women lag behind men in scientific education and careers because their feminine minds are just more focused on families and relationships, he was giving credence to that prejudice. Ten years later, when Nobel Laureate Tim Hunt announced to the World Conference of Science Journalists that "girls" don't belong in science labs alongside men ("Three things happen when they're in the lab: you fall in love with them, they fall in love with you, and when you criticize them they cry"), he was asserting the same ideas in an even more ham-fisted way. (Hunt later tried, unsuccessfully, to pass his words off as a failed attempt to satirize himself.) It's not a secret that there are tons of people who are smart and accomplished and progressive and who nevertheless think this way. The issue isn't that they exist, but that they are continually offered media airtime and/or validation simply because the combination of gender essentialism and feminist antagonism translates into attention, readership, and sales.

This goes the other way too, in a spate of recent books, talks, and self-help seminars that urge women to harness some of the worst features of men's supposedly hard-wired personalities to succeed in traditionally gendered spheres. 2014's *The Confidence Code: The Science and Art of Self-Assurance* was penned by Katty Kay and Claire Shipman, two female news professionals who theorized that a "confidence gap" among women was responsible for their inability to get to the highest echelons of the corporate sphere. The authors admitted that a vicious cycle was at play: the persistence of gender essentialism means that girls are socialized differently than boys, which makes them look less confident than male colleagues who—to pull from one of their examples—might just drop by a boss's office to make a pitch rather than scheduling an appointment. Men's socially approved tendency toward confidence, even when it's at odds with competence, fuels their sense that they're capable of anything; that go-getting attitude in women is frequently a source of suspicion or dislike.[7]

And yet the thrust of *The Confidence Gap*'s self-help prescription was "Be more like guys who may not know what the hell they're doing but just act like they do." This directive bypassed over a crucial complicating factor: almost every problem in current American economics was caused by arrogant, overconfident attitudes like those the authors were encouraging. But having as much unearned female confidence at the top as there is unearned male confidence isn't progress, it's just a recipe for more jackasses of all genders with the power to do untold damage to everyone below them.

The rise of the difference industry results in a lot of contradictory ideas and directives. Women are take-charge, Third Metric-ing, networking career powerhouses who can bloviate with the big boys, as the new prevalence of lady-power conferences and advice books would have it. But according to the allegedly maverick biological determinists of neuroscience, our innate empathy and passivity make us poor risks for workplace longevity. The career executives among us should be pushing to emulate male colleagues, but we should also revel in our pink sphere, enjoy our women's granola and Bic for Her pens, and bask in our glorious, Venusian womanity. Media and pop culture phenomena, meanwhile, seem increasingly to suggest that not only is gender essentialism a good basis for happiness in work, love, and family, but that embracing such essentialism is, in fact, a thoroughly modern and superior form of feminism that women reject at their peril.

Bizarro Feminism

Marketplace feminism, as a buffet of adjectives and at-will definitions, has fostered a media realm in which the word "feminism" is used as a stand-in for "strength," "authority," "wealth," "happiness," and any number of other characteristics and descriptors that exist independent of a larger ideology. Pop star Katy Perry was reluctant to call herself a feminist, for instance, until she decided that feminism, for her, was defined as "lov[ing] myself as a female and lov[ing] men." *Elle UK*, in its December 2014 "Feminism" issue, asked a handful of contributors to share their definitions of feminism, to which one writer (the husband of British author Caitlin Moran), offered the truly head-scratching response, "good manners." A blog post published on *Huffington Post Women* asserted, in defense of a recently-gone-public Caitlyn Jenner, that "We get to choose how we define what it means to be a woman and we also get to define feminism." It's a fill-in-the-blank approach to feminism that has in recent years found an unlikely new home: the realm of right-wing conservative politics.

Take Sarah Palin, whose choose-your-own-feminism adventure began after the 2008 election in which a cynical GOP ploy—get a woman, any woman, on the ticket—backfired spectacularly. During the run-up to the election, Palin had demurred when she was asked about feminism in an interview with NBC's Brian Williams, saying that she wasn't "going to label [her]self anything." By 2010, however, Palin had pivoted, most notably with a breakfast-meeting address to the antichoice advocacy group the Susan B. Anthony List. In a speech larded with references to "grizzly mamas" and "pro-woman sisterhood," Palin urged supporters to join her in shaping an "emerging, conservative, feminist identity"—an identity which specifically involved only backing candidates who took a strong antiabortion stance.

Headlines like *The Economist*'s "Sarah Palin: Feminism Is for Everyone" suggested that Palin was valiantly exposing the hypocrisy of Democratic feminists in claiming the term and watching them freak out. Within days, pundits who had never invoked feminism except to rail against it could not get enough of what Palin was peddling. "Pro-life Feminism Is the Future!" enthused the *Washington Post*. "Is the Tea Party a Feminist Movement?" queried *Slate*. "Sarah Palin, Feminist," announced the *L.A. Times*. It was a full-tilt Opposite World media moment. By the strange magic of conservative logic, feminists working toward policy that prioritized such things as reproductive autonomy, access to contraception, informed and comprehensive sex education in schools, fair family and medical leave, a living wage, marriage equality, law enforcement oversight, financial institution oversight, and prison reform—were exposed as, in fact, working *against* women's interests, all because of their interest in keeping abortion legal. Nutty, right?

Yes, actually, it was. As writer Kate Harding asked, "In a series that begins with 'anti-choice feminism,' 'Tea Party feminism,' and 'Sarah Palin feminism,' what comes next? 'Phyllis Schlafly feminism?' 'Patriarchal feminism?' 'He-Man Woman Hater Feminism?' I mean, how long until the *Washington Post* publishes a 'feminist' argument for repealing the 19th Amendment (there's no truly pro-woman party anyway, don't you know?), or widening the pay gap (so more men can be sole breadwinners again and more women can *freely choose* to stay home) or, I don't know, reclaiming the word 'chattel'?"[8] While that hasn't happened yet, there remains a conservative push for women to recognize that the *real* feminists are those who don't believe in abortion. This argument blames Big Abortion for selling women a bill of goods: "the result," wrote one earnest male columnist, "of a systematic effort by abortion activists to mislead vulnerable women. They're waging an emotional and psychological 'war on women.'"[9]

Carly Fiorina's adoption of an opportunistically feminist identity found much of the press greeting her with the same credulity. The former Hewlett-Packard CEO threw her hat in the presidential ring alongside Hillary Clinton in 2015 with a campaign that, she boasted, would "rende[r] the Democratic 'war on women' baloney sort of neutral."[10] While a presidential campaign based on a glaring fallacy ("I am a woman; therefore, there is no war on women") might not sound promising, the media adored the catfight potential of this Hillary-meets-her-match angle. *The Week* noted in a fawning profile, "[Fiorina] has no use for laws mandating 'equal pay' or paid maternity leave or contraceptive coverage that movement feminists espouse and Clinton laps up—for the obvious reason that they'll backfire by making women more expensive and hence less employable." "Here's How Carly Fiorina Wants to Redefine Feminism," offered a blog post at *Time* in which Fiorina was quoted saying "a feminist is a woman who lives the life she chooses. . . . A woman may choose to have five children and home-school them. She may choose to become a CEO, or run for President." "What Kind of Feminist is Carly Fiorina?" asked *Newsweek*, and at least partially answered its own question by noting that the candidate had, months earlier, called feminism "a weapon [used] to win elections."

Fiorina had honed her image as a "pro-woman" candidate in a 2010 California Senate campaign against Democratic incumbent Barbara Boxer that was infused with the same rhetoric as her presidential bid. At the time, Susan B. Anthony List president Marjorie Dannenfelser crowed that Fiorina-vs.-Boxer would be "a test of all the dogmas of feminism and women in political life, because we'll have perfect contrast between these two women." But ironically, both Dannenfelser and Fiorina did exactly what they expected those dogmatic feminists to do—assumed that voters would define "feminism" as narrowly as they did. Boxer didn't take California for a third term because she conformed to the straw-feminist image that her opponent had conjured up; she won largely on issues that are crucial to all genders: the economy, clean energy, and health care for everyone. (It also may be worth noting that Fiorina's comment, captured by a hot mic, about her opponent's hair—"so yesterday"—painted more of a mean-girl picture than a pro-woman one.)

And then there's the Independent Women's Forum, a Washington D.C. think tank funded by right-wing and conservative foundations whose focus is on what member and author Christina Hoff Sommers terms "equity feminism." Positioning the group in direct opposition to established feminist lobbying organizations like NOW and the Feminist Majority, the IWF has denounced "radical" feminism as damaging to families and women themselves, and its members take a hard line on everything from the wage gap (it doesn't exist; women simply make choices that merit a different pay scale than their male counterparts) to the so-called boy crisis in schools (Sommers has written extensively that "feminization" of public education is leaving male students in peril). And though the IWF's mission statement doesn't mention feminism (it names "greater respect for limited government, equality under the law, property rights, free markets, strong families, and a powerful and effective national defense and foreign policy" as key goals), its name piggybacks on independence as a feature of traditional feminism.

There's a lot to be said for an expansive approach to feminism, especially given the movement's historical blind spots around race, class, and religion. Palin's attempted hijacking of the term in 2008 exploited, if inadvertantly, an existing apprehension about dictating what constituted "real" feminism. The primary season had found longtime feminist leaders Gloria Steinem and Robin Morgan chastised for their decidedly nonintersectional belief that women should vote for Hillary Clinton over Barack Obama because, per Steinem, "Gender is probably the most restricting force in American life." After Palin joined the Republican ticket, NOW's Kim Gandy drew ire for opining that Palin wasn't an "authentic" woman because of her antiabortion values. These gaffes justified some of the resistance to categorically calling bullshit on Palin, or even suggesting that her feminism might be little more than tactical spin. In her *L.A. Times* column, Meghan Daum wrote that "If [Palin] has the guts to call herself a feminist, then she's entitled to be accepted as one," which seems about as useful as saying that anyone who is willing to call themselves a personal injury lawyer (an equally despised term in many circles, after all) should go ahead and set up shop. Palin's, and now Fiorina's, wish to deny abortion rights and/or contraceptive access to her fellow women can't seriously be considered in line with an ideology that for decades has put bodily autonomy at the top of its priorities. A big tent is great and all, but there has to be a line in the sand, and I'm pretty sure the desire to legislate other women's bodies is it. Media outlets don't see it that way, though, and why would they? Debating the feminism of Palin or Fiorina equals pageviews on a silver platter.

Since the advent of the 24-hour news cycle, the issue of what feminism means in a political context has become particularly subjective. It's notable that neither Palin nor Fiorina's performative embrace of feminism has stopped Democratic female politicians like Hillary Clinton, Nancy Pelosi, and Elizabeth Warren from being demonized by right-wing pundits and politicians as feminazis who hate families and eat babies and want to take their giant feminist sledgehammers to the moral bedrock on which America was founded. Yet when politicians on the other side of the aisle embrace their own interpretations of feminism, those same pundits are all of a sudden attentive to feminism. This is not just transparently contrived branding that serves a narrow set of interests; it's ideological narcissism.

Learning from Lilith

In the late 1990s, there was a magical place, a place where being a woman was just about the most special thing you could be. A place where blissed-out white ladies with long, flowing hair strummed guitars and crooned wistfully into crowds of people, many of whom were wearing blackhead-removing strips on their noses (just go with it). It was a place called Lilith Fair, and it was both a very successful and very disappointing effort to harness the power of gender essentialism for the greater corporate good.

The all-female music festival was founded by Canadian musician Sarah McLachlan, in a stretch of the '90s that overlapped with Riot Grrrl on one side and Girl Power on the other. It was a time when corporate airwaves saw an influx of female musicians with radio hits—Tori Amos, Joan Osborne, Missy Elliot, Fiona Apple, India.Arie—and wide appeal. But the industry's prejudice against women as revenue killers was as strong as ever: McLachlan conceived Lilith as a retort to risk-averse radio DJs and concert promoters who acted as though any man who had to sit through more than one female act at a rock festival or two female artists back-to-back on the radio was in danger of drowning-by-estrogen. Lilith Fair was a big-ticket summer tour in the guise of a welcoming oasis, fusing music and community with civic awareness. (A portion of ticket sales went to organizations like Planned Parenthood and the Rape and Incest National Network, as well as local nonprofits in cities around the country.) In its first year, Lilith was an undeniable success, outselling such summer-festival staples as Lollapalooza and the H.O.R.D.E. festival and proving that women and girls were a market force that the music men were foolish to ignore. "In a sense, we're talking more to the industry than the public," noted McLachlan. "Because the industry thinks the public only responds to the lowest common denominator, and I think the public deserves more credit than that."[11]

Lilith Fair was just as successful in breaking ground in an emerging difference industry where being female was no longer a recipe for consumer marginalization. The corporations that Lilith partnered with over its run—among them the Jergens Company (makers of those Bioré blackhead strips), Luna women's nutrition bars, and Volkswagen—were thrilled to be reaching a captive market. That such sponsors had chosen to put their brands behind a tour attended largely by politically progressive, female-identified people earmarked them as companies that women should subsequently think of when buying cars, nutrition bars, and blackhead strips.

By the third year of Lilith Fair, though, there was something cloying about it. For one, the sheer sameness of a majority of its performers wore thin—though the festival did try to book acts beyond the white-lady singer-songwriter category, the lineups were still thick with them. The profusion of flowy skirts and gentle sounds made Lilith kind of the festival version of a tampon or yogurt commercial in which women are *just so darn psyched* to be female that they're practically levitating. Author Sarah Vowell had this entertainingly blistering critique: "Just because I have ovaries doesn't make me feel solidarity with horrid Tracy Chapman and her obvious, hippie-dippy songs like 'The Rape of the World'; or claim sisterhood with wimpy, meek-voiced Lisa Loeb; or cheer ditzy Sheryl Crow, whose song about how 'If it makes you happy, it can't be that bad' was probably meant as a defense of eating ice cream or sleeping around or something, but I can't hear it without imagining Joseph Stalin lip-synching it as a defense of all things evil."[12]

But the festival's girly sounds had implications beyond annoying Vowell and others who shared her Lilith animosity. Rock festivals that had previously made at least halfhearted efforts to include female musicians on their rosters suddenly didn't even have to do that. It was as though because Lilith Fair existed, every other mainstream music festival was off the hook for gender diversity: Lollapalooza, Warped, Ozzfest, and others had already been sausage parties, but in the wake of Lilith Fair's success they became even more so. By the summer of 1999, it seemed as though an invisible wall had been erected between Lilith Fair and all other festivals, with each side sinking deeper into the worst of their respective stereotypes. Seeping out from the reviews of Woodstock 99—a reboot of the classic festival of peace, love, and bad acid—were reports of women being assaulted and raped in the cheering crowds for Limp Bizkit and Insane Clown Posse. Performer Sheryl Crow and emcee Rosie Perez were greeted with entreaties to show their tits. (Perez, at least, zinged back: "Go rent *Do the Right Thing*!")

In the wake of Woodstock, rock critic Ann Powers suggested that while Lilith Fair's success was notable, it may have heightened gender tensions that have always permeated rock music and "confine[ed] mainstream female artists within the gilded cage of the pop songbird."[13] The festival, which had begun as an assimilated kind of separatism, now seemed like proof that separatism itself was assimilated past the point of no return. Certainly, the numbers of female musicians and bands on summer-festival rosters, twenty years later, haven't changed much, and considering women these days are consistently at the top of charts across almost all genres, it's a striking discrepancy. It's even become a summer tradition for music–festival coverage to include at least one image of the posters from Coachella, Reading, Lollapalooza, and others with the all-male acts Photoshopped out—leaving a handful of all-female, mixed-gender, and genderqueer names suspended in suddenly-empty spaces.

Empowering Who?

There's a feminist legacy of gender essentialism that, in some cases, has profoundly changed our culture. In the early days of radical feminism, for instance, there was a call to not simply theorize about a world remade by feminism, but to make one. The idea was that a "counter-reality," as the women of one group known as The Feminists called it—a literal construction of alternatives to every institution in mainstream culture, owned and operated by women—was the only viable way to live without mainstream culture's half-measures and stutter steps toward liberation. To start women's schools, health centers, publishing companies, credit unions, and cultural centers from scratch would allow for prioritizing women rather than shoehorning them in alongside men, and also allow women marginalized by "straight" society—working-class women, women of color, women with disabilities, and lesbian women—to flourish financially and socially.

The utopia was never realized in a complete sense, but some of its projects definitely were. The women's health movement, for one, was an upending of medicine's paternalistic approach to women's health brought about by activist groups like the Boston Women's Health Book Collective, the Black Women's Health Project, and Chicago's underground network of abortion providers, Jane. They shared one big idea: that women had the right to know about their bodies, control their reproductive destinies, and make decisions about their health care in a time when the medical establishment was characterized by a disdain for "female problems" that left women misdiagnosed, pathologized, mistreated, and forcibly sterilized. On a much smaller scale, the rise of a "women's music" genre created and supported by lesbian artists led to cultural successes like that of Olivia Records, a lesbian record label–turned–fancy cruise line. And intentional communities where women live simply and collectively are, though well off the mainstream radar, still surviving in parts of the country.

In some places, of course, these visions of a female utopia hardened into a distrust of anything (and anyone) that wasn't explicitly female. The now-defunct Michigan Womyn's Music Festival, for one, was the longest-running institution in women's music, but its gender rigidity—it refused to grant entry to anyone who wasn't a "woman-born-woman"—came to symbolize the ideological conflict between second-wave radical separatists (now called simply "radfems") and more intersectionally aware activists.

Women's music and lesbian collectives and all-female intentional communities are often portrayed as a hippie holdover that, if viewed at all by the mainstream, seem like a gendered variation on the Pet Rock, hardly the fearsome threat to American wholesomeness they once were. But the same narrow picture of what a woman is has, in this new marketplace-feminist reality, been shined up and refashioned into "empowerment" events and political campaigns that hijack these terms to refer to an identity of power, rather than a process of social and political change. Defining "feminist" as "a woman who lives the life she chooses" is great if you're a woman who already has choices. But it does nothing for the vast majority on the outside of the conference hall, waiting in vain for that empowerment to trickle down.

CHAPTER 9

Creeping Beauty

"Looks are the new feminism, an activism of aesthetics." —Alex Kuczynski, *Beauty Junkies*

The power of erotic capital has been explicit in culture since culture has existed. How many narratives in literature, theater, film, and contemporary popular culture have featured women undergoing physical, sartorial, and temperamental changes to leverage their looks into a better station in life, even temporarily? (I'll start: Scheherazade, *Cinderella*, *Pygmalion* and its countless updates, *The Taming of the Shrew*, *Little Women*'s indelible "Vanity Fair" chapter, *Pretty Woman*, *Miss Congeniality*, ZZ Top's "Legs" video . . .) And how much tragedy has resulted from cultural messages that some bodies, colors, and sizes are simply worth more than others? The works of Toni Morrison, Edith Wharton, James Baldwin, and many more testify.

Erotic capital was once a matter of coy artifice ("Only her hairdresser knows for sure . . . "), but these days there are more and more ways to find out just how, and why, to deploy it. A 2011 *New York Times* article titled, "Up the Career Ladder, Lipstick in Hand," offered evidence that women who wear makeup increase their likability and trustworthiness in the workplace. This finding might seem a likely conclusion to a study funded by Procter & Gamble, manufacturers of   **221** both the drugstore staple CoverGirl and the high-end beauty line by Dolce & Gabbana. But the article hurried to assure readers that the authors of the study were unaffiliated with P&G, and thus legit; one of them was Nancy Etcoff, Harvard professor, author of the 1999 book *Survival of the Prettiest*, and consultant to the Dove Campaign for Real Beauty. (We'll get to that shortly.) Etcoff, responding to a query about whether individuals should be judged on competence rather than appearance, made the case that a "cultural shift" in women's attitudes about their own appearance must be taken into account. She argued, "Twenty or thirty years ago, if you got dressed up, it was simply to please men, or it was something you were doing because society demand[ed] it. . . . Women and feminists today see this is their own choice, and it may be an effective tool."

Author and London School of Economics professor Catherine Hakim popularized the name of this effective tool via her 2010 book *Erotic Capital*. Hakim's thesis is that where gender inequality persists, women should make better use of their one clear advantage—erotic capital—to level the playing field. Some of Hakim's pronouncements were deliberately provocative (for instance, the suggestion that erotic capital is, for women, possibly more useful than a college degree), but most of her theory was a case of same rabbit, different hat. The "beauty premium" and its effect on workplace hiring has been a regular subject of study for academics over the years. Results have generally varied: one report found that good-looking male study subjects in Europe and Israel who included a photo when applying for jobs had a significantly higher response rate than both unspectacular men and those whose CV didn't include a photo at all. The same experiment with female subjects found that women without a photo were, somewhat surprisingly, more likely to be called back than those with one, whatever the level of attractiveness. An earlier study, meanwhile, found that people considered attractive earned at least 5 percent more than their plainer colleagues—and, conversely, that those labeled ugly found their earnings penalized to the tune of 5 percent less (women) and 10 percent less (men) than their more comely coworkers. In other words, there is a beauty premium, but since nobody can say for sure when or how it will come into play, it's safer to proceed through life with the switch set firmly to "on."

With *Erotic Capital*, Hakim brought not only a coinage with an intellectual pedigree—the phrase built on sociologist Pierre Bourdieu's identification of multiple forms of capital—but also a use-it-or-lose-it attitude regarding negotiations of sex and power in daily life. Though her book emphasized that erotic capital is not exclusively effective for women, Hakim put special emphasis on the need for them (as well as anyone "with less access to economic and social capital, including young people, ethic minorities, and working-class groups") to deploy it. The acknowledgment that white men, for the most part, still disproportionately hold the reins of power translated into the book being shilled as a high-minded, if politically incorrect, how-to for women, a twenty-first century version of Helen Gurley Brown's *Sex and the Office*.

The argument for prioritizing erotic capital is that most of us are naturally more confident when we look good, so why not look good first, harness that confidence, and then move on to doing the thing you want to do that changes the world/gets you a promotion/increases your opportunities for success. In some parts of the world, this plan has become part of a larger economic strategy. Brazil, until recently the world's leader in cosmetic surgeries performed (South Korea now surpasses it), is home to dozens of public hospitals that offer free or discounted cosmetic procedures to low-income citizens, with the belief that conforming to the country's famously stringent beauty standards gives underprivileged people a leg up in the job market (preferably one with no spider veins). And while procedures like facelifts, nose jobs, and butt implants are performed regardless of gender, women are the ones featured in most media coverage of the subsidized surgeries, giving the impression that the management and leverage of erotic capital is primarily a woman's concern.

Most women don't need a corporate-funded study to inform them that erotic capital is an uneasy and often thankless negotiation. The Procter & Gamble study profiled in "Up the Career Ladder" noted that while makeup in general may positively affect how a woman's colleagues and superiors assess her worth, too much makeup, or "high-contrasting" colors—a vampy, dark lip, say—risked making a woman come across as "untrustworthy." Women's-magazine guides on dressing appropriately for the workplace have long warned that button-up shirts or pencil skirts that look perfectly chic on A-cup breasts and mini backsides risk looking "tarty" when worn by bustier, bootier women. The message, ultimately, is that erotic capital is incredibly useful, assuming your existing body already lands in the sweet spot between attractive but not intimidating, sexual but not oversexed, feminine but not Jessica Rabbit.

Like many people who have attempted the almost impossible feat of finding that sweet spot, I was absorbed back in 2010 by the story of a New York City–based former Citibank employee named Debrahlee Lorenzana who brought suit against her employer's parent company, Citigroup, claiming that she'd been fired for being too sexy for her job. Lorenzana's lawsuit asserted that her bosses complained that her body was just too distracting for her male colleagues. They forbade her to wear, among other things, turtleneck shirts, pencil skirts, fitted suits, and three-inch heels. When Lorenzana pointed out that her attire was no different from that of other female Citibank employees, she was told that "their body shapes were different than mine, and I drew too much attention."[1] In the end, Lorenzana was awarded no damages, and since she went on to become serially litigious—between 2011 and 2013, she sued a cab company and a medical lab—media coverage has more or less voided the substance of the Citigroup suit. But the question of whether there's a beauty penalty as well as a premium has been answered resoundingly in recent years.

In 2013, a Florida high-school teacher was asked to resign from her job after photos from her side gig as a model (for which she used a different name) were sent to the school's principal; in 2014, a recruit at the Port Authority Police Academy was singled out as a "Barbie Doll" and "American Girl Doll" by her instructors, repeatedly harassed, and ultimately fired after she refused to resign.[2] Before he was ousted as CEO of American Apparel, the list of harassment allegations and rumors accrued by now-legendary garment-industry douchebag Dov Charney included the claim that he had fired employees he deemed insufficiently fuckable.[3] And the Iowa Supreme Court ruled in 2013 that it's fair for a woman to be fired from her job if her appearance is distracting enough to threaten the marriage of her superior—a decision spurred by the case of a dentist who fired his hygienist because even in head-to-foot scrubs, she was simply too irresistible. In the court's finding, this was totally legitimate: employers "can fire employees that they and their spouses see as threats to their marriages." It's not up to employers, you see, to be more professional and appropriate in such cases, it's up to female employees not to unwittingly lead them on by doing nothing other than having the gall to show up for work with their god-given faces and bodies. (If you're wondering where you've heard this narrative of women as temptress and man as hapless accessory to his desires before, just check out, oh, the past few thousand years of history, art, literature, and music.)

When the lines between acceptable and unacceptable deployment of erotic capital are drawn and redrawn at will by others—employers, peers, state judicial bodies—the "choice" Etcoff spoke of in the *New York Times* seems pretty hollow. Furthermore, erotic capital is indelibly racialized, making proclamations about its power inevitably subject to white-centric standards. Consider the incident at a 2007 *Glamour* magazine event held at a law firm and called "The Dos and Don't of Corporate Fashion," where one of the magazine's editors instructed the assembled female lawyers that Afros, dreadlocks, and other "political" hairstyles were "inappropriate" and a definite "don't." Seven years later, the U.S. Military, as part of an overhaul of grooming regulations, prohibited styles significant to African-American hair, including dreadlocks, two-strand and flat twists, and Afros. The new-do rules, issued to "maintain uniformity within a military population," according to their wording, also made reference to "matted and unkempt" styles which seemed to further point a finger toward black service members. (The unwelcome publicity about the changes prompted an official response by the Congressional Black Caucus and an eventual rollback of the provisions.) These examples speak to the entrenched belief that words like "appropriate," "professional," and "uniform" refer only to white baselines of attractiveness; this can't help but suggest that people of color who don't strive for that standard squander the erotic capital they might otherwise use for professional and social advancement.

Adding to the problem of erotic capital is that its trappings—clothes, makeup, even shoes—are often the first things to come under review in cases of sexual harassment and rape, as anyone who's ever read a media account of those incidents knows. It's only very recently that "Well, what was she wearing?" has ceased to be the first question posed (though it's often the second or third). The woman who in 1991 accused William Kennedy Smith of rape had both her story and her credibility questioned in part because of the undergarments she wore on the night in question—a pearl-studded lace bra and underpants from Victoria's Secret. Though the bra was admitted into evidence ostensibly to counter the plaintiff's claim that she was tackled and raped by Kennedy, it was treated in the media as proof that its wearer was a wanton opportunist, with photos of similar garments splashed across the covers of supermarket tabloids as the televised trial played out.

Even those women who are arguably the most successful in trading on their erotic capital—those whose careers depend on it—ultimately have less choice than the likes of Etcoff and Hakim would have us believe. In late 2014, when a massive hack of Sony Entertainment revealed email exchanges between the film company's top executives, one of the more notable revelations was the discrepancy in salaries between men and women working on equal footing. Jennifer Lawrence was revealed to have been paid less than both her male costars in the ensemble movie *American Hustle*. Charlize Theron, after finding out via the leaked correspondence that she made significantly less than her *Snow White and the Huntsman* costar Chris Hemsworth (who doesn't, by the way, have an Oscar to his name), demanded a pay increase.

An even more depressing example comes via the fashion models who in the past decade-plus have spoken up about the sexual coercion they've experienced working with star fashion photographer Terry Richardson. Richardson's patented creepy-uncle approach to young female models—involving on-set requests for hand- and blow jobs, often in front of roomfuls of people—was for years an open secret in the industry. Starting in 2004, however, multiple current and former models began coming forward (some anonymously, some not) in online spaces including *Jezebel*, *The Gloss*, and *BuzzFeed* to denounce Richardson's predatory m.o. Their tales underscored how the alleged power of female beauty and sexuality can be easily *over*powered in a career where young models' ability to earn a living may well rest in the hands of a man who once said, "It's not who you know, it's who you blow." An extensive 2014 profile in *New York* magazine revealed what seemed to be Richardson's willful ignorance of the power imbalance between a celebrity photographer and unknown models who knew that walking out of a shoot could end their careers before they started. A photography agent quoted in the piece was blunt: "Kate Moss wasn't asked to grab a hard dick. Miley Cyrus wasn't asked to grab a hard dick. H&M models weren't asked to grab a hard dick. But these other girls, the nineteen-year-old girl from Whereverville, [she] should be the one to say, 'I don't think this is a good idea'? These girls are told by agents how important he is, and then they show up and it's a bait-and-switch. This guy and his friends are literally like, 'Grab my boner.' Is this girl going to say no? And go back to the village? That's not a real choice. It's a false choice."[4]

In other words, if there's a difference between the women who make the "choice" to leverage erotic capital in their careers—fittingly, the one place where erotic capital favors women over men is in the commercial sex industry—and the millions of those who are coerced or forced to in order to simply survive, it's pretty minimal.

Navel (and Nasal) Gazing

"I did it for me," reads the plaque held by the woman in a Botox ad. There's a sense that she's presenting the plaque to us, the audience, and it's kind of unnerving. The makers of the ad are conversant in the basic language of both body acceptance and choice feminism, and this ad is an attempt to make an end-run around any existing skepticism about cosmetic surgery, by appealing to free, market-savvy choice and its result, empowerment. This woman who paid a tidy sum of money for a smooth forehead and nonexistent nasolabial folds is not a dupe of the patriarchy, dammit! She's not doing it for a man; she's not doing it for a woman; she's doing it *for herself*, and those are the magic words. Variations on "I did it for me" appear and reappear in ads for Botox and breast implants; they're present when *Vogue* suggests—you know, just puts it out there—that you *could* shorten your toes in order to better fit them into Jimmy Choos; they exist whenever morning talk-radio hosts give away free breast implants to the woman with the best small-boobs sob story. "I did it for me," "I did it to feel better about myself," and, "I'm not doing it for anyone else" are defensive reflexes that acknowledge an imagined feminist disapproval and impatiently brush it away.

It's been twenty-five years since Naomi Wolf wrote, in her best-selling book *The Beauty Myth*, that "The ideology of beauty is the last one remaining of the old feminine ideologies that still has the power to control those women whom second-wave feminism would have otherwise made relatively uncontrollable." For all the gains that various women's movements have made possible, rigidly prescribed, predominantly white beauty standards are one site where time has not revolutionized our thinking. Concurrently, it's also where the expansion of consumer choice has made it possible to bow to such standards in countless new ways.

Choice has become the primary way to talk about looks, a phenomenon that journalist Alex Kuczynski called "an activism of aesthetics" in her 2006 book *Beauty Junkies*. In the book, the cosmetic surgery industry in particular is portrayed as a kind of Thunderdome where the waiting lists for a new injectable climb into the double digits, impeccably spray-tanned celebrity doctors jostle for prime soundbite space in women's magazines, and speakers at surgeons' conventions end their speeches with a call to "Push plastic surgery." With a rise in options—more doctors, more competing pharmaceutical brands, the rise of cosmetic-surgery tourism that promises cheap procedures in tropical locations—the landscape of sculpted noses and liposuctioned abs has been defined by choice. The "activism," too, is one of individual choice—it refers to being proactive about one's own appearance, vigilant enough to be able to head off wrinkles, droops, and sags at the pass. Framed within our neoliberal discourse, an activism of aesthetics doesn't dismantle the beauty standards that telegraph worth and status, but advocates for everyone's right to purchase whatever interventions are necessary to achieve those standards. The individual world shrinks to the size of a doctor's office; other people exist only as points of physical comparison.

Though we often think of beauty and body imperatives in their prefeminist form—the hobbling footbinding, the lead whitening powders, the tapeworm diet—the ostensibly consciousness-raised decades since the 1970s have brought a mind-boggling array of dictates, standards, and trends to all genders, but most forcefully to women. When capri pants were the move of the moment in the 1990s, *Vogue* was there to suggest quick surgical fixes for knobby knees and undefined calves. Less than ten years later, the clavicle was the body part du jour, balancing the trend of voluminous clothing with reassuring proof that, under all that material, the wearer was appropriately thin. (One clavicle-boasting woman stated to *The New York Times* that the clavicle was the "easiest and least controversial expression of a kind of sex appeal"—not as obviously sexy as breasts, but evidence of a physical discipline coveted among the fashion set.[5]) A handful of years after that, the focus moved south again, to the "thigh gap" coveted by a largely young audience, some of whom blogged about their pursuit of the gap with diet journals and process photos.

Though certain types of bodies have historically come in and out of fashion—the flapper dresses of the 1920s required a boyish, hipless figure, while the tight angora sweaters of the '50s demanded breasts, or at least the padded semblance of them—the pace with which bodies are presented as the "right" ones to have has quickened. The beachy girls-next-door of the 1970s were elbowed out by the Amazonion supermodels of the 1980s, who gave way to the heroin-chic waifs of the '90s, who were knocked off the editorial pages of the early 2000s by the Brazilian bombshells, who were then edged out by the doll-eyed British blondes. Meanwhile, the fashion industry selectively co-opts whatever "ethnic" attributes can be appropriated in the service of a trend. Black and Latina women with junk in the trunk who have been erased by mainstream glossies, overlooked as runway models, and ill-served by pants designed for comparatively flat rears were rightly annoyed to hear from *Vogue*, in 2014, that "We're Officially in the Era of the Big Booty" thanks to stars like Iggy Azalea, Miley Cyrus, and Kim Kardashian. "There is no wrong way to have a body," wrote author and size-positive sage Hanne Blank, but that sentiment will always be contradicted by a market, and a media, that depends on people not believing it.

Pubic Property

Joan Jacobs Brumberg, in her 1997 book *The Body Project: An Intimate History of American Girls*, used the diaries of young women past and present to trace the role of families, medicine, nutrition, and consumerism in increasing body- and beauty-focused anxiety in girls. One conspicuous takeaway was that girls of the 1900s, living as they did with limited consumer choices in less urbanized areas, were rarely inclined to equate their bodies or looks with their worth, but contemporary girls were positively obsessed with both. One comparison of New Years' resolutions written a hundred years apart is jarring: An adolescent girl's diary from the 1890s reads, "Resolved . . . to think before speaking. To work seriously. To be self-restrained in conversations and actions. Not to let my thoughts wander. To be dignified. Interest myself more in others." From her 1990s counterpart: "I will try to make myself better in any way I possibly can . . . I will lose weight, get new lenses, already got new haircut, good makeup, new clothes and accessories." The equation of "better" with "more physically attractive" is echoed everywhere, and it affects girls in particular sooner than ever. If you don't believe it, there's a t-shirt for tweens reading "I'm Too Pretty to Do Math" that might convince you.

Increasingly, the tenets of choice feminism, combined with an ever-lengthening menu of choices for taming, firming, filling, reducing, smoothing, softening, darkening, lightening, and otherwise prettying up various body parts, have become a justification for this obsession. You've got your high-tech cosmetic fillers—collagen, hyaluronic acid, Restylane—to smooth out laugh lines, crow's feet, and other signs that women eventually age. There are serums to make eyelashes more voluminous, and, failing that, eyelash-implant and -dyeing procedures. If you're not quite ready for full-on breast augmentation, you can opt for "vacation breasts" created by an injectable substance whose effects last two or three weeks. And, of course, there's the surfeit of treatments to spruce up the downstairs, from "vajazzling" (the application of crystals and other adornments to the bare mons pubis) and "vajacials" all the way to labiaplasty and the pithily euphemistic "vaginal rejuvenation," also known as tightening. Some of this stuff comes off as Hollywood hype—it was actress Jennifer Love Hewitt who first put vajazzling on the map—but the amount of places that offer the service suggest that increasing numbers of regular women are buying into the repairing and redecorating game.

So what, though? Haven't women always felt compelled to use the materials at their disposal in the service of beauty? With a graveyard of products that have failed to unfrizz my hair, and a drawer full of cosmetics that will never give me actual cheekbones, I definitely have and will no doubt continue to. Botox injections, when you think about it, are no weirder than poisons like arsenic, lead, and deadly nightshade that ladies of the past consumed, patted on, and dropped in their eyes to make their complexions more comely and their peepers more doe-like; shapewear is just a less barbaric descendant of the whalebone corset. Women may be showing up at emergency rooms with painful waxing and vajazzling injuries and infections (estimates from emergency rooms showed a 50 percent increase in such injuries in the years 2002 to 2008),[6] but that's just how things are now. Get with the times! It's her choice!

Yes, women were suffering for beauty long before the rise of consumer culture as we know it. And once advertising, marketing, and mass media got in on the action, such suffering was deemed crucial to their self-worth, happiness, and ability to find lasting love. Women's magazines of the 1950s urged women to douche with Lysol and Listerine to maintain "feminine daintiness," lest they drive away their husbands. (From one Lysol ad: "Often a wife fails to realize that doubts due to one intimate neglect shut her out from happy married love.")[7] In the 1950s and '60s, women were explicitly instructed to never reveal their bare faces to their husbands, which necessitated—according to *The Cosmo Girl's Guide to the New Etiquette*—keeping a stash of foundation, lipstick, and eyeshadow under the marital bed so they could wake up early and "survey the damages."[8]

The tonal shift in the advertising of clothing, beauty products, and surgical and topical procedures, wherein they're reframed as choices rather than imperatives, is a fairly recent one. Until well into the 1970s, women's-magazine ads and editorial were almost exclusively prescriptive, though the language did change through the years. In the 1920s, ad copy warned that the wrong consumer choices would doom a young woman's future by making her unlovable, while in the 1940s women with sweethearts overseas at war were urged to stay as young-looking as possible for their returning heroes. In post–second wave times, prescriptions were leavened with suggestions ("Why not try blue eyeshadow?"). And soon, it wasn't a matter of having to buy any one thing, but choosing among many. ("Take this quick quiz to find the right scent for you!") But as choice has become a default assumption, the belief that women's individual choices regarding what to do with their bodies and appearance occur on a level, postfeminist playing field has changed too. It's a seductive narrative and, fittingly, it's the site of some of mainstream feminism's most tiresome arguments.

Take pubic hair, which over the past two decades has likely been discussed more than at any known time in history, in a dialogue that can regularly approach near-nuclear levels of vitriol and self-righteousness. Most of the debates stem from an incontrovertible fact: female pubic hair, once considered a desirable marker of adolescence (recall Judy Blume's Margaret, who, when not addressing God, is standing anxiously in front of her mirror searching for evidence of growth), and, for boys, an even more desirable erotic frontier, is now a disappearing phenomenon. Its extinction has been driven variously by the easy availability of porn, the mainstreaming of lingerie marketing, and a 24/7 culture of celebrity surveillance. Though waxing defenders are quick to remind us that pubic hair removal has enjoyed popularity throughout history as far back as the ancient Egyptians and Greeks, the contemporary world has seen an unmistakable uptick in both the practice and the available services since the 1990s.

In heterosexual porn, hairlessness is the norm for female performers: not only does it showcase more stuff, but it serves a disconcertingly blatant market for women who look as underage as possible. A once-unremarkable feature of women's bodies is now considered a fetish, and women with pubic hair are one of porn's many niche properties, marketed with the same frisson of sensationalism as granny porn, pregnancy porn, and plushie porn (I don't recommend Googling any of those, by the way). Porn isn't solely to blame for recasting what Amy Poehler once rhapsodically called "the ladygarden" as a bushy burden; shrinking bathing-suit and underwear styles have also played a role. As one Brazilian-wax devotee said, "[I]f you have hair sticking out the sides of your underwear, that's just kind of, like, unkempt."[9] And celebrities like Spice Girl–turned–fashion mogul Victoria Beckham (who, in 2003, asserted that Brazilian waxes "ought to be compulsory at 15, don't you think?") and Kim Kardashian ("Women shouldn't have hair anywhere but on their heads") have largely taken over from fashion magazines when it comes to the business of grooming dictates.

The central pubic-hair argument that's raged in mainstream feminism for more than a decade is that pubic deforestation is either a capitulation to patriarchal, pornified beauty standards or is, by contrast, a bold declaration of the feminist freedom to choose. Either way, it has been made inherently, and depressingly, political. It's worth noting here that men haven't been immune to the message that the hair down there is passé. Gay porn has always had categories for body hair havers and the dudes who love them, but many hetero male porn performers began to regularly go bald at the same time as their female colleagues. This has certainly affected the grooming choices of laymen: The "back, sack, and crack" wax has become a popular choice among men of varying tastes and orientations. But there's no apparent political significance attached to men's decision to de-pube or not. For women, however, the quarrel continues online and off, with no sign of stopping. A writer for London's *Telegraph* argued, in 2013, that for the young women she knows, the main feminist conundrum isn't reproductive rights or the wage gap, but how they groom their nethers—a statement that is either great or completely terrifying, depending on how you look at it.

When British feminist Caitlin Moran argued strenuously for keeping one's pubic hair in her best-selling 2012 memoir *How to Be a Woman*—devoting seven pages to her self-admitted didacticism on the subject—much of her audience felt annoyed by what they saw as the substitution of one sort of prescriptiveness for another. Moran had already offended almost as many readers as she'd charmed (via the book's tossed-off references to "trannies" and some casually racist asides on Twitter), and that might have had something to do with the animosity toward her position in the Great Pubic Hair Debate. Still, her point—that an unholy convergence of capitalism, cultural pornification, and ongoing gender inequality has normalized pubelessness such that female adolescents are waxing it off almost as soon as it appears—got a little bit lost. Since then, Moran has spoken in interviews about women who now see her as some sort of pubic-hair Mother Confessor: "I've had a couple of women come up to me and guiltily, drunkenly confess that they still wax and they like it and that works best for them and it makes sex better for them and all this stuff, and they're expecting me to just reach into my handbag and grab a pubic hair and shove it on them going, 'No, no. You must be hairy forever.' In my own most benign and lovely way, I don't care what women do if it makes you happy."[10]

Even having the luxury of time to spend debating the liberatory dimensions of pubic hair might suggest that more pressing feminist issues have been resolved; people engaging in these dialogues, after all, probably aren't taking time out from working three minimum-wage jobs to hop online and weigh in. This debate is one that happens in a quite privileged sphere where individual actualization has prevailed over collective work. That's not to suggest you can't be engaged in both, but consider Moran's reassurances: "If it makes you happy" and "If it's your choice" are similar sentiments in that both focus on personal feelings and choices, aiming to decontextualize them from larger questions about why these choices are being debated at all. The fact that women feel the need to confess the details of their nethers to Moran in the first place speaks to how charged the debate is, but also points out that assigning feminist value to subjective grooming regimens is a pretty unstable base for ideology. And yet, along with high heels and makeup and underpants, pubic hair has become a feminist issue that depends on the invocation of choice as an unquestioned defense. It's also had more ink devoted to it than more urgent issues—say, violence against women and the need for decent family-leave policies. We can care about all these issues, but it seems worth asking why ones that foreground appearance and desirability are amplified above the others.

"Am I a Bad Feminist?"

Looking around the blogosphere in the past few years, there seems to be a massive crisis of conscience among young, female, and generally white women who consider themselves feminist . . . *except*. One writer wonders, "Does Waxing Make Me a Bad Feminist?" (See what I mean?) Another asks "Can a Feminist Wear High Heels?" Another: "Can a Beauty Editor Be a Feminist?" And still another: "I'm Engaged and It Makes Me Feel Like a Bad Feminist." Everywhere you turn, there's a woman wringing her virtual hands over the prospect of not conforming to a mythical ideal, admitting to what she has self-diagnosed as feminist failure, and imagining the wrath of her strident foremothers raining down hellfire. (Or menstrual blood, maybe.)

"Sometimes I do stuff which I'm frightened Germaine Greer will find out I like doing," muses one conflicted soul, who then goes on to confess to loving high heels and kitschy 1950s-housewife apparel. It's become a formulaic script: whatever the topic—push-up bras, cheesy romance novels, gonzo porn, etc.—there's a woman out there pondering whether her interest in it somehow negates her basic belief in gender equality. There's a performativity to it, as though public self-flagellation is equivalent to thorough analysis. Yet all of these pieces conclude with some familiar sentiments: *It's my choice. I do it for me. So it is feminist.* But if that's the case, writing 1,500 words on it for a public forum seems like an odd choice. Like the girls who wobble up to Moran to confess their pubic sins, such personal essays seem like a somewhat pointless bid for absolution. If you like high heels, wear them. If you want to get married in a white dress or watch women get choked with a bunch of penises, go on with your bad self. But don't use a personal essay about it as a hair shirt.

This content genre is one of marketplace feminism's biggest triumphs: women who act on the illusion of free choice offered by the market, and then offer themselves up for corporate media to capitalize on. Most of these essays are written for very little money, and almost all of them are published because they are guaranteed clickbait: they appear on Web sites that rely on numerous daily updates and increasing pageviews as a way to fill space that's demanded by the constant need for new content. And young women are, by and large, the ones who answer this demand by mining their perceived failures. In doing so, they perpetuate the idea that feminism is a deeply heteronormative, white- and middle class–centric movement that's become hopelessly stuck up its own ass. And, you know, sometimes it's hard to argue against that. Someday, perhaps, we'll start seeing essays by men with titles like "Does My Back-Sack-and-Crack Wax Betray My Marxism?" But so far, we don't, and that seems like a good enough reason to cool it with the dramatics.

These essays help drive marketplace feminism not only because they omit other topics—keeping the focus firmly in the realm of the sexy and easily sellable—but also because they invariably conclude with an invocation of choice that forecloses on the possibility of deeper exploration. To be clear, this is not a condemnation of women for feeling confused and bombarded by mixed messages about what they need to do to be successful or desirable or happy. It's not a condemnation of women who get Botox or style their pubic hair just so. There are countless reasons that all kinds of people enjoy dressing up, making up, pursuing styles, following trends: family and cultural traditions, rebellion from or adhesion to religion, and personal expression are only a handful among them. But what the bad-feminist genre reveals is that the personal, the individual, and the appearance-centric are the most likely both to be elevated as sites for empowerment and pointed to as things that betray a monolithic idea of feminism. Cultural critic Susan Bordo has pointed out that this kind of rationalization reflex acts as a "diversionary din" that shifts focus from its cause—consumer culture, persistent inequality—to its symptoms.[11] We don't exist in a vacuum, and neither do our choices. The cultural ideals created and delivered by profit-driven media and corporations have a massive impact on the supposedly free choices we make with our bodies, and rationalizing that away for the length of a personal essay is much easier than trying to change it.

Meet the New Beauty, Same as the Old Beauty

It's a paradox that as more and more women are steered toward a cosmetically-enhanced sameness, a key feature of marketplace feminism is its earnest dialogue about broadening beauty standards. That brings us to Dove, a brand which in the past decade has made itself empowertising's top banana with its Campaign for Real Beauty.

Beginning in 2004, women across North America and the UK began seeing something new in advertisements for Dove soap: namely, nothing. Replacing the humble, curved bar of white soap the brand was known for were stark photos of women of all ages, colors, and sizes, with checkboxes next to them. "Oversized? Outstanding?" asked the boxes placed next to a photo of a plump, smiling woman, arms raised in a black strapless dress. "Flawed? Flawless?" asked those alongside a fantastically freckled redhead. "Half empty? Half full?" was the query for a woman whose small chest was highlighted by a white tank top. Instead of a product, there was a Web site URL and an entreaty to "join the beauty debate."

More than 1.5 million women were inspired or curious enough to visit Dove's site on the strength of the "Tick Box" campaign. But that was nothing compared to the exposure that came with phase two, when billboards featuring women in white bras and panties began appearing in New York, Chicago, Washington, D.C., and other major U.S. cities. The women were big—bigger than "normal" models, and, perhaps more surprising, they didn't look miserable about it. They smiled, they laughed, they leaned against one another. In contrast to high-fashion billboard ads in which models looked contorted, pained, or simply frozen, these women looked alive. It shouldn't have been such a shock to see happy-looking women of varying sizes and skin tones standing twenty feet tall above Times Square, but it was, and within days the media was buzzing about Dove's newest coup on behalf of "real" beauty.

The Campaign for Real Beauty combined its body boosterism with lush, striking images by big-name female photographers Annie Leibovitz and Peggy Sirota, and with the institutional heft conferred by a 2004 study commissioned by Dove and developed in part by Harvard University's Nancy Etcoff and the London School of Economics' Susie Orbach. Both women had authored popular books about women and body/beauty image—Orbach was best known for her foundational 1978 manifesto *Fat Is a Feminist Issue*, and Etcoff's 1999 *Survival of the Prettiest* broke down the biological basis for what's considered beautiful. Conducted in the United States, Canada, Great Britain, Italy, France, Portugal, the Netherlands, Brazil, Argentina, and Japan, *The Real Truth About Beauty* study boasted of being "global," though the exclusion of the entire continent of Africa and the Asian subcontinent seems like a big omission in a survey of women and beauty standards. Its questions sought to gauge how women in different countries and cultures value beauty—both in themselves and in others—and how their perceptions of their own bodies are affected by conventional beauty standards.

In disseminating the study's findings, Dove focused less on the negative findings of the study—for instance, the fact that only about 2 percent of women interviewed used the word "beautiful" to describe themselves—and more on the section titled "Perceptions About Beauty." Here, interviewees indicated how strongly they agreed with statements such as "A woman can be beautiful at any age" (89 percent strongly agreed); "I think that every woman has something about her that is beautiful" (85 percent); and " If I had a daughter, I would want her to feel beautiful even if she is not physically attractive" (82 percent). The overall picture that informed the ads was one in which women were bonded in an urge to celebrate the beauty of capital-W Women while not quite able to testify to their own pulchritude. Thus was born the campaign's stated mission—to "start a global conversation about the need for a wider definition of beauty"—and the Dove woman herself, bravely putting herself out there as a beacon for all womankind. One billboard model, Gina Crisanti, told the Associated Press that "I grew up not being happy with my body shape and size at all. . . . In my 20s, I realized all those [ideas] were simply self-destructive. Once I started to develop an alternative definition of beauty, all of it started to fall into place. It's all about how you shine."

Well, that and the firming cream. What? Oh, yeah, those beaming women on Dove's groundbreaking billboards were shilling a line of lotions and creams meant to smooth out cellulite. As Jennifer L. Pozner wrote in a September 2005 consideration of the Real Beauty campaign, "[Dove's] feel-good 'women are okay at whatever size' message is hopelessly hampered by the underlying attempt to get us to spend, spend, spend to 'correct' those pesky 'problem areas' advertisers have always told us to hate."[12] (Not to mention the previously nonexistent problem areas created by the brand itself: a later entry in the Real Beauty ad juggernaut proposed that women "turn armpits into underarms" with Dove's Advanced Care line of whitening deodorants.)

But if Dove was a case of same story, slightly different-sized models, it still put much of its target audience—average, diverse, cosmetics-buying women—in a bind. It seemed important to support the brand's effort to recognize that not all women are a white, paper-smooth size 2—and even more important not to give credence to people worried that seeing a size-12 woman in her underwear would fuel America's obesity crisis (a worry put forth, in all seriousness, in articles like one titled "When Tush Comes to Dove"). It was equally tempting to support Dove in the face of male critics who protested the billboards on the grounds that having to look at underwear-clad women bigger than size 4 posed a grievous threat to their erections. Among these were film critic Richard Roeper, who penned an anti-Dove screed for the *Chicago Tribune* that read, in part, "When we're talking women in their underwear on billboards outside my living room windows, give me the fantasy babes, please. If that makes me sound superficial, shallow, and sexist—well, yes, I'm a man." In Chicago's competing *Sun-Times*, as if trying to outdo Roeper, Lucio Guerrero cracked, "The only time I want to see a thigh that big is in a bucket with bread crumbs on it."

The ads were both a symptom and an effect of marketplace feminism. By addressing something feminism had long sought to remedy—the narrow prescriptiveness of mainstream beauty standards—Dove positioned itself as a progressive brand, even while performing its "firming" bait-and-switch. And those who identified it as a blatant shill were accused of letting the perfect be the enemy of the good. Dove was part of a multinational corporation, after all, went the rationalization. We can't exactly expect them *not* to want to move units. At least they're trying to do it in a way that nods to size positivity and women's confidence. Right? Consumers, in any case, responded: in 2006, two-thirds of Dove's sales were generated by people who bought more than one Dove product, double the number from 2003 before the start of the campaign. And ten years in, revenues had grown from 2.5 billion to 4 billion.[13]

In the years since the Campaign for Real Beauty launched, Dove has continued to tread the line between consciousness-raising and co-optation. The company's 2007 video "Onslaught" is an example of the former: In it, the camera zooms in on the peachy face of a young white girl, allowing our gaze to linger for a moment before the screen is strafed with a montage of women's bodies and body parts—breasts, lips, bikini lines, hips, clavicles. A woman on a scale grows and shrinks rapidly; surgeon's scalpels and cannulae cut and suck at mortified flesh. It's a riot of mediated images, and that's exactly the point; at video's end, a message appears: "Talk to your daughter before the beauty industry does." "Onslaught" borrowed heavily from the work of Jean Kilbourne and Sut Jhally, two media critics whose films make explicit and unsettling connections between women's images in advertising and the treatment of women in culture more broadly.

"Onslaught," along with an earlier video called "Evolution" that used time-lapse photography to track how makeup and Photoshop transform everyday models to ad-ready Amazons, were early viral sensations, unrecognizable as ads until one dug a bit further to find that they were projects of the Dove Self-Esteem Fund, one of the Campaign for Real Beauty's initiatives. Both videos set the tone for the Upworthy era, using frank, discomfiting visual cues, urgent music, and spare copy to make viewers question what they thought they knew. Discovering that Dove was behind them added a layer of perceived legitimacy: this wasn't the work of some crazed feminist activists, after all, but that of a company that had a lot to lose if women and girls were to reject the supremacy of beauty ideals. If *they* cared, then shit must really be bad.

But if the viral videos did help jumpstart the global dialogue that Dove desired, some of the company's actual ads eventually derailed those same conversations. Take the "Sketches" video, which premiered in 2013 as both a TV spot and a longer video meant to be shared on social media. In "Sketches," women in a spacious, sunny loft are asked to describe their features to a forensics artist, who later asks strangers to describe the same women to him. The women are then presented with two sketches each, which inspire shock, startled laughter, and sheepishness. The game, you see, is to point out how women are their own worst beauty critics—invariably, the sketch based on the woman's own description of herself is much less attractive than the sketch based on the stranger's description.

More than 135 million people watched the video, and if the number who shared it on Facebook is any indication, "Sketches" resonated as a real truth bomb. *Advertising Age* even named it the Viral Campaign of the Year. And yet, as a number of critics pointed out, the video arguably failed in its larger mission as part of the Campaign for Real Beauty—not only because it did little to expand the definition of what constitutes "beautiful," but because it upheld the idea that "beautiful" is the most important word that can be used to describe a woman. As Ann Friedman pointed out at style-and-culture blog *The Cut*, "What if Dove had filmed a woman who looked exactly like one of the 'negative' self-descriptions—maybe someone with a heavy brow line and a prominent mole and deep, dark circles under her eyes? Someone who wore a size 14? And what if that woman had said to the sketch artist, 'Well, first off, I'm really pretty?'"

The prevalence of young, thin, white women in the video also hinted that diversity of all kinds had become less of a priority for Dove (or at least for the agency that created the ad, longtime Dove partners Ogilvy & Mather) than the Campaign had suggested. In contrast to the brand's past use of real people—gray-haired women, dreadlocked women, wrinkled women—the main subjects of "Sketches" are homogenous. Not one is a woman of color, all are conventionally thin, and all except one are under the age of forty. Given that both women of color and women over forty already see themselves reflected less in mainstream media than white women—and far less as avatars of beauty of any kind—this was significant.

The campaign's next video was even more of a head-scratcher: titled "Patches," it featured unsuspecting women being offered "beauty patches," nicotine patch–like adhesives that they've been told will help them feel more beautiful. What happens next will not shock you in the least: The placebo effect of the patches lasts even after the women are told they've been duped and that—cue the swelling music—*true beauty comes from within.* "Knowing that I don't need something to make me feel that way—that it's just who I am and it was hidden and now it's not anymore," says one satisfied hoaxee, "that's very empowering." In just under ten years, Dove had gone from presenting women as straightforwardly confident in their own actual beauty to deeply gullible in service to the ideal of beauty itself. Not exactly progress—and yet, as with other ads, "Patches" received a largely favorable response: an *Advertising Age* survey of social-media reaction recorded a 91 percent favorable response in the first two days of the video's release in sixty-five countries.[14]

Success aside, both "Sketches" and "Patches" revealed the limitations of a marriage between true body acceptance and market status quo. Dove's stated goals might be sincere, but the company is still part of a system whose bottom line depends on perpetuating female insecurity—and subtly encouraging women to blame themselves for it. And yet, simply because few other companies have dared to engage with the subject of mediated beauty standards, Dove continues to be seen as the company that cares. The fact that it cares just enough not to put revenues in jeopardy (and not enough to cease inventing new insecurities and products to address them) isn't important in a marketplace where simply flirting with body acceptance still seems radical. Unilever funded a follow-up survey in 2014 to measure the effect of the Campaign for Real Beauty; in it, survey consultant Etcoff found that 62 percent of woman interviewed agreed that they were "responsible for influencing their own definition of beauty"—triple the number who had agreed with that statement ten years earlier. The beauty-focused media those interviewees consumed hadn't changed their messages; they had simply gotten savvier at delivering them with a feminist-inspired twist.

It's clear there's at least some self-awareness in the larger scope of campaigns like these. And anticipating charges of talking out both sides of their mouths, such brands increasingly pair their advertising with opportunities for their consumers to help "join" or "shape" social media conversations sparked by their market activism. In 2013, for instance, Special K—a brand that has long boasted of its cereal's singular power to slim women down enough to fit into a snug red frock—launched #fightfattalk, a hashtag campaign designed to bring awareness to the phenomenon of women using self-hating language when talking about their bodies. "From 'joking' about cankles to destructive self-deprecation, fat talk has become part of ordinary conversation, spoken without a second thought," read the ad copy, which went on to state, "Words are powerful. Let's make sure they're positive."

So far, so good. Special K was on point about the phenomenon of fat talk as a staple of women's self-deprecatory arsenal, especially the fact that it's by now ingrained as an ordinary topic of conversation, particularly among white women in commercial culture. From female stand-up comedians for whom cutting self-observation has for decades been among the acceptable riffs (see Phyllis Diller's observation that "My Playtex Living bra died. . . . of starvation," or Janeane Garofalo's reference to having "the physique of a melting candle"), to celebrity profiles in which starlets admit to being "caught" eating like humans by the paparazzi, apologizing for simply having visible bodies is part of many women's average day. And for many women of color, the dynamic of self-deprecation might not only look like apologizing for having the audacity to inhabit a living body that requires food to function, but can also include an awareness that not conforming to ethnic stereotypes—the bountiful butts of Black and Latina women, or the birdlike delicacy and long limbs of East Asian ones—renders them either invisible or "wrong."

And yet. Where Special K's site proclaims, "99 percent of women fat talk, are your friends among them?" and invites readers to "find out now" by clicking a link, the resulting page is not a revelation about "your friends" at all, but a slideshow ad for several Special K products, including one that urges you to "Outsmart Those Temptations" by buying Protein Cinnamon Brown Sugar Crunch cereal. In other words, Special K *is itself* fat-talking to the consumer by positioning non–Special K food as a "temptation." The press release for the campaign revealed the true impetus behind #fightfattalk: it wasn't that the brand wanted women to stop trash-talking their bodies for its own sake, but rather because such talk is "a destructive and significant barrier to weight-management success." It was a deceptive feminist hook for a decidedly unfeminist campaign: shut up about why you *think* you need to lose weight and just lose it, already. Model/TV personality and #fightfattalk ambassador Tyra Banks inadvertently summed up the campaign's mixed message when she stated, "I'm excited to partner with Special K to help empower women to not only feel confident about their bodies, but also to remove those negative thoughts and show them how to employ tips and tricks to make their least-liked physical attributes look better."

Similarly, as feminism's popular profile began to rise in 2014, Cover-Girl got in on the beauty-positivity action with its own hashtag campaign, #GirlsCan, announcing a five-year campaign to "empower [girls] to be the next generation to rock the world" and an estimated $5 million donation to individuals and organizations focused on developing girls' potential. (One of the brand's first donations was $500,000 given to Girls Who Code, a nonprofit whose mission is training and encouraging girls to enter technology fields.) The campaign enlisted celebrities including Ellen DeGeneres, Katy Perry, Pink, Janelle Monae, and Queen Latifah, all of whom spoke inspiringly in ads about the things they were told they couldn't do and did anyway.

What CoverGirl didn't do as part of the campaign, however, was change its point-of-sale appeals to girls and women. Thus we have Katy Perry in a #GirlsCan promotional video, discussing the meaning of empowerment ("confidence, inner confidence") and enthusing that

"Girls can own the word," but there she is in a store display along with the question, "What kind of bombshell are you?" (The options, in case you're wondering, are "sweet," "flirty," and "wild.") It's a textbook example of a brand trying to have its empowerment both ways, telling girls they can be anything they want, and then advising them to fit themselves into a limited range of boxes.

Almost all the brands that push female empowerment with their products have charitable arms, whether it's breast-cancer research (Avon, Revlon, and Estée Lauder, among others), girls' education (Dove, CoverGirl, Gillette), or domestic-violence awareness (The Body Shop, Mary Kay). It's hard to argue with that, and these brands know it. But when you look at the business practices, ingredients, and parent companies associated with these empowering brands, the cracks are difficult to ignore. If Estée Lauder and Revlon care so much about preventing breast cancer, for instance, you'd think they might do a better job of making sure their products are free of known carcinogens. If Dove truly wants to broaden how we think about beauty globally, parent company Unilever might want to reconsider the skin-lightening creams like Fair & Lovely that it hawks across the Middle East and South Asia. It would be hard to make the case that corporate brands' co-option of tacitly feminist attitudes has changed their appeals to female consumers. In deepening the connection between external good looks and happiness/fulfillment, Dove and Cover-Girl and Special K have just further allied their brands with a cultural vision that equates youth, thinness, and whiteness with self-esteem and success.

The fact that these feminist issues are the ones that again and again float to the surface of a deep well of gender inequality makes sense, in the saddest way. As Susan J. Douglas points out, we live in a time where "fantasies of power . . . assure girls and women, repeatedly, that women's liberation is a fait accompli and that we are stronger, more successful, more sexually in control, more fearless, and more held in awe than we actually are."[15] In this context, attending to what one can feasibly control—body, clothing, grooming, consuming—can seem like less of an uphill climb. It's certainly much easier than calling out the people and the systems that are actively opposing our freedom and humanity. Erotic capital is real, and in many places, in many individual lives, it pays off. But what's found at the end of a needle, a razor, and a lipstick tube is a quick fix, not a sustained strategy.

EPILOGUE

The End of Feel-Good Feminism

By the time this book comes out, it will have been two years since feminism broke into the American mainstream. And as I've written, edited, and rewritten this epilogue over the span of a few months, I'm not quite sure how to bring it to a natural conclusion. Do I point to the many successes that have resulted from a more politicized popular culture, and a corporate media that is increasingly informed by the more enlightened—or "politically correct," if you're not a fan of enlightenment—outlets that report on it? I could definitely do that, since these two years have indeed seen a striking change in public attitude toward intrinsically feminist issues.

Bill Cosby's penchant for drugging and raping women under the guise of offering "mentorship," for instance, was an open secret for years among the showbiz people and media figures who knew about it (and, of course, among the more than four dozen women who eventually came forward with their stories). The video of comedian Hannibal Burress condemning Cosby might not have sparked a new interest—and, perhaps, some justice for Papa Pudding Pop's victims—if not for a media landscape that's become, since Cosby's TV heyday, more conscious of how popular culture reflects and creates real-life biases and beliefs.

I could also list the ways that an awareness of media and pop culture's influence has inspired a wealth of grassroots activism, **247** organizing, and creativity. For this, credit goes mostly to the Internet, which as a transformative tool has been unparalled in amplifying discourses, disseminating facts, and mobilizing activism that has actually made a difference. Think of organizations like Know Your IX, an advocacy initiative that informs college rape and abuse survivors of their rights under Title IX. Or Hollaback! which grew quickly from a smartphone app to a global initiative to confront racist and sexist street harassment. There are well-funded organizations dedicated to preparing girls for careers in STEM fields, like Girls Who Code, Black Girls CODE, and the Girlstart. There's The National Domestic Workers Alliance, which helps organize on- and offline, caregivers, nannies, and other domestic workers across the country. The girl-run organization and summit SPARK! (Sexualization Protest, Action, Resistence, Knowledge) campaigns against media sexualization of girls, while the Women's Media Center monitors the gendered language often deployed in political journalism. And there's a slew of media and pop culture-specific projects and initiatives, from hackathons to Twitter hashtags, that have raised the profile of media literacy and resurrected "If you can see it, you can be it" as a mantra for reform.

I could certainly talk about the way that current feminist movements have effected changes in how mainstream media and pop culture talk about all manner of bias and bigotry, nudging terms like "rape culture," "cisgender," and "colorism" into public spaces and dialogues. This shift has brought with it flashbacks to the early 1990s, with headlines bemoaning "thought police" and "political correctness gone mad"—but it's also brought forward the voices of people for whom safety, justice, and humanity are not rhetorical thought experiments. Two thousand and fifteen's college-campus protests against police violence pushed the feminist-born term "safe space" into contact with jeering mainstream pundits, but it also started a conversation about why such a lampoonable term needs to exist. As Roxane Gay noted, "Those who take safety for granted disparage safety because it is, like so many other rights, one that has always been inalienable to them. They wrongly assume we all enjoy such luxury and are blindly seeking something even more extravagant."[1]

The confrontation of campus rape as a systemic issue has become a national talking point; the necessity of an intersectional lens on feminist issues a global one. The long-held contention that representation matters—in leadership, on TV, in Hollywood, in literature, in politics—is finally getting through, and pop culture is at the forefront of more complex, more nuanced conversations about it. The importance of workplaces that not only recruit but retain diverse staff has become a talking point among economists and human-resources professionals; and studies asserting that companies with more gender and race diversity see concrete financial gains are highlighted in the likes of *Forbes* and *Scientific American*. In short, more and more people are realizing what feminists have been saying for years: Equality makes things better for everyone, if we can get past fears and stereotypes and embrace it.

And yet, where the loose ends of feminism are concerned, we're not much further along than we were in 1971, when then-president Richard Nixon quashed the Comprehensive Child Care Bill, a bipartisan measure that called for the establishment of child care centers open to everyone, and for every community in the United States to establish early-education programs. Once the bill was approved by both houses of Congress, it landed on Nixon's desk—where he promptly vetoed it on the grounds that it was part of a stealthy Communist plot to rend America's delicate moral fabric. He claimed that, if implemented, the bill "would commit the vast moral authority of the National Government to the side of communal approaches to childrearing" and undermine the sanctity of family and, especially, mothers' roles. "The goal," wrote *New York Times* columnist Gail Collins, "was not just to kill the bill but also to bury the idea of a national child-care entitlement forever."[2]

Child care remains one of the overwhelming unfinished projects that feminist movements set out to fix over and over again; even modest proposals, like the tax credits for working parents proposed by Barack Obama in 2015, are met with outraged echoes of Nixon's appeal to "traditional" values. The lowest-paying jobs—cashiers, waitresses, line workers in factories—are some of the only jobs available to women lacking a high-school or college degree; one in five fast-food workers lives below the poverty line.[3] Where abortion and bodily autonomy are concerned, we're actually moving backward. (Three words: *mandatory transvaginal ultrasounds*.) The Equal Rights Amendment was never ratified, which means that while we may feel and look equal to our male counterparts, women are still, officially, legally, not considered full citizens of the United States.

The phrase "no going back" has become a global mantra for feminist movements, used in the context of everything from state-sanctioned violence to LGBT rights to children's television programming. The toothpaste is out of the tube, the genie's out of the bottle, the ocean refuses to be held back by a broom. And yet, in our current pattern of two-steps-forward-one-step-back (or vice versa, depending on the week), there's also no guarantee of a steady, sustained path forward. And this is why marketplace feminism—and, more to the point, our embrace of it—matters.

Celebration vs. Co-optation

Feminism these days really does look brighter and funnier, cooler and easier than ever before. Posting a video of Amy Schumer using a faux–boy band to take on "natural beauty" is a simple way to signify that you, too, are tired of bullshit bait-and-switch beauty standards. Watching a politician with shoddy facts and ahistorical opinions—on how uteruses work, say—get schooled by a million quick-thinking Internet wags can be intensely gratifying. That gamers can now play FIFA's videogame as Alex Morgan and other world soccer stars is a big step forward for sports-game franchises. Perusing Etsy for "Riot Don't Diet" pins and t-shirts proclaiming "Ovaries Before Brovaries" is an excellent way to spend a few minutes. (I will happily accept the Feminist Sloth Sticker Set from anyone who wants to buy it for me.) All of these things reflect feminism's inroads into mass culture, but it's still unclear what happens once it's there. Marketplace feminism is seductive. But marketplace feminism itself is not equality.

The narrative that feminism has succeeded because it's all over the Internet, because it's a marketing buzzword, because there's a handful of famous people happy to serve as its icons is as wrongheaded as the notion that feminism succeeded when (white) women got the vote or when the first female CEO stepped a sensible shoe into her spacious office. That doesn't mean that these things aren't important, or that they haven't made a difference in people's lives, because of course they have. But some women gaining some ground in many areas is not a wholesale feminist victory, especially since even that incremental progress has resulted in a disproportionate amount of fear.

If feminism has succeeded, for instance, why have state restrictions on abortion skyrocketed in the last half-dozen years, with fifty-one new restrictions enacted in the first half of 2015 alone?[4] If we're all equal now, why are women of all races underrepresented as advocates and experts in mainstream news outlets? If feminism has changed the culture so thoroughly, why are tabloids still worrying over which woman has the best beach body or concerned with what's happening in Jennifer Aniston's lonely old uterus? If women's voices matter as much as anyone else's, why do women receive rape and death threats on Twitter when they merely express an opinion on sports or video games, when millions of men express the same opinions with no one calling them a stupid whore or threatening to hack their phones or rape their lifeless bodies? And if feminism is something people are truly on board with, why is the first reaction to feminist discussions of gendered violence or structural inequality either, "But this happens to men too," or "Not *all* men!"?

The problem is—the problem has always been—that feminism is not fun. It's not supposed to be fun. It's complex and hard and it pisses people off. It's serious because it is about people demanding that their humanity be recognized as valuable. The root issues that feminism confronts—wage inequality, gendered divisions of labor, institutional racism and sexism, structural violence and, of course, bodily autonomy—are deeply unsexy. That's a hard sell for fast-moving content streams that depend on online clicks and consumer appeals that exist to serve the bottom line. Even more difficult is that feminism is fundamentally about resetting the balance of power, and it makes people who hold that power uncomfortable because that's what it has to do in order to work. So when we hear from those people—and, oh, do we hear from them—that feminism should modulate its voices, ask nicely for the rights it seeks, and keep anger and stridency out of the picture, let's remember that large-scale social change doesn't result from polite requests and sweet-talking appeasements. But make no mistake, that's what marketplace feminism is: A way to promise potential detractors that feminism can exist in fundamentally unequal spaces without posing any foundational changes to them.

In the course of writing this book, I talked with, listened to, and eavesdropped on a lot of people about what feminism's rise to cultural prominence means and why it matters. I heard optimism and excitement. I saw skepticism and eye-rolling. I listened to white college students talk about how Beyoncé could be a "gateway drug" that led to mainlining pure, unadulterated feminist theory. I listened to nonwhite feminists worried that a cultural embrace of only the least critical aspects of feminism won't rectify erasures that are both historical and extremely current. I witnessed giddy recollections of feminist "click" moments from people of all ages. I saw the universal obscene hand gesture that asks "*This* self-indulgent media circle jerk again?"

And I asked how feminism's high profile can be leveraged for concrete change, but almost nobody had an answer that suggested that there *was* only one answer. One thing almost everyone could agree on however, was this: there is a very fine line between celebrating feminism and co-opting it.

The central conflict, which I hope has been made clear throughout this book, is that while feminist movements seek to change systems, marketplace feminism prioritizes individuals. The wingwoman of neoliberalism, marketplace feminism's focus is on casting systemic issues as personal ones and cheerily dispensing commercial fixes for them. You *could* focus on bummers like the lack of workable family-leave policies for low-wage workers, but wouldn't it be a lot easier to seize your power and tap into your inner warrior? Marketplace feminism presumes that we can be clean, blank slates with no residue at all of the sexism or racism that defined the lives of those who came before us. It encourages us to believe that if we hit walls at school, at work, in relationships, in leadership, it's not anything to do with gender, but with problems that can be resolved with better self-esteem, more confidence, maybe some life coaching.

Certifiably Feminist

So here we are. We've got feminist underpants and feminist romance novels, feminist gifs and feminist jokes. We've got 12 feminist cocktails to make the world a better place, 10 reasons why *The Mindy Project* is a feminist masterpiece, and 9 quotes that explain why *Game of Thrones* is actually empowering. We know how many people flocked to the movies that have been heralded as game-changing feminist statements, but we don't know whether those numbers will change deeply gendered systems that make game-changing feminist movies a necessity to begin with. Beyoncé's claim to a feminist identity that people sought to deny her was undeniably powerful, and there's no doubt that she (and Emma, and Lena, and Taylor) inspired people to claim that identity as well. But what happens next?

Feminism as a product, as a discrete measure of worthiness or unworthiness, as a selling point for products that have no animate capabilities, is a deeply imperfect way to assess whether feminism is "working" or not because it's less about feminism than about capitalism. The companies that make feminist body lotion, feminist energy drinks, and feminist t-shirts are not interested in putting themselves out of business by actually changing the status quo.

The branding of feminism, meanwhile, is not a new phenomenon. The feminist movements we're all most familiar with are ones that were able to be easily understood by outsiders with a minimum of difficulty. Optics mattered: First-wave feminists didn't want the presence of women of color to put the kibosh on gaining suffrage; second-wave feminists didn't want lesbian and transgender women "tainting" the movement with fringe identities. Both movements were selling a branded image to wary buyers. And the fractures in feminism that exist now exist in part because of the inability to broaden the scope of those brands—a mistake that can't happen again if feminism wants to be a movement that serves more than an elite class.

Feminism has to evolve, and capitalizing on its ideology without any action effectively stunts that process. What we might see as liberatory is liberatory only within the already circumscribed goals of capitalism. More ways to consume fashion products that are "empowering" does not change the fact that the industry of fashion is demonstrably harmful to women at every level of production. Lionizing a male porn star as a feminist because of one offhand remark about respecting women does not magically change the exploitative economics of the sex industry. More female TV writers in a system that then says, "We've got enough female TV writers" after hiring two is not a triumph for diversity in that industry. Three black women winning Emmy Awards in 2015 does not mean that racist representations of black women now live only in Hollywood's past. Making things less bad is not the same as making them good. Subtracting misogyny from pop culture is not the same as adding feminism to it.

But currently, marketplace feminism tells us to take what we can get. It tells us that we should be happy with what we've got, because we still don't have enough power to ensure that what we've got won't be taken away if we push for too much more. That's not feminism, that's Stockholm Syndrome.

There was a time, early on, when I was pretty adamant that people, especially women, who believed in the equal value and treatment of women had a responsibility to call themselves feminists; otherwise it was an insult to the people who helped build a world in which feminism was even an option. I forwarded Sarah D. Bunting's now-famous blog post "Yes, You Are"—a great piece of writing—to countless people and grimaced when I heard women start their sentences with "I'm not a feminist, but . . ." I know now that this was a shortsighted, non-intersectional perspective; I had failed to acknowledge the millions of women who were erased by movement feminism, who saw their issues sidelined, or who just didn't know the language of feminism to begin with.

These days, I'm much less interested in who labels themselves feminist and more interested in what they're doing with feminism. I no longer see mainstream acceptance of the term as the end goal, but as a useful tool for activism. These days, I want to see people interested in learning more than what's printed in a *BuzzFeed* listicle. I want to hear the women I meet at college campuses ask questions that can't be answered by publicity-wizened celebrities like Beyoncé or Emma Watson. I want idealism to be more than a passing fad. I want feminism to be meaningful long after no one is singing about it, or name-checking it on red carpets, or printing it on granny panties.

Marketplace feminism has made equality look attractive, sexy, and cool. It's transformed everyday behaviors and activities into "bold feminist statements"; it's endowed unremarkable celebrities with fascinating new dimensions; it's allowed Taylor Swift to somehow convince us that having a squad of gorgeous friends by our sides at all times is the pinnacle of female equality. It's made us more likely to honor a Muppet's feminist bona fides than pay attention to a human woman's less synergistic efforts. It's convinced people that feminism can be accomplished by dressing up the status quo in slogan t-shirts and I-do-it-for-me heels. It's moved boatloads of consumer product. It's been a good run. But I hope—and I hope that you, too, hope—we can retain the excitement and joy that's come from seeing a more feminist culture take shape, and bulk up the resolve that's required to continue shaping it. A post–marketplace-feminism world may not be as headline-worthy, but it will be a world that benefits more than a commercially empowered few.

ACKNOWLEDGMENTS

This book would not have become what it is without Jill Grinberg, my agent. She deserves much more than an acknowledgment, so hopefully by the time she reads this I will have sent her a basket of muffins or a very expensive wine that someone who knows about wine picked out.

I talked to a number of authors, journalists, scholars, activists, and all-around smarties for this book, and though I wasn't able to quote all of them, each was full of fantastic insight. I thank them for taking the time to talk with me, and for the crucial work they do: Veronica Arreola, Jennifer L. Pozner, Linda Hirshman, Phoebe Robinson, Susan J. Douglas, Anna Holmes, Feminista Jones, J. Maureen Henderson, Leslie Bennetts, Leora Tanenbaum, Nicki Lisa Cole, Allison Dahl Crossley, Tamara Winfrey Harris, Jaclyn Friedman, Soraya Chemaly, Inkoo Kang, Melissa Silverstein, Jessica Bennett, Anne Elizabeth Moore, Mary Dore, Gloria Feldt, Jessica Valenti, Zeba Blay, Sarah Banet-Weiser, Lisa Wade, and Susan Brownmiller. Special thanks to Susan J. Douglas and bell hooks, the authors who first helped me understand that loving popular culture could be both immensely rewarding and endlessly frustrating.

Many thanks to my editors at PublicAffairs, Clive Priddle and Maria Goldverg, whose thoughtful guidance and editing made writing and revising this book as much of a pleasure as writing and revising a book can be. Thanks to Marco Pavia, my production editor, for moving things along and being patient as I procrastinated like hell on these acknowledgments. And thanks in advance to the publicity and marketing team at PublicAffairs—Lindsay Fradkoff, Emily Lavelle, Kristina Fazzolaro, and Jaime Leifer.

Thanks to my editors at *Salon* and *Oregon Humanities*, two publications in which I first explored some of the topics in this book. Also, since I don't want to go out like Jonah Lehrer, I will note that I reworked sections of those pieces, but some of the phrasings remain the same.

Thanks to every one of my colleagues at Bitch Media, a group of people whose smarts, commitment, optimism, and humor are unparalleled, and whom I feel very lucky to spend my days with. Extra thanks to our Executive Director, Julie Falk, who tolerated both my absences and my neuroses over the past few years, and who also read early drafts of some of these chapters; and to Kate Lesniak and Ashley McAllister for helping to organize my life in ways that I consistently forget to.

Thanks to Rabbi Danya Ruttenberg, my writing pal from Evanston to Jerusalem; to Paul Fischer, who loaned me his couch on several occasions as I researched the book; and to Rollene Saal, a woman I am just generally proud to know.

All kinds of thanks to the members of Little Justice Media Club Portland Original for their friendship, moral support, procrastination fodder, and cheese. Extra-strength gratitude to Briar Levit, whose creativity, steadiness, and curiosity about the world always inspire me to do more and be better.

Thanks to Dawn Jones and Hearts + Sparks Productions.

Thanks to all my Zeisler siblings for their long-distance support. Beyond thanks to Jeff Walls, for his love and his patience with the nonsense that comes with being married to someone with a book deadline; and to Harvey Zeisler-Walls, for reminding me to take breaks.

And finally, thank you to all the feminists who have been, are, and will be.

NOTES

Introduction

1. The phrase "Montreal Massacre" is an alternative name for the 1979 mass murder at École Polytechnique, when a male student assassinated fourteen women, calling them "a bunch of feminists."

Chapter 1

1. In theory, at least. Since then, there's plenty of evidence that banks continue to discriminate on the basis of race.

2. Slade, Giles, *Made to Break: Technology and Obsolescence in America* (Cambridge: Harvard University Press, 2007) page 19.

3. http://www.mediainstitute.edu/media-schools-blog/2014/02/edward-bernays/

4. http://www.ncbi.nlm.nih.gov/pmc/articles/PMC1748044/pdf/v014p00172.pdf

5. Sherrie A. Inness, *Disco Divas: Women and Popular Culture in the 1970s*, University of Pennsylvania Press, 2003, page 21.

6. https://fcpfragrance.wordpress.com/2013/04/17/successful-brands-charlie/

7. http://marketing-case-studies.blogspot.com/2008/07/raise-your-right-hand-campaign.html

8. "The Alluring Right-Hand Diamond Ring," NBCnews.com, Jan. 20, 2004

9. Kiran Adhikam, "Behind-the-Swoosh: The-Making of Nike's Greatest Commercials," *MediaBistro*, Jan, 25, 2010

10. http://scholarship.law.marquette.edu/cgi/viewcontent.cgi?article=1150&context=sportslaw

11. An entire category called "Sadvertising" has flourished in the viral age, partly as a response to a referential, too-cool-for-school trend that defined the late 1990s and 2000s.

12. Liz Leyden, "Barbie Gets Career Advice From Feminists," *Columbia Journalism Review*, March 28, 1999

13. Ophira Edut, "Barbie Girls Rule?" *Bitch,* Winter 1999, page 16

14. Douglas, Susan J., *Where the Girls Are: Growing Up Female with the Mass Media* (New York: Times Books, 1994) page 247

15. Bianca London, "Model Eva Herzigova says her iconic Hello Boys Wonderbra ad didn't 'degrade women' but left them 'empowered' instead," MailOnline.com, Nov. 21, 2014

16. http://adage.com/article/cmo-strategy/marketers-soft-feminism/294740/

Chapter 2

1. Director George Miller acknowledged in interviews that the feminist import of the film came largely from its main plot point, which was an extended chase to save the wives. "I needed a warrior. But it couldn't be a man taking five wives from another man. That's an entirely different story." He also credits the film's editor, his wife, Margaret Sixel, for the film's feel.

2. Mahar, Karen Ward, *Women Filmmakers in Early Hollywood* (Baltimore: JHU Press, 2008) page 190

3. Michelle Goldberg, "Where Are the Female Directors?" *Salon*, Aug. 27 2002 4. Ibid 5. Laura Hertzfeld, "From Sundance to the multiplex: Women directors are taking the spotlight," *Entertaiment Weekly*, Aug. 16, 2013

4. http://www.theguardian.com/film/2002/sep/08/features.review1

5. http://www.ew.com/article/2013/08/16/women-directors-to-do-list -sundance

6. Wilson, Marie C., *Closing the Leadership Gap: Add Women, Change Everything* (New York: Penguin Books, 2004).

7. Brent Lang, "Theater Chief Says 2015 Will Be 'Year of Women' at Box Office," *Variety*, April 21, 2015

8. Megan Angelo, "The *Bridesmaids* Effect: 6 Hollywood Changes The Chick-Comedy's Big Weekend Will Trigger," Business Insider, May 16, 2011

9. "'Bridesmaids' Effect: Funny women flourish in female-written comedies like 'Pitch Perfect'," Associated Press, September 28, 2012

10. "Swedish cinemas take aim at gender bias with Bechdel test rating," *The Guardian*, November 6, 2013

11. Aja Romano, "The Mako Mori Test: 'Pacific Rim' inspires a Bechdel Test alternative," *The Daily Dot*, August 18, 2013

12. http://www.dailydot.com/opinion/guardians-of-the-galaxy-fails-women/

Chapter 3

1. We don't, but—not to brag—our recent batch of tees reading "Outsmart the Patriarchy" sold out within a week.

2. The year 2003 was also when Planned Parenthood began selling t-shirts printed with the statement, "I Had an Abortion," created by feminist activist Jennifer Baumgardner as a companion piece for her documentary of the same name.

3. Davis, Angela Y., "Afro Images: Politics, Fashion, and Nostalgia," Critical Inquiry Vol. 21, No. 1 (1994).

4. http://tressiemc.com/2012/06/23/the-atlantic-article-trickle-down -feminism-and-my-twitter-mentions-god-help-us-all/

Chapter 4

1. http://rocunited.org/new-report-the-glass-floor-sexual-harassment-in- the-restaurant-industry/

2. Bryce Covert, "43 Sexual Harassment Cases That Were Thrown Out Because of One Supreme Court Decision," *ThinkProgress*, Nov. 24, 2014

3. Armstrong, Jennifer Keishin, *Mary and Lou and Rhoda and Ted: And All the Brilliant Minds Who Made The Mary Tyler Moore Show a Classic* (New York: Simon and Schuster, 2013).

4. Faludi Susan, *Backlash: The Undeclared War Against American Women* (New York: Crown Publishers, 1991).

5. Amanda D. Lotz, *Redesigning Women: Television After the Network Era* (Champaign: University of Illinois Press, 2006).

6. http://scholarship.law.duke.edu/cgi/viewcontent.cgi?article=3311 &context=dlj

7. Susan J. Douglas: "Patriarchy, New and Improved," *In These Times,* Nov. 22, 2002

8. Pozner, Jennifer L., *Reality Bites Back: The Troubling Truth about Guilty Pleasure TV* (Berkeley: Seal Press, 2010).

9. http://morningafter.gawker.com/unreal-creator-sarah-gertrude-shapiro -talks-feminism-an-1721758299

10. http://livefromthetrail.com/about-the-book/speeches/chapter-18/vice-president-dan-quayle

11. http://www.scpr.org/programs/the-frame/2014/09/23/39476/geena-davis-institute-study-shows-gender-gap-in-fi/

12. Zeba Blay, "How Feminist TV Became the New Normal," *The Huffington Post*, June 18, 2015

13. https://medium.com/@mariskreizman/game-of-thrones-and-the-threatening-fantasy-ec8767758cda

Chapter 5

1. Tamara Winfrey Harris, "All Hail the Queen? What do our perceptions of Beyonce's feminism say about us?" *Bitch*, May 2013

2. STOP ERA was an acronym for "Stop Taking Our Privileges," and was, among other things, concerned with the specter of unisex bathrooms as the result of an equality-filled future—not unlike anti-transgender crusaders these days who center public bathrooms in their own scare tactics.

3. Mia McKenzie, "Why I'm Not Really Here For Emma Watson's Feminism Speech At the U.N." Sept. 24, 2014

4. Barth, Ramona, "The Feminist Crusade," *The Nation*, July 17, 1948.

5. Katherine Cross, "Words, Words, Words: On Toxicity and Abuse in Online Activism," January 2014

6. "Mo'Nique: I Was 'Blackballed' After Winning My Oscar," *The Hollywood Reporter,* February 19, 2015

7. Roxane Gay, "Emma Watson? Jennifer Lawrence? These aren't the feminists you're looking for," *The Guardian*, Oct. 10, 2014

Chapter 6

1. Jennifer L. Pozner, "The Big Lie: False Feminist Death Syndrome, Profit, and the Media," from *Catching a Wave: Reclaiming Feminism for the 21st Century,* Rory Dicker and Allison Piepmeier, eds., 2003, page 31

2. "Reagan Is Shortchanging Women, Says GOP Feminist Kathy Wilson, and He May Pay for It Next Year at the Polls," *People*, August 1983

3. Faludi, Susan, *Backlash: The Undeclared War Against American Women* (New York: Crown Publishers, 1990).

4. Douglas, Susan J., *Where the Girls Are: Growing Up Female with the Mass Media* (New York: Times Books, 1994).

5. Faludi, Susan, *Backlash: The Undeclared War Against American Women* (New York: Crown Publishing, 1990).

6. Cora Harris, "*She's Gotta Have It*: A comedy in error," http://socialism .com/drupal-6.8/?q=node/2643

7. Abcarian, Robin, "Clarence Thomas vs. Anita Hill: She's Still Telling the Truth," *Los Angeles Times*, March 12, 2014

8. Kimberlé Williams Crenshaw, "Black Women Still in Defense of Ourselves," *The Nation*, Oct. 24, 2011

9. Walker, Rebecca, *To Be Real: Telling the Truth and Changing the Face of Feminism*, (New York: Anchor Books, 1995).

10. Elizabeth Sweet, "Toys Are More Divided by Gender Now Than They Were 50 Years Ago," *The Atlantic*, Dec. 9 2014

11. http://www.thebaffler.com/salvos/the-selling-of-katie-roiphe

12. Herman, Kristine, "Demands from the Women of Antioch," in *Just Sex: Students Rewrite the Rules on Sex, Violence, Activism, and Equality* (Jodi Gold and Susan Villari, eds.; Lanham, MD., Rowman and Littlefield, 1999).

13. "Are You a Card-Carrying Feminist?" *BUST*, Winter 2000

14. Barbara Ehrenreich, "Are women getting unhappier? Don't make me laugh," *Los Angeles Times*, Oct. 14, 2009

15. http://articles.latimes.com/2009/oct/14/opinion/oe-ehrenreich14

Chapter 7

1. https://www.opendemocracy.net/article/putting_power_back_into _empowerment_0

2. Elona Jones, "Go Ask Alice: A Q&A with author and punk veteran Alice Bag," *Bitch,* Summer 2012, page 38

3. Sara Marcus, *Girls to the Front: The True Story of the Riot Grrrl Revolution*, (New York: HarperCollins*Publishers*, 2010) page190.

4. Solinger, Rickie, *Beggars and Choosers: How the Politics of Choice Shapes Adoption, Abortion, and Welfare in the United States* (New York: Hill & Wang, 2002).

5. Summer Wood, "On Language: Choice," *Bitch,* Spring 2004

6. Hirshman, Linda, "Homeward Bound," *The American Prospect*, November 21, 2005.

7. Al Norman, "Woman-Owned Vest Company Gets Soaked by *Shark Tank* and Walmart," *The Huffington Post*, Jan. 26, 2015

8. "The Most Pointless, Pretentious, and Useless Business Jargon," *Forbes*, January 6, 2012.

9. http://www.techweekeurope.co.uk/workspace/microsoft-convergence
-satya-nadella-keynote-164565

10. Gay male authors were a part of the sex-work memoir boom as well, including David Henry Sterry (*Chicken: Portrait of a Young Man for Rent*) and Rick Whitaker (*Assuming the Position: A Memoir of Hustling*), but garnered considerably less media attention.

Chapter 8

1. http://www.makers.com/conference/2014

2. Christine Haughney and Leslie Kaufman, "The Rise of Conferences on Women's Empowerment," *The New York Times*, Oct. 6, 2014

3. Melissa Harris-Perry, "Nightline Asks Why Black Women Can't Get a Man," *The Nation*, April 22, 2010

4. Sanders, Joshunda, *How Racism and Sexism Killed Traditional Media: Why the Future of Journalism Depends on Women and People of Color* (Westport, CT, Praeger Press, 2015).

5. http://recode.net/2014/10/09/neurosexism-brains-gender-and-tech/

6. Eliot, Lise, *Pink Brain, Blue Brain: How Small Differences Grow Into Troublesome Gaps—And What We Can Do About It* (Boston: Mariner Books, 2009).

7. Katty Kay and Claire Shipman, "The Confidence Gap," *The Atlantic*, May 2014

8. http://kateharding.net/2010/05/26/5-ways-of-looking-at-sarah-palin
-feminism/

9. Aaron Breitkrutz, "With abortion, feminists are waging war on women," HutchinsonLeader.com, Oct. 3, 2015

10. Melinda Henneberger, "What Brought Carly Fiorina Down at HP Is Her Greatest 2016 Asset," *Bloomberg Business*, April 30, 2015

11. http://articles.philly.com/1997-07-24/entertainment/25549106_1
_sarah-mclachlan-lilith-fair-music-festival

12. Vowell, Sarah, "Throwing Ovaries," *Salon*, July 11, 1997.

13. Powers, Ann, "Critic's Notebook: A Surge of Sexism on the Rock Scene," *The New York Times*, August 2, 1999.

Chapter 9

1. Elizabeth Dwoskin, "Is This Woman Too Hot to Be a Banker?" *The Village Voice*, June 1, 2010

2. Nicole Hensley, "Port Authority cops said female recruit was 'too feminine' to be a police officer: lawsuit," *New York Daily News*, Dec. 10, 2014

3. Jim Edwards, "Inside the 'conspiracy' that forced Dov Charney out of American Apparel," *Business Insider*, Aug. 21, 2015

4. Benjamin Wallace, "Is Terry Richardson an Artist or a Predator?" *New York*, June 15, 2014

5. Kara Jesella, "The Collarbone's Connected to Slimness," *The New York Times*, May 10, 2007

6. http://www.stylist.co.uk/people/lucy-mangan-our-grandmas-had-corsets -we-have-vajazzling

7. A secondary, off-label use for Lysol douches was birth control, though as historian Andrea Tone has noted, when put to the test in a 1933 study, the germicide failed to prevent pregnancy in almost half of the 507 women using it for birth control.

8. Lynn Peril, *Pink Think: Becoming a Woman in Many Uneasy Lessons* (New York: W.W. Norton: 2002).

9. Lorraine Berry, "Caitlin Moran: Women have won nothing," *Salon*, Oct. 16, 2012

10. http://www.salon.com/2012/10/16/caitlin_moran_and_bitch/

11. http://www.public.iastate.edu/~jwcwolf/Papers/Bordo.pdf

12. Jack Neff, "Ten Years In, Dove's 'Real Beauty' Seems to Be Aging Well," *AdvertisingAge*, Jan. 22, 2014

13. Jack Neff, "Dove's 'Real Beauty' Hits a Rough Patch," *AdvertisingAge*, April 14, 2014

14. http://adage.com/article/news/dove-s-real-beauty-hits-a-rough-patch /292632/

15. Douglas, Susan J., *Enlightened Sexism: The Seductive Message That Feminism's Work Is Done* (New York: Times Books, 2010).

Epilogue

1. Gay, Roxane, "The Seduction of Safety, on Campus and Beyond," *The New York Times*, November 13 2015

2. Collins, Gail, *When Everything Changed: The Amazing Journey of American Women from 1960 to the Present* (Boston: Little, Brown, 2009).

3. Hayley Peterson, "McDonald's Hotline Caught Urging Employee To Get Food Stamps," *Business Insider*, Oct. 24, 2013

4. http://www.guttmacher.org/media/inthenews/2015/07/01/

INDEX

Andi Zeisler is a writer, editor, and cultural critic. She is the cofounder of Bitch Media and the editorial director of *Bitch* magazine. Zeisler's writing on feminism, popular culture, and media has appeared in *Ms.*, *Mother Jones*, *BUST*, the *San Francisco Chronicle*, the *Los Angeles Review of Books*, and the *Washington Post*. She has been interviewed in various national publications, such as the *New York Times*, and radio programs nationwide. She lives in Portland, OR.

PublicAffairs is a publishing house founded in 1997. It is a tribute to the standards, values, and flair of three persons who have served as mentors to countless reporters, writers, editors, and book people of all kinds, including me.

I. F. STONE, proprietor of *I. F. Stone's Weekly*, combined a commitment to the First Amendment with entrepreneurial zeal and reporting skill and became one of the great independent journalists in American history. At the age of eighty, Izzy published *The Trial of Socrates*, which was a national bestseller. He wrote the book after he taught himself ancient Greek.

BENJAMIN C. BRADLEE was for nearly thirty years the charismatic editorial leader of *The Washington Post*. It was Ben who gave the *Post* the range and courage to pursue such historic issues as Watergate. He supported his reporters with a tenacity that made them fearless and it is no accident that so many became authors of influential, best-selling books.

ROBERT L. BERNSTEIN, the chief executive of Random House for more than a quarter century, guided one of the nation's premier publishing houses. Bob was personally responsible for many books of political dissent and argument that challenged tyranny around the globe. He is also the founder and longtime chair of Human Rights Watch, one of the most respected human rights organizations in the world.

•   •   •

For fifty years, the banner of Public Affairs Press was carried by its owner Morris B. Schnapper, who published Gandhi, Nasser, Toynbee, Truman, and about 1,500 other authors. In 1983, Schnapper was described by *The Washington Post* as "a redoubtable gadfly." His legacy will endure in the books to come.

Peter Osnos, *Founder and Editor-at-Large*